Acting White

ALSO BY RON CHRISTIE

Black in the White House

Acting  White

The Curious History of a
RACIAL SLUR

Ron Christie

THOMAS DUNNE BOOKS
ST. MARTIN'S PRESS ≋ NEW YORK

THOMAS DUNNE BOOKS.
An imprint of St. Martin's Press.

www.thomasdunnebooks.com
www.stmartins.com

ISBN 978-0-312-59946-1

First Edition: October 2010

10   9   8   7   6   5   4   3   2   1

Dedicated to the pioneers of the civil rights era who fought for an American society in which citizens would be judged on the content of their character rather than the color of their skin.

Contents

Go into any inner-city neighborhood, and folks will tell you that government alone can't teach kids to learn. They know that parents have to parent, that children can't achieve unless we raise their expectations and . . . eradicate the slander that says a black youth with a book is acting white.

BARACK OBAMA, From a speech delivered in Boston, July 27, 2004

■ ■ ■

Always dream and shoot higher than you know you can do. Don't bother just to be better than your contemporaries or predecessors. Try to be better than yourself.

WILLIAM FAULKNER

Acting White

Prologue

A New Day or Déjà Vu?

All this time the eyes of the thousands present looked straight at the [black] orator. A strange thing was about to happen. A black man was to speak for his people, and with none to interrupt him. . . . As [he] strode to the edge of the stage, the low, descending sun shot fiery rays through the windows into his face. A great shout greeted him. He turned his head to avoid the blinding light, and moved about the platform for relief. Then he turned his wonderful countenance to the sun without a blink of the eyelids, and began to talk.

There was a remarkable figure; tall, bony, straight as a Sioux chief, high forehead, straight nose, heavy jaws, and strong, determined mouth, with big white teeth, piercing eyes, and a commanding manner. The sinews stood out on his bronzed neck, and his muscular right arm swung high in the air. . . . His voice rang out clear and true, and he paused impressively as he made each point. Within ten minutes the multitude was in an uproar of enthusiasm—handkerchiefs were waved, canes were flourished, hats were tossed in the air.[1]

The preceding newspaper account of an eloquent and influential black orator taking the stage to the cheers of thousands could have been taken from the inauguration of the forty-fourth president of the United States. Except that it wasn't. Instead, it was the report James Creelman filed with the *New York World* on September 18, 1895, to describe the captivating manner in which Booker T. Washington electrified the predominately white audience as he outlined his vision of a new America where blacks and whites could live and work together in harmony. A new day? Or did the event foreshadow events yet to come?

Booker T. Washington, like President Barack Obama, possessed remarkable oratory skills. He was also, like Obama, the most famous and recognizable black man in the United States during his career. Both men have also been accused of acting white and selling out members of their own race to advance their own remarkable careers. And yet the notion that a black man who works hard, receives an education, and seeks to depart from the conventional social and political norms is one who is acting white has been a slur rooted in American history for well over a hundred years. This isn't a theoretical exercise; this is a reality faced by many blacks who refused to accept the conventional wisdom of how they were supposed to think, act, and dress. The reward for such dangerous behavior? One is labeled a sellout, an Uncle Tom, a betrayer to his or her race. Famous men such as Booker T. Washington, Martin Luther King Jr., and Barack Obama have been tagged with such a slur. And, sadly, so have I.

FALL 1991: I was offered and I accepted a position as a junior legislative assistant to a member of Congress representing the fourth congressional district of Florida, an area rich with armed-forces personnel and retired veterans. My boss, the Honorable Craig T. James (R-FL) served as a member of the House Veterans Affairs Committee—a position that gave him the best opportunity to look after the needs of his constituents. One of my first responsibilities as a member of Congressman

James's staff was to serve as his legislative aide for the committee—a position that placed me in a seat directly behind him when the committee was in session.

The night before my first hearing I could hardly sleep. I was proud of how my years of hard work and intense sense of purpose gave Representative James the confidence in my ability to advise him. I had just turned twenty-two years old, and I was right on track. The next morning, I was the first staffer in the room, eager, excited, and prepared. I assumed my seat behind the congressman's seat on the dais and looked out upon the ornate hearing room before me. This was a moment to cherish, and I couldn't help but smile. For me, it was the equivalent of getting a roster spot on the New York Yankees.

A few minutes later, Representative Maxine Waters (D-CA) entered the room and sat in her seat on the dais. She was positioned directly across from me. I felt a rush of excitement as Ms. Waters prepared for the meeting. Ms. Waters is a woman just about every Californian admires. She began her political career in the California State Assembly in 1976 and was instrumental in getting the state's pension funds to divest from any businesses active in South Africa during the apartheid era. In 1990, she ran for Congress when Augustus Hawkins retired and won 79 percent of the popular vote. She was a true inspiration, and I felt some serious butterflies in my stomach being in her presence.

As I watched the congresswoman settle in, I noticed she was watching me watching her. With a smile on her face, she rose slowly and walked directly to where I was seated. I was nervous but excited to see her. Awesome—my first day on the job and I'm already making connections. My great aunt and uncle lived in her district, so I prepared a "my family is proud to have you as their representative" speech.

"Good morning, young man."

I didn't have time to reel off my calm and collected small talk:

"Are you serving on the Veterans Affairs Committee?"

"No, ma'am," I assured her. "I am a new legislative aide."

"Oh, fine, what Congressman are you working with?"

"For Mr. James from Florida."

With a neutral look Waters turned around and walked back to her seat. I wondered what that exchange was all about—a conversation that would soon permanently become part of the *Congressional Record*.

Moments later, the courtly chairman of the Veterans Affairs Committee, G. V. "Sonny" Montgomery, gaveled the hearing into order. Montgomery, a hero of World War II, was the namesake of the landmark program providing scholarships for returning veterans seeking to enhance their education. As the hearing commenced, Ms. Waters asked to be recognized by the chairman. While slightly out of protocol, the gracious chairman recognized Ms. Waters and opened her microphone.

CONGRESSWOMAN WATERS questioned the genial chairman of the Veterans Affairs Committee and asked why there were no persons of color working for the committee other than me. As I watched in horror, Ms. Waters raised her hand and pointed her finger straight in my direction. I should note that the role of a junior staffer is to be seen and not heard while in the presence of their member of Congress. And yet every eye in the room was fixed firmly in my direction. The worst glance came as Mr. James turned around slowly to meet my gaze. Nearly my first day on the job could end up being my last, I thought.

Ms. Waters continued her diatribe, and the chair promised to look into increasing the numbers of persons of color who worked on the committee. The hearing continued without further incident.

Walking back to the office with Congressman James, he said nothing of the drama. A few hours later the intercom on my desk rang and our receptionist announced that Congresswoman Waters was on the line looking to speak with me. "Yeah, right," I thought as I picked up.

"Young man, this is Congresswoman Maxine Waters, and I would like to speak with you. Immediately." As I headed from our office on the fourth floor of the Longworth House Office Building to hers, I wondered what she had in mind. Perhaps she wanted to apologize?

Walking into the congresswoman's office, I was quickly ushered into her sanctum sanctorum. Then the door shut firmly behind me. Up close and personal, Waters's presence was an intimidating one, and the look she gave me withering. "What are you doing working for Mr. James?"

I told her that my grandmother lived in his district and that he was the first member of Congress to offer me a job. "No, I want to know why you're working for a Republican," she continued. "Are you confused?"

"No ma'am, I'm not confused. I work with Congressman James because I share his values. I am a Republican."

"You are a sellout to your race! White people work for Republicans! Not African-Americans! You're nothing but an Uncle Tom!" Waters thundered.

I was stunned. A respected member of Congress called me an Uncle Tom and accused me of acting white for the mere offense of aligning myself politically with the party of Abraham Lincoln. A strong black woman who I admired and who professed to look out for the interests of those whose voices were not heard had no interest in listening to mine. I wasn't naïve. I expected black democrats to have strong philosophical differences with my choice of party, but I trusted that my right to make that choice was one they would not only respect but also fight for to their core. How many decades did black Americans weather with no choices? After several minutes of yelling at me, she announced I was free to go. I bit my tongue and left.

Working hard, educating yourself, and communicating effectively is a color-blind value. The power of our nation is in our differences, not our conformity, and respecting others with differing opinions is critical to our form of democracy. Behaving the way others demand you behave because of the color of your skin is repellent and a betrayal of the men and women who fought tooth and nail for civil rights.

Sadly, Ms. Waters's point of view, which holds that any black person who chooses to serve the Republican Party is an "acting white Uncle Tom" is not an anomaly. It's a pervasive belief among African Americans, and, not only that, it has crossed over into Hispanic communities too; it has even breached white households enveloped in hip-hop culture. For over eighteen years of my political and personal life, I've found this belief shared by just about every other person of color who did not share my party affiliation. And it's not just Republican blacks who get labeled with the acting white slur, either.

Hard work, diligent study, and eloquent communication skills worked for many other young blacks climbing the ladder of power in our nation's capital. There's the case of a senator who plowed past adverse economic conditions in the South Side of Chicago, got into Columbia for his undergraduate work, and then walked through the gates of Harvard Law School. After earning his seat in the United States Senate at age forty-five, Barack Obama was sworn into office as the forty-fourth president of the United States on January 20, 2009. But let's not forget that even before he assumed the most powerful job in the world, the then senator Barack Obama (D-IL) was accused by none other than Reverend Jesse L. Jackson Sr. of "acting like he's white"[2] as Obama sought his party's nomination for president in 2008.

SEPTEMBER 2010: Since that harrowing encounter with that prominent black member of Congress years ago, I never stopped thinking about what "acting white" is really all about. The slur is so counterintuitive that there must be some deep-rooted emotionally charged origin. Hard work, dressing well, speaking well, and ambitiously pursuing a fulfilling life is not a "white" thing. It's the way our society achieves. We teach our children to respect people who reach the highest levels of their profession in order that we as a society can better our world. And those core social conventions are essential to communicating across personal and professional cultures.

So where did the idea come from that working hard and dressing well is "selling out to the white world"? Is it really a pervasive attitude in the black community? Who has propagated the attitude? What do they gain by doing so? At what point can African Americans stop self-segregating and join the great American dream?

The time has come to bury the acting white slur with a broad historical examination of its origins. Once the truth about how it took hold and spread from one community to the next is revealed, we can strip it of its power and bury the slur once and for all.

For me, the inspiration for tackling the acting white puzzle is the culmination of more than fourteen years of agonizing over the words a precious first grader had uttered to me, which have circled in my mind ever since. When I worked on Capitol Hill, I was asked to participate in the HOSTS mentoring program. HOSTS, an acronym for Help One Student to Succeed, was an opportunity to work as a tutor and mentor for at-risk children at a local elementary school within the District of Columbia. On my first day of the program I crossed the Anacostia River and headed south.

South of the Anacostia River, unlike near the gleaming federal buildings along Pennsylvania Avenue or the power corridor of K Street, where lobbyists line "Gucci gulch," the population is overwhelmingly poor, illiterate, and black. I passed liquor store after liquor store and check-cashing store after check-cashing store along the way and thought of the kids who had to walk past them on their way to school. What a message—cash your welfare check and spend it on booze. Hardly inspirational, I thought.

I felt better when I arrived at my final destination, Elm Elementary School.* Struck by its neat and orderly appearance—in marked contrast to the dilapidated structures across the street, where several young men smoked glass pipes—I was comforted by the familiar sound of children laughing and talking. It was lunchtime, and young boys dressed in matching slacks and white shirts and little girls wearing similar shirts and skirts were seated at numerous benches eating their lunches and chatting amiably. I was then escorted to a smaller room in the rear of the school were only a dozen or so students waited to meet with their tutors.

I asked the program's administrator why there were more mentors

---

* I have changed the name of the school to protect the confidentiality of the students and staff.

present than students? "These are the students we believe have the best chance to make it to high school."

"That sounds like you're writing the rest of the other kids in the cafeteria off . . ." I obviously echoed scores of other mentors who had come before me.

"These are the best behaved and the students who have the best chance of making it through the system." With a real look of resignation and despair in her eyes, she continued, "It isn't fair; it isn't right; but that's how it is."

These were kindergarten through second-grade children! Why were the rest of the students written off as unreachable? If my introduction to the mentoring program wasn't jarring in and of itself, the questions my young pupil asked me over the months we worked together were soul wrenching. Justin was a quick study and readily took to our reading sessions together.* Yet there wasn't a week in the program where he didn't ask me a penetrating question or present an insightful observation. One question has stayed with me: "Is it cool to study and sound and act white like you do?"

When I pressed him on the subject, he told me that everyone in school knows that if you study, pay attention in class, and do well, you're "ACTING WHITE." After that I noticed that as much as he enjoyed reading and poring over new ideas alone with me, when he was outside of our one-on-one environment, Justin was careful not to appear to his friends like he was ACTING WHITE. He'd pretend not to see me or move quickly away when he did, putting as much distance between himself and the black man dressed in a suit.

At the end of the school year, the HOSTS program tutors and their students are invited to a reception held on Capitol Hill, where the children are able to dig in to pizza at a party held beneath the dome. When I asked Justin whether he and his mother would like to attend the pizza party with me, he looked at me without malice, just confusion. Why would he want to go to *White Washington*? He had never left the south

---

* Name changed to protect the identity of my young mentee.

side of the Anacostia River. Then he shrugged. "Our folks aren't welcome over there in White D.C., anyway."

I vowed from that day forward I would do my best to eradicate the slur of acting white once and for all. I wanted to trace where the slur came from and how we could eliminate the thought that black children studying hard, applying themselves, dressing well, and getting ahead was nothing more than acting white. This is a slur that has been flung at me over the years, and it is one that I believe we can eliminate over time with greater racial understanding and tolerance of the views of others.

1

Uncle Tom's Cabin

The Genesis of Acting White

March 1862—the White House, Washington, D.C. With the nation consumed by civil war, the sixteenth president of the United States broke away from his duties as commander in chief one day that spring to receive a visitor to the White House. According to a variety of accounts, when President Abraham Lincoln received Harriet Beecher Stowe that day, he is said to have exclaimed to the author of *Uncle Tom's Cabin:* "So you are the little woman who wrote the book that started this great war!"[1]

Whether or not Stowe's landmark novel generated the spark that ignited into war between southern states, which endorsed slavery, or the states in the north, which opposed the practice, the author started yet another war with her words in *Uncle Tom's Cabin*. This was a war waged both between blacks and whites and between blacks and fellow members of their race for what it meant to be black in the United States at the midpoint of the nineteenth century. These battles were not waged for territory or possession but instead for personal identity, ideology, and freedom.

Unwittingly or not, with the publication of *Uncle Tom's Cabin* in

1852 Stowe began a war of words in America about what it meant to be acting white while one was black, whether free or enslaved—a turmoil that still rages well past the turn of the twenty-first century. While certainly a work of fiction, *Uncle Tom's Cabin* drew its power and inspiration from the real-life struggles for freedom, dignity, and identity confronting blacks during the middle of the nineteenth century—a legacy that remains with us to the present day.

During the first year of publication, *Uncle Tom's Cabin* sold 300,000 copies and was the bestselling novel of the nineteenth century.[2] In fact, the novel was the second-bestselling book of the nineteenth century, surpassed only by sales of the Bible. Stowe's work had a tremendous impact on American culture, an impact whose legacy resonates in contemporary society today. For one, while the author intended that her title character be perceived as a noble hero worthy of praise by her audience—Uncle Tom fought for his beliefs and refused to be exploited by his detractors—many instead found that Tom was subservient and all too willing to please whites. This stereotype—a black man who curries favor with whites by acting white is a sellout to his race—is one whose seeds were planted in 1852 and it has grown steadily over the decades such that an African-American believed to be acting white is treated to the derogatory moniker of being an "Uncle Tom" in contemporary society.

While ostensibly a work of fiction, *Uncle Tom's Cabin* provides an interesting starting point to ascertain what it meant for blacks to be acting white in the American cultural mind-set of the 1850s. Before one can ascertain what it meant to be acting white during this time period, however, one must first establish a baseline from Stowe's novel of what it meant to be black during this era both from a legal and stereotypical perspective. This is where our examination begins.

Harriet Beecher Stowe knew the legal definition of what it meant to be a Negro in several southern states: a person with a black parent or grandparent. Certain states, such as Louisiana, legally denoted one as being black even if they were one-eighth black—an octoroon. This legal distinction of being black with just one-eighth's percentage is examined in chapter 3, which discusses the separate but equal precedent established in *Plessy v. Ferguson*.

Here, however, we examine how Stowe moved beyond the sterility of legalistic formalities to breathe life into her black characters in *Uncle Tom's Cabin* by cleverly allowing blacks to be perceived and defined by the reader through the prism of three distinct vantage points: whites looking upon blacks, blacks looking upon fellow blacks, and both blacks and whites looking upon Uncle Tom himself. In order to best arouse the passion of sympathy of abolitionists in the North, who sought to eradicate slavery from the shores of America, Harriet Beecher Stowe often portrayed blacks in her novel—as viewed from the prism and perspective of whites—in the most negative light possible. To this end, one prevalent depiction of being black as viewed from the eyes of whites in *Uncle Tom's Cabin* was that blacks were subservient and existed only to please the whims of whites rather than exercise any independent control over their mind or bodies.

From the opening pages of the novel, Stowe introduces her reader to the young slave Harry in the most subservient and demeaning manner possible. As his master, Mr. Shelby, calls Harry forth to introduce the boy to the slave trader Haley, Stowe writes:

> "Come here, Jim Crow," said he. The child came up and the master patted the curly head, and chuckled him under the chin.
>
> "Now Jim, show this gentleman how you can dance and sing."[3]

"Jump Jim Crow," well known to Harriet Beecher Stowe and other social observers of the time, was a derogatory song and dance routine created in 1828 by the white comedian Thomas Dartmouth Rice that was performed in blackface. This routine was supposedly inspired by a dance of a crippled African immigrant in Cincinnati, Stowe's adopted hometown from 1832 to 1851. On more than one occasion, Stowe introduces the reader to a young black slave for the first time by referring to him or her as Jim Crow in the presence of whites. The introduction of the term "Jim Crow" into the lexicon at this point in American history is significant given that it would soon characterize a pattern of oppressive and discriminatory behavior from whites toward blacks well into the middle part of the twentieth century. "Jump Jim Crow" would soon devolve from a derogatory song and dance to symbolize the oppressive discrimination that enveloped the American South for more than one hundred years.

In the novel, however, consider the following derisive comments made by the slave owner Augustine St. Clare when he introduces Topsy, the poor yet clever slave girl, to the reader:

> "I thought she was rather a funny specimen in the Jim Crow line. Here, Topsy," he added, giving a whistle, as a man would to call the attention of a dog, "give us a song now, and show us some of your dancing."[4]

It is significant that the author uses the derogatory term "Jim Crow"—a term that would later be used to identify racial-discriminatory practices such as prohibiting blacks from using the same railway cars as whites or from sharing the same lunch counters, a practice that would extend well into the 1960s in contemporary American society.[5]

Beyond viewing blacks as subservient, many white characters in *Uncle Tom's Cabin* consider blacks unintelligent—incapable of performing such basic tasks as reading, writing, and speaking clearly. Literacy was an important aspect of being a full and well-informed member of society during the eighteenth and nineteenth centuries. Blacks were legally denied the opportunity to become literate in several southern states. Alabama, Georgia, and Virginia joined several other states in enacting statutes that prescribed fines, flogging, and imprisonment for those who taught African-Americans how to read and write during this era.

Blacks were to remain uneducated and illiterate to the greatest extent possible during this era of American history since literacy and the ability to communicate clearly and intelligently were the province of whites; blacks who attempted to read and write were deemed as acting in the manner of a proper member of white contemporary society—behavior that was discouraged or forbidden.

Consider the following speech in Stowe's novel between two slaves, George and Eliza Harris. While the characters themselves are clearly fictional, Stowe infused life into the struggles faced by blacks during this era both enslaved and free. In railing against the oppressive treatment at the hands of his master, George proclaims the following in regard to his station in life:

> My master! And who made him my master? That's what I think of—what right has he to me? I'm a man as much as he is. I'm a better man than he is. I know more about business than he does; I am a better manager than he is; I can read better than he can; I can write a better hand,—and I've learned it all myself, and no thanks to him, I've learned it in spite of him.[6]

There is an interesting dichotomy of thought among blacks in *Uncle Tom's Cabin* in regard to literacy and academic achievement that persists today. On the one hand, there are blacks who agree with the sentiments expressed by George; they believe reading and writing are critical assets one must possess to be successful—even if such skills must be self-taught in order to be acquired. On the other hand, some blacks in the 1850s as well as today believe that education and literacy is only the province of whites. This perspective thus extended law to an ideology. It holds that blacks, unable to receive a proper education or become literate in the 1850s, are only acting according to a white man's prerogative when they achieve such things—a black man doing so would be acting white.

Illustrative of the sentiment that literacy and success should be limited only to whites is what Tom says to young Master George, the son of his previous owner as Uncle Tom is led away after being sold to a new master:

O, Mas'r George, you has everything,—l'arnin', privileges, readin', writin',—and you'll grow up to be a great, learned, good man, and all the people on the place and your mother and father'll be so proud on ye![7]

Apparently, the notion that blacks would apply themselves to become literate and educated, even in the face of antiliteracy statutes, was a foreign concept to someone of Uncle Tom's mind-set since these attributes applied only to whites rather than blacks. This subservient and inferior ideology about education—then and now—holds that African-Americans seeking to emancipate their minds from the chains of illiteracy act as do whites.

As Harriet Beecher Stowe further reveals in her work, blacks who possessed such advanced skills as literacy, ingenuity, and independent thought were perceived not only as acting white but also as a threat to whites. Consider once more the description of the slave protagonist George, who was relegated by his master to work in a bagging factory. Rather than complete his tasks in a plodding and uninspired manner, George was instead viewed by his fellow slaves and factory owner alike as being adroit and thoughtful—it should not be lost on the reader that Harriet Beecher Stowe reveals that George has created an invention that could rival the genius of Whitney's cotton gin.*

Rather than revel in the ingenuity of an enslaved black man's creativity, the white slave owner in this instance feels threatened by a display of intelligence by a black man who was perceived to be property, not a person, under the laws of the era in question:

George, who in high spirits, talked so fluently, held himself so erect, looked so handsome and manly, that his master began to feel an uneasy consciousness of inferiority. What business had

---

* As Stowe herself noted in *Uncle Tom's Cabin,* a young colored man from Kentucky had created just such an invention in real life. The fact that her fictional character George is described as having created such a machine in the book—and hailed from Kentucky—is not to be overlooked.

his slave to be marching round the country, inventing machines and holding himself up his head among gentlemen? He'd soon put a stop to it. He'd take him back, and put him to hoeing and digging, and "see if he'd step about so smart."[8]

While *Uncle Tom's Cabin* was fiction, Stowe's snapshot of life in America in the 1850s proved all too real. In the discrimination depicted by Stowe, as well as that suffered by blacks today, whites believe that a person of color speaking well, holding themselves high, and possessing intelligence threatens society.

As Augustine St. Clare discusses the notion of educating blacks in the South, he articulates a fear prevalent at the time that has yet to be fully extinguished from certain segments of American culture today:

Yet our laws positively and utterly forbid any efficient general educational system [for blacks], and they do it wisely, too; for just begin and thoroughly educate one generation, and the whole thing would be blown sky high. If they would not give them liberty, they would take it.[9]

The infraction committed by the proper education of blacks? That blacks would become successful, intellectual, influential—in other words, that they would act equally as whites—while being black.

It is important to recognize, however, that not all the depictions of blacks acting as whites from the perspective of whites in *Uncle Tom's Cabin* were to be perceived in a negative light. Instead, Harriet Beecher Stowe subtly used the characters George and Eliza Harris to portray blacks in a different light altogether—strong, determined, and intelligent. To this end it is fascinating to observe that Harriet Beecher Stowe's representation of all major black characters in *Uncle Tom's Cabin* (save Uncle Tom himself) could *pass* as white—in other words, they possessed fair complexions, spoke well, were literate, and could assimilate as whites without arousing suspicion of their true racial identity.

Given the era in which *Uncle Tom's Cabin* was published, Stowe's subterfuge is remarkable. George and Eliza could pass as white and move freely in society because they were treated as human beings rather than as black—or rather than as blacks accused of acting white. Instead of building on racial prejudices and stereotypes of the time, Stowe created black characters that not only were perceived sympathetically by her audience but also further instilled the notion that blacks and whites could interact as relative equals, an equality based not on the color of one's skin but on the content and strength of one's character.

In this vein, the author subtly yet overtly moves beyond the physical descriptions of George and Eliza to focus on those character attributes that allowed them to succeed in very difficult circumstances. For example, George and Eliza were each able to read, write, and speak clearly. Each possessed a strong sense of purpose, moral compass, and love for God and family.

More demonstrably, Stowe sought to instill the same character and value attributes of well-to-do members of white society within these two black characters to illustrate that blacks could successfully integrate into society not by acting white but by enjoying the freedom and emancipation brought on by hard work, morality, and a foundation built on education and literacy. George and Eliza symbolize the essence of freedom, and their quest in the novel is to be free from oppression, free to live their lives without castigation and to assimilate in society not as blacks acting as whites but as individuals who can choose their own destiny.

This quest for freedom and emancipation shone as a beacon of hope in a novel wrought with personal tragedy and despair brought about through the evils of slavery in the United States. Following his escape from slavery in Kentucky, George encounters Mr. Wilson, the kind white foreman from his job in the bagging factory. Stowe adroitly reunites the two men in a tavern where white "gentlemen" had congregated to discuss the flight from slavery of a young man who could pass as white; his return, dead or alive, held the promise of a reward. The slave in question here of course is George, and Wilson spies his former employee acting and passing as white among a group of whites eager to recover him and return him to slavery. As the two men retire to a more discreet area of the tavern to speak, Mr. Wilson makes the following observation:

> "George, something has brought you out wonderfully. You hold up your head, and speak and move like another man," said Mr. Wilson.
>
> "Because I'm a *freeman!*" said George, proudly. "Yes sir; I've said Mas'r for the last time to any man. *I'm free!*"[10]

This freedom to integrate and assimilate in society is demonstrated shortly thereafter. George travels farther north on his journey to freedom in Canada and receives sanctuary from a benevolent Quaker family along the Underground Railroad.

Unbeknownst at first to George, the same family also rescued his wife, Eliza, and their small son, Harry. Following their joyous reunion, George has the opportunity to sit down to breakfast with his family in the home of the Quaker conductors who had brought them one step closer to freedom. As Harriet Beecher Stowe describes the happy reunion around the breakfast table, she writes:

> It was the first time that George had sat down on equal terms at any white man's table; and he sat down, at first, with some constraint and awkwardness; but they all exhaled and went off like fog, in the genial morning rays of this simple, overflowing kindness.[11]

One should recognize, however, that George and Eliza are not the only black characters in *Uncle Tom's Cabin* that are treated as human beings by whites in the novel. Eva, the daughter of the slave owner St. Clare, is one of the only major white characters that refuses to castigate blacks who sought physical and intellectual freedom as acting white. Topsy, the comical slave girl, and Eva are brought together in one of the most symbolic and allegorical scenes in the novel. Assessing the void between blacks and whites in the South at the midpoint of the nineteenth century, Harriet Beecher Stowe writes:

> Eva stood looking at Topsy. There stood two children, represen-
> tatives of the two extremes of society. The fair, high-bred child,
> with her golden head, her deep eyes, her spiritual, noble brow, and
> prince-like movements; and her black, keen, subtle, cringing, yet
> acute neighbor. They stood the representatives of their races. The
> Saxon, born of ages of cultivation, command, education, physical
> and moral eminence; the Afric, born of ages of oppression, sub-
> mission, ignorance, toil and vice![12]

And yet, despite the racial, social, and educational dichotomy Stowe outlines above, the two children soon develop a bond of trust and friendship that transcends their racial difference—a remarkable depiction just before a civil war that would nearly destroy the country and that was waged in large measure to secure the rights of blacks and whites to act as equals rather than as subservient and dominant members of society who were at odds with one another.

Thus far we have observed how whites perceived blacks throughout *Uncle Tom's Cabin*. At this juncture it is important to recognize that, while many whites in *Uncle Tom's Cabin* perceived blacks who sought to educate themselves, speak clearly, and free themselves from the yoke imposed by slavery as acting white, it is further illustrative to examine how blacks, then as now, negatively perceive fellow members of their race who seek similar emancipation.

Prejudice, then as now, is not merely confined to whites treating blacks poorly; black-on-black prejudice is rampant in *Uncle Tom's Cabin*—prejudice that is particularly manifested in the derogatory manner in which lighter-skinned blacks perceive those whose complex-ions are darker than their own. As we shall also see, darker-skinned blacks in *Uncle Tom's Cabin* often accuse lighter-skinned members of the same race as acting white—based merely on skin color. This form of discrimination that Harriet Beecher Stowe brought vividly to life in her work of fiction more than 150 years ago remains in certain black communities across America today.

Harriet Beecher Stowe introduces this form of black-on-black prejudice most eloquently in her depictions of the slaves in the household of the New Orleans slave owner Augustine St. Clare.

First, the reader is introduced to the kitchen ruled by Dinah—best described as a dark-skinned and malevolent Aunt Jemima–like figure— who runs her kitchen with a tart mouth and iron fist. When two of the light-skinned black servants discuss their desire to dress up handsomely and attend a ball, Dinah remarks,

> Don't want non o' your light-colored balls . . . cuttin' round, makin' b'lieve you're white folks. Arter all, you's niggers, much as I am.[13]

Harriet Beecher Stowe is prescient in her observation that blacks used the word "nigger" both as a form of greeting as well as a derogatory expression to describe other blacks—a practice that sadly continues today. When the light-skinned slaves in the St. Clare home are introduced to the young slave girl Topsy for the first time, they recoil at her dark appearance, instigating an admonishment from the darker-skinned Dinah that the niggers should not think of themselves as white people:

> "Don't see what Mas'r St. Clare wants of [a]nother nigger!" said Dinah, surveying the new arrival with no friendly air. "Won't have her round under *my* feet, *I* know!"
>
> "Pah!" said Rosa and Jane, with supreme disgust; "let her keep out of our way! What in the world Mas'r wanted another of these low niggers, for, I can't see!"
>
> "You go long! No more nigger [th]an you be, Miss Rosa," said Dinah, who felt this last remark a reflection on herself. "You seem to t[h]ink yourself white folks. You an't nerry one, black *nor* white. I'd like to be on or [the other]."[14]

The reader is reminded here of the prescient observation made by Booker T. Washington in his 1901 biography *Up from Slavery*, where he likens the plight of blacks to those of crabs seeking to escape a barrel. In Washington's view, all too often blacks pull other blacks down into the barrel with them rather than let one another escape from similar despair. Rather than comfort a young slave girl who arrived from the lash of a cruel master, the character exchange above indicates a mindset that unfortunately remains to the current day: some blacks view themselves as superior to other blacks based merely on their lighter pigmentation. In the novel, one "crab" pulls another down into the barrel of slavery based merely on skin color rather than recognizing their identical predicament; most whites viewed all blacks as inferior and subservient based on skin color.

Perhaps most poignantly we arrive at the negative manner in which both blacks and whites in *Uncle Tom's Cabin* perceived the novel's namesake—Uncle Tom himself. While Harriet Beecher Stowe intended that the protagonist around whom the entire story was cast be a strong and noble man, many blacks and whites from the nineteenth century to the current day instead took a less than complimentary view of Uncle Tom's behavior.

Sadly, it is a common pejorative for both blacks and whites today to castigate a black man by labeling him an Uncle Tom—ironically, for different reasons. Many blacks use the slur today to cast aspersions on blacks who allegedly act subservient before whites or, more commonly, who are perceived as ingratiating themselves to whites by speaking, dressing, and acting white—that is, acting and thinking differently from the accepted social and political norms adhered to by many blacks across the United States. Similarly, there are certain whites in America today who also use the derogatory expression to denigrate blacks for the alleged affront of acting white.

Unwittingly, the author created both a character and a negative pejorative in Uncle Tom that has become synonymous with a black man acting white. I turn in this chapter to how Uncle Tom evolved from being a heroic fictional character to an expression of disgust used toward blacks in contemporary America who seek to exercise differing social, cultural, and political opinions. This expression asserts such a black man is nothing more than one who is acting white—an Uncle Tom. I should know: I've been labeled an Uncle Tom for all of my adult and professional life.

In his foreword to the annotated *Uncle Tom's Cabin,* the Harvard professor Henry Louis Gates Jr. remarks on the unintended derogatory manner in which the novel's namesake would be regarded throughout American literary and cultural history. Rather than be remembered and described as a strong leader who held firm to his convictions and beliefs, Tom instead was transformed over time into a reviled slur by both blacks and whites alike to criticize those blacks who, through their dress, demeanor, or independent freedom of thought, were deemed to be acting white. As Gates first observes:

> My sense of the book soon became inextricably intertwined with the negative stereotype of an "Uncle Tom," the black man all too eager to please the whites around him. Accordingly, Uncle Tom became for us the most reviled figure in American literary history. He was the embodiment of "race betrayal" and an object of scorn.[15]

From the opening pages of the novel, Tom is described as being an honest, hardworking, and a pious man. This is the sympathetic impression Harriet Beecher Stowe intended her audience to maintain throughout Tom's difficult odyssey. Intentionally or not, however, Stowe portrayed an Uncle Tom throughout the novel who appeared more content with currying favor with whites than one who possessed the spirit and zeal to break free of the chains that bound him.

The meek, subservient Tom is a more prevalent figure throughout the novel than the strong, hardworking man that Stowe had intended. For example, as Tom is led away after being sold to another master, Tom appears more distraught by his separation from the son of his former slave owner than he does by his being sold and forever removed from his family. To this end, Tom appears meek, subservient, and all too willing to seek favor with whites rather than with the black family mourning his departure and standing beside him:

> Tom rose meekly, to follow his new master, and raised up his heavy box on his shoulder. His wife took the baby in her arms to go with him to the wagon, and the children, still crying, trailed on behind.[16]

And yet as he was led away, Tom not only failed to express emotion or remorse for his predicament, he was instead distraught by his inability to express his love for the son of his former master:

> "I'm sorry," said Tom, "that Mas'r George happened to be away. . . . Give my love to Mas'r George," he said, earnestly.[17]

This is only one of dozens of occurrences in the novel in which Tom expresses empathy and compassion for a white family that had enslaved him and denied him an opportunity of life, liberty, and the pursuit of happiness instead for a black member of his immediate family. The impotent and subservient manner in which Tom subjugated his own best interests to gain favor with his white "benefactors" is perhaps best manifested in an exchange between Tom and St. Clare on the occasion of Tom's potential release from the bonds of slavery. St. Clare elects to sign papers giving Tom his freedom and the ability to return home to his wife and family, and yet Tom refuses to leave his master: "'Not while Mas'r is in trouble,' said Tom. 'I'll stay with Mas'r as long as he wants me,—so as I can be of any use.'" St. Clare's response was predictable: "'Ah, Tom, you soft, silly boy! I won't keep you till that day. Go home to your wife and children, and give my love to all.'"[18] And yet Tom would rather remain in the care and protection of the white family that enslaved him rather than return home to Kentucky to resume his life in freedom with his own wife and children.

Intentionally or not, Harriet Beecher Stowe's Uncle Tom does not develop strong bonds or relationships with other black characters in the novel. Tom is solicitous of his masters and other white people throughout the work but fails to establish a physical or cultural connection with other blacks in the story. Perhaps this is where the fictional Uncle Tom became the real-life pejorative in American society today. Over the decades, blacks began to associate fellow blacks perceived to be eager to assist whites as those who had turned their backs on their own cultural and racial heritage.

While a work of fiction, *Uncle Tom's Cabin* planted the seeds of the idea that black inferiority is the result of blacks seeking favor with whites, an idea that would grow with each successive generation in American culture. Over time, blacks began to associate fellow members of their race perceived as giving assiduous attention to whites as being an Uncle Tom—a black person acting white to gain the white person's approval. As Henry Louis Gates Jr. notes:

> The label "Uncle Tom" became such a potent two-word brand of impotence that nobody really cared how far the public perception had traveled from the literary reality. We knew what an "Uncle Tom" was, and it was not good.[19]

Ironically, the fictional character originally created to be a figure of strength and piety instead evolved into a contemporary expression of disdain for both blacks and whites alike. A black man who elected to congregate socially, academically, and professionally with whites became an Uncle Tom in the minds of many blacks and whites in America. Blacks elected to denigrate their fellow blacks for the infraction of thinking, acting, and living differently from how they did. As for certain whites, "Uncle Tom" became a term used to describe a black man who appeared to be acting white through speech, dress, or vocation.

Harriet Beecher Stowe will long be remembered in American history as the little woman who wrote the book that helped bring about the Civil War. At the same time, she is also the unwitting creator of a character that has long been reviled by blacks and whites alike. Stowe's

Uncle Tom evolved into a slur denoting a black man acting white rather than a black man exercising the very freedoms of life, liberty, and the pursuit of happiness denied both to her fictional character as well as to millions of black Americans who had endured the evils of slavery—an unintended consequence of her legacy, perhaps, but I believe the genesis of the acting white slur hails from the namesake found in Harriet Beecher Stowe's *Uncle Tom's Cabin.*

2

Booker T. Washington

A Turn-of-the-Century Uncle Tom Acting White?

Who best to represent the Negro race? The directors of the Cotton States and International Exposition posed this question to themselves as they searched for someone to take to the podium and represent the Negro race. The year was 1895; Reconstruction had long since ended and Jim Crow and segregation had enveloped the South like a thick fog of oppression, yet a Negro was needed to address the Atlanta Exposition that year—a man who could symbolize the "good feeling" that prevailed between the two races. After several days of reflection, the Negro was found who would address the crowd. The man who would take to the podium on September 18, 1895, more than a hundred years ago, has been the subject of fierce discussions, primarily within the African-American community, over the decades. This man, who rose from the horrors of slavery to a role of prominence in America and who would mingle freely among whites and dine at the table of the president of the United States, has mainly been described in one of two ways: as a man of vision and reverence who was a pioneer of the civil rights movement or as an Uncle Tom appeaser who preferred the subjugation of blacks to whites while he was busy thinking and acting white himself. Whether Booker T. Washington deserves to be hailed as a leader or ridiculed as a black man who acted white to survive at the turn of the twentieth century is where we begin our discussion.

Booker T. Washington was born a slave to a black mother and a white father he knew little about in Franklin County, Virginia, around 1856. Freed from the bonds of slavery by the Emancipation Proclamation during the Civil War, Washington later moved to the coalfields of West Virginia, where he worked as a young boy. At the age of sixteen, in 1872, Washington returned to Virginia, where he attended the Hampton Institute (present-day Hampton University), which had been established to provide freed blacks with an education. Washington later completed his studies at the Wayland Seminary in Washington, D.C., before returning to Hampton as an instructor.

Soon after his return to Hampton, Booker T. Washington was recommended by Hampton University president Samuel Armstrong to become the first head of what was to become the Tuskegee Institute in 1881—a position Washington held until his death in 1915. Washington set July 4, 1881, as the opening day for his new school in Tuskegee—an event that was met with interest by both blacks and whites.

As noted in his autobiography, *Up from Slavery,* the notion of educating blacks in the Deep South in the era following Reconstruction was not met with universal approval by whites in the surrounding area. First, there was a sense that educating blacks would bring about trouble between the races; the rationale for this position held that the more educated blacks became, the less economic value they provided to the state of Alabama. The assertion here, of course, is that blacks belonged in the fields working the plantations rather than in the halls of academia learning—they couldn't pick cotton while sharpening their minds with knowledge.

Second, a caricature of the "Educating Negro" had been created and perpetuated by whites. As Washington describes in his autobiography:

The white people who questioned the wisdom of starting this new school had in their minds pictures of what was called an educated Negro, with a high hat, kid gloves, fancy boots, and what not—in a word, a man who was determined to live by his wits. It was difficult for these people to see how education would produce any other kind of coloured man.[1]

What Washington helped many of the whites in the community surrounding Tuskegee envision was an institution that would teach blacks, freed from the bonds of slavery and menial agrarian servitude, to act and live just as freely as whites. Ironically, Washington moved the campus of the school shortly after its founding to an abandoned one hundred–acre plantation, which became the site of the Tuskegee Institute to the current day.

As the Tuskegee Normal and Industrial Institute gained prominence across the South as a beacon of inspiration to blacks who had been marginalized through the darkness of illiteracy, Washington's name soon became a household commonplace for both blacks and whites in the United States. The lessons of hard work and economic self-reliance for blacks who he taught at the Tuskegee Institute elevated Booker T. Washington to become the most recognizable and famous black man in the United States during the early 1900s. However eminent he was because of his deeds and accomplishments, Washington's rise to prominence was not without abundant criticism, since many blacks accused him then and continue to accuse him today of currying favor with whites at the expense of blacks: he was a sellout, an Uncle Tom, a black man acting white to advance his own personal agenda.

Some might equate Booker T. Washington to the contemporary figures the Reverend Jesse Jackson Sr. and the Reverend Al Sharpton since all three men purport—and in their own minds believe they do and in the minds of whites are perceived—to speak for black America. In doing so, all three men have been criticized for taking to the stage to speak for the hopes, views, and aspirations of one race and for thereby conveniently allowing whites the opportunity to concentrate their outreach efforts and solicit opinions from one black person rather than many. For Booker T. Washington, his moment to speak on behalf of black America on a sweltering day in Atlanta, Georgia, would forever enshrine him both in praise and controversy.

On September 18, 1895, Booker T. Washington ascended the stage before a predominately white audience at the Cotton States and International Exposition in Atlanta, Georgia, where he was introduced by the former governor, Rufus Brown Bullock, as a "Representative of the Negro enterprise and Negro civilization."[2] These remarks, later known as the Atlanta Compromise, sought to quell white fears about black progress in the South by promoting the notion that blacks would be content to work and live by the production of their hands. Put another way, blacks would be content to only study industry and agriculture and to toil in blue-collar positions, leaving whites to prosper through higher education and white-collar occupations.

However controversial at the time, the Atlanta Compromise speech would later be regarded as one of the most influential and important speeches in American history. One question has remained unanswered since he delivered the speech: did Booker T. Washington seek to advance the condition of blacks in America at the turn of the twentieth century through his speech at the Atlanta Exposition, or was he merely trying to position himself favorably, acting white to gain personal fame and fortune at the expense of the black folks he claimed to represent?

Whether one is a supporter or a critic of Washington's Atlanta Compromise address, in several passages it portrays blacks as subservient, if not inferior, to whites. Two passages in particular drew the ire of blacks then as much as they do today for the manner in which Washington appeared to put down members of his own race as being second-rate citizens—to the applause and fanfare of the whites in attendance for his remarks.

First, Booker T. Washington discussed how blacks would prosper if whites gave them the opportunity to succeed. At the same time, to assuage any fears of any intellectual or professional dominance by blacks, Washington added:

While doing this, you can be sure in the future, as in the past, that you and your families will be surrounded by the most patient, faithful, law-abiding, and unresentful people that the world has ever seen. As we have proven our loyalty to you in the past, in nursing your children, watching by the sick-bed of your mothers and fathers, and often following them with tear-dimmed eyes to their graves, so in the future in our humble way, we shall stand by you with a devotion that no foreigner can approach, ready to lay down our lives, if need be, in defence of yours, interlacing our industrial, commercial, civil, and religious life with yours in a way that shall make the interests of both races one.[3]

Even taking into account the era and the difficulties blacks and whites in the Deep South encountered while trying to coexist at the turn of the twentieth century, Washington's articulation of a society in which blacks must prostrate themselves at the feet of whites makes one cringe. While arguing for blacks' assimilation into society, Washington also believed that blacks should be patient and nonresentful in caring "in our own humble way" for the same people who had enslaved them. In today's vernacular this would be akin to saying: "Don't rock the boat. The white man will reward us over time, but we must not press too hard or ask for too much."

And yet I believe even the most ardent defender of Booker T. Washington would note that he was hardly patient or humble in his disposition toward others. How could he claim to be speaking for the Negro race, a group of some eight million blacks in the South who were barely away from the horrors of slavery, when he failed to act as he instructed other blacks to act? Or, why did Booker T. Washington walk, speak, and act as did educated whites at the same time as he very subserviently called for blacks to integrate into southern society—a practice he failed to preach himself?

Booker T. Washington's apparent "do as I say, not as I do" position is particularly manifest in the most famous yet controversial line from his address before the Atlanta Exposition. Commenting on how blacks and whites could interact in society on a professional and social basis,

Washington promised that, "In all things that are purely social we can be as separate as the fingers, yet one as the hand in all things essential to mutual progress."[4] Scholars have long sought to define exactly what Booker T. Washington meant with this historic phrase. There are some who maintain he sought to assuage fears of social assimilation between the races and that any relationships maintained between the two races would be strictly professional rather than personal. Others believe that Washington sought to imply the inferiority of blacks to whites—hence the call for separation between the races.

In other words, blacks would best assimilate in American society by remaining inferior and not seeking to act white or uppity by undertaking activities that had long been the prerogative of whites. Moreover, Washington advocated that blacks would remain segregated from whites in their social interactions, remaining as separate as the distinct fingers of a hand.

While the Atlanta Exposition speech was widely hailed in white quarters across the United States, it was hardly met with universal acceptance and praise from the black community. W. E. B. Du Bois would emerge as the most famous and influential critic of both the Atlanta Compromise speech as well as the singular dominance centered on the Tuskegee Institute's belief that blacks should receive an industrial rather than a comprehensive and well-rounded education.

While Du Bois and his transformational Niagara Movement will be discussed in greater detail in chapter 4, it is important to comment for a moment on the lone significant voice that rose up to challenge Booker T. Washington and his assertions in the Atlanta Exposition address on the manner in which blacks should assimilate in American society as less than equals of whites.

In a stinging essay entitled "Of Mr. Booker T. Washington and Others," Du Bois challenged and rejected the vision articulated by the Atlanta Exposition address:

His programme of industrial education, conciliation of the South and submission and silence as to civil and political rights, was not wholly original. . . . But Mr. Washington first indissolubly linked these things; he put enthusiasm, unlimited energy, and perfect faith into this programme, and changed it from a by-path into a veritable Way of Life."[5]

Mr. Du Bois continued his critique of Washington's address by commenting on the impact the Atlanta Exposition remarks had had thus far upon the American psyche:

It startled the nation to hear a Negro advocating such a programme after many decades of bitter complaint; it startled and won the admiration of the South, it interested and won the admiration of the North; and after a confused murmur of protest, it silenced if it did not convert the Negros themselves.[6]

In Du Bois's view, many blacks and whites accepted the notion that blacks could not compete intellectually or professionally or interact socially with their white counterparts in society. Whites welcomed the separation and segregation, while many but not all blacks silently acquiesced—either conditioned or resigned to the belief that blacks were inherently inferior. To this end, Du Bois asserted that blacks could only empower their status in society by demanding the right to vote, self-respect, and the value of an education. He wrote:

They do not expect to see the bias and prejudices of years disappear at the blast of a trumpet; but they are absolutely certain that the way for a people to gain their reasonable rights is not by voluntarily throwing them away and insisting that they do not want them; that the way for a people to gain respect is not by continually belittling and ridiculing themselves; that, on the contrary, Negros must insist continually in season and out of season, that voting is necessary to modern manhood, that color discrimination is barbarism, and that black boys need education as well as white boys.[7]

Du Bois did not accept the notion that treating people with respect while working hard and receiving an education was only the province of whites in America at the turn of the twentieth century. Blacks were not inherently inferior, Du Bois argued, but they would remain inferior in society if they could not challenge the status quo by improving their economic and social standing.

To this end, Du Bois further remarked of Booker T. Washington and his Atlanta Compromise speech that "Mr. Washington represents in Negro thought the old attitude of adjustment and submission—[His] programme practically accepts the alleged inferiority of the Negro races."[8] For Du Bois and an emerging group of new black leaders, for blacks to receive a proper education and hold themselves up with dignity and respect was not acting white. To the contrary, these new leaders believed it was critical for blacks to advance in a society that made prejudiced and stereotypical assumptions about blacks based merely on the color of their skin and that did not take their academic, intellectual, and professional skills into account.

Moreover, it was not without irony to contemporary critics of Booker T. Washington such as Du Bois that Washington failed to uphold the very declarations and admonitions he had urged fellow blacks to follow in his Atlanta Exposition address—the most prominent of which was the belief that blacks and whites should remain as separate as the fingers of the hand and not interact as social equals. Not only did Washington associate freely with philanthropists with prominent names such as Carnegie, Mellon, and Rockefeller, he also made his company with current and former presidents of the United States.

Many critics over the decades have accused Washington of hypocrisy because he assuaged white fears by promoting social segregation while refusing to adhere to the very same rules he postulated that other blacks should follow. Consider, for example, Washington's repeated professional and social engagements with Presidents Grover Cleveland and Theodore Roosevelt. An examination of Washington's relationships with these two presidents leads to a very different conclusion about

Washington and blacks being as separate as the fingers of a hand when it came to social interaction.

Both personal and media accounts show that Washington was particularly enamored with his personal and professional relationship with President Grover Cleveland. For example, immediately following his address at the Atlanta Exposition, Washington mailed the president a copy of his remarks; Washington would later recount with relish in his autobiography, *Up from Slavery*, the favorable response he received from President Cleveland shortly thereafter.

Following his salutary greetings, Cleveland would write to Washington on October 6, 1895:

> Your words cannot fail to delight and encourage all who wish well for your race; and if our colored fellow-citizens do not from your utterances gather new hope and form new determination to gain every valuable advantage offered them by their citizenship, it will be strange indeed.[9]

There is an inherent contradiction in the words spoken by Washington in the Atlanta Exposition address for which President Cleveland lavished praise, and the subsequent actions taken by Washington are directly incongruent to his stated views. If the point of the Atlanta Exposition speech was to mollify the fears of whites by telling them that blacks would apply themselves to vocations that posed no threat to whites and that blacks would undertake these vocations while being subservient, humble, patient—all while refusing to integrate socially and while remaining as separate as the fingers on a hand—how can one explain how Washington acted subsequent to his famous speech?

Far from segregating himself from the company of whites as he encouraged other blacks to do, Washington actively sought to be in their company and confidence at the highest social and political circles. Or, put another way, Washington promoted a tranquil American society with blacks acting separate and subservient to whites while he could act as freely as whites and consider himself their equal.

Shortly following the receipt of President Cleveland's letter congratulating him on his speech, Washington invited the president to tour the Atlanta Exposition in person—an invitation that Cleveland accepted. In his memoirs Washington reflected, "Mr. Cleveland has not only shown his friendship for me in many personal ways, but has always consented to do anything I have asked of him."[10] One can hardly find fault or criticism with President Cleveland for his friendship with Washington. To the contrary, the former president's willingness not only to proclaim his friendship with Washington but also to call repeatedly for improved relations between the races was remarkable. Their relationship only underscored that blacks and whites could live together as equals—even as Washington professed that blacks should not do so.

The incongruence between Washington's stated view that blacks should not interact socially with whites while he maintained his own prerogative to do so is particularly striking. Or, Washington could act as an equal to whites since his view was that the reason other blacks should not be able to do so was because of their inferior educational, social, and political status. As contemporary author Debra Dickerson would note in this regard: "[Booker T. Washington] most assuredly accepted the white man's version of him, he also decided to be the best damned version of the white man's version that he could be."[11]

President Cleveland was public about his friendship with Washington while he himself advocated solutions to address the "Negro problem" in America at the beginning of the twentieth century. During a joint appearance and speaking opportunity with Washington at New York City's Madison Square Garden on April 15, 1903, Cleveland declared:

> I have come here to-night as a sincere friend of the negro; and I should be very sorry to suppose that my good and regular standing in such company needed support at this late day either from certificate or confession of faith. . . . Inasmuch, however, as

there may be some differences of thought and sentiment of those who profess to be friends of the negro, I desire to declare myself as being part of the Booker Washington–Tuskegee section of the organization. I believe the days of "Uncle Tom's Cabin" are past.[12]

In my mind, Washington perpetuated the dark days and visions presented in *Uncle Tom's Cabin* through his remarks at the Atlanta Exposition in 1895. While proclaiming to seek advancement and opportunities for blacks, I believe he put forth a vision where blacks would be inherently separate and unequal in society—words spoken just months before the Supreme Court would codify the separate but equal doctrine in *Plessy v. Ferguson,* which will be discussed in the following chapter.

Unlike the overt warm and public relationship shared between Cleveland and Washington, President Theodore Roosevelt would treat Washington in a manner that was decidedly separate and not entirely equal. Shortly upon assuming the presidency following the assassination of William McKinley, Roosevelt sought out Washington to advise him on matters of race.

Although Roosevelt had initiated the counsel of Washington, the president's description of the famed black orator was decidedly less than complimentary. While Roosevelt had once described Washington as "the most useful, as well as the most distinguished member of his race," he also added the less than laudatory description of Washington as an example of a black man who was "occasionally good, well-educated, intelligent and honest."[13]

According to Kenneth O'Reilly in *Nixon's Piano: Presidents and Racial Politics from Washington to Clinton,* the courtship and cultivation of the relationship between President Roosevelt and Washington was mutual. And yet, unlike the social relationship shared between Washington and President Cleveland, President Roosevelt took strides to ensure their social relationship was as separate and distinct as the fingers of a hand—connected yet distinctly separate—following an infamous dinner shared by the two men on October 16, 1901, little more than a month after Roosevelt had first assumed office.

Both Washington and President Roosevelt were subjected to blister-ing criticism from blacks and whites for their decision to break bread and dine together at the White House on October 16, 1901. Washing-ton was assailed as a hypocrite by the Harvard-educated lawyer William Monroe Trotter, given the thrust of the Atlanta Exposition remarks in which blacks and whites were to remain socially segregated. Trotter would remain a constant critic of Washington and joined forces with Du Bois in 1905 to form the Niagara Movement and later the NAACP as an alternative school of thought to Washington's—a subject exam-ined in greater detail in chapters to follow.

For his part, Roosevelt was criticized by hard-line segregationists who took a dim view of blacks and whites socializing together—the identical view held by Washington. As the Mississippi senator, James K. Vardaman, would acidly remark: "The White House," following the Roosevelt-Washington dinner, was "so saturated with the odor of the nigger that the rats have taken refuge in the stable."[14]

Initially Roosevelt shrugged off criticism of his decision to dine with Washington. In a Gridiron Club dinner in December 1901, for example, guests were given a cartoon meant to be humorous with a smiling Teddy Roosevelt depicted as the "Ace of Hearts" dining with Booker T. Washington, the "Ace of Spades."[15] As the criticism intensi-fied, President Roosevelt and his allies engaged in a combination of spin and damage control: the dinner was downgraded to being a lun-cheon, and, true to the form of segregation advocated by Washington, the president's team reminded those concerned that white women did not dine, sit, and eat with the black man in the White House.

In the aftermath of repeated criticism, Roosevelt took steps to en-sure that his relationship with Washington would be largely confined to an exchange of correspondence through the mail rather than in so-cial settings where a black man could act as an equal to his white coun-terpart. Thus the black man would remain as distinct as the separate fingers of the hand; Roosevelt was unwilling to draw more ire from southern segregationists, who took strong exception to a white presi-dent entertaining a black man in the White House.

As their relationship evolved, Roosevelt would call upon Washington to assist him in filling patronage positions that, in the words of Roosevelt, would be for

[N]ames of one or two first-class colored men, the kind of colored man who reflects credit upon his people—the kind that I want to see given the recognition to which they are entitled; that is, given the recognition which would come to them naturally if they were not colored.[16]

Once again, it is interesting to note that in 1901, just as today, there were whites in significant positions of influence who believed that one black man could speak for an entire race of people—in this case, Washington—which paved the way for the Reverends Jesse Jackson and Al Sharpton to assume similar roles with relish in the decades to follow.

Contemporaries of the one black man anointed to speak for the entire race, then as now, did not universally accept the notion that Washington spoke for them. In response to President Roosevelt calling upon Washington to assist him in filling patronage positions in his administration with blacks Washington deemed qualified, Trotter noted with scorn: "It is simply an insult to every Negro to have such a trimmer made a boss by President Roosevelt."[17]

Contemporary African-American scholarship on the importance of Washington's Atlanta Exposition speech is both vigorous and divided as to whether he was a man of vision or an Uncle Tom apologist content to act white while treating fellow members of his own race with disdain. Rebecca Carroll attacked this question head-on with her recent work, *Uncle Tom or New Negro? African Americans Reflect on Booker T. Washington and "Up from Slavery" 100 Years Later.* Carroll invited twenty prominent African-Americans from academia, the arts, business, and elected public service to discuss the positive and negative aspects of Washington's legacy—with a particular emphasis on the importance of the Atlanta Exposition speech.

In her introduction to the book, Carroll discusses how many

African-Americans have described Washington as an Uncle Tom—the docile and dutiful character passive in nature that is eager to please white people. To this Carroll notes:

> But over the years, *passive* became *house nigger* became *spineless* and finally became *sellout.* In some ways there is a kind of involuntary reflex among African-Americans, particularly in the twentieth and twenty-first centuries, to brand one of our own— usually one of our famed own—as an unforgivable sellout. From Clarence Thomas to Colin Powell and Henry Louis Gates, black people (most often men) who negotiate with white people are frequently labeled "sellouts" no matter what they are selling.[18]

While I agree with Carroll's assessment, Washington's deeds and actions were dramatically different from those of the three pioneers discussed above. None of the three men have sought to be the representative spokesman for an entire race of people: Justice Thomas never purported to be America's black jurist, General Powell America's black soldier and later diplomat, or Gates the preeminent black scholar to interface with white America. Instead, Washington held himself out to be the representative of an entire race of people—all the while acting as freely in society as a white man of upstanding social and political status and explicitly denying other blacks the very opportunities that he personally availed for himself.

Washington's work to improve the condition of African-Americans through the Tuskegee Institute and his network of financiers, philanthropists, and politicians was considerable until the time of his death in 1915. Whether he was a true visionary, self-possessed opportunist, or perhaps a combination of both, one thing may be said about Washington that will long be debated in the days to follow: whether by accident or by design, his portrayal of blacks during the Atlanta Exposition address in 1895 planted a seed in the minds of blacks and whites that the Negro race was inferior by way of vocation, education, and social interaction. His call for blacks to remain as separate from whites in society as fingers on a hand led for many segregationists in the South and those sympathetic to blacks in the North to endorse the concept that blacks and whites could segregate themselves in separate but equal accommodations—a decision codified by the Supreme Court, which has had resounding and lasting ramifications on the educational development of blacks in America.

Whether lauded or loathed, Booker T. Washington is one of the most important and transformative figures in black American history. While keenly interested in providing blacks with the industrial skills to make a living for themselves, Washington may well be best known for his Atlanta Exposition or "Compromise" speech, in which he prescribed that blacks segregate themselves from whites in contemporary society. Yet he spurned his own edict and acted as an equal of whites by keeping company with presidents of the United States and famous philanthropists of the day. Whether pioneer or hypocrite, Booker T. Washington certainly believed in his own dealings that he was free to act as a peer and a contemporary of whites, even as he decried the ability of fellow blacks to do the same.

3

Plessy v. Ferguson

A Long Journey Toward Equality

On the morning of June 7, 1892, the thirty-year-old shoemaker Homer Plessy boarded the first-class cabin on the East Louisiana Railroad line between New Orleans and Covington, Louisiana. Plessy looked just like the other passengers. In his nicely pressed shirt and summer suit, he behaved with the manners of a seasoned New Orleans businessman. As the train chugged out of Press Street Station, the porter collected tickets. Plessy sat in his plush seat prepared to make history.

Homer Adolphe Plessy was born three months after the Emancipation Proclamation to Adolphe Plessy and Rosa Debergue on Saint Patrick's Day, March 17, 1862. His parents were classified as free people of color since their forebears were of African and French descent. As is true today, New Orleans was a unique stew of people. "One source of leadership and strength that Louisiana Negroes enjoyed that Blacks in no other states shared was a well-established upper class of mixed racial origin in New Orleans with a strong infusion of French and other Latin intermixtures," the historian C. Vann Woodward wrote in *American Counterpoint*. "Among these people were descendants of the 'Free

People of Color,' some of them men of culture, education, and wealth, often with a heritage of several generations of freedom. Unlike the great majority of Negroes, they were city people with an established professional class and a high degree of literacy."[1] Raised among these free-thinking city people during Reconstruction (1865–77), Plessy assumed the values of his community. Through education and perseverance, a man of any color could now take his place at the American table.

At twenty-four, Plessy stood beside his values and became vice president of the Justice, Protective, Educational, and Social Club, a group dedicated to reforming public education in New Orleans. A year later, in 1888, he married his sweetheart, Louise Bordenave; scouted a home for his family; and settled into 1108 North Claiborne Avenue, in the Faubourg Treme section of New Orleans. He then walked the third precinct and registered to vote in the sixth ward. Like most Americans, Plessy would work his hardest to make a better life for his unborn children, and securing them an education was his first priority.

The man who provided Plessy an equal opportunity paid a heavy price. President Abraham Lincoln made the ultimate sacrifice when he was assassinated less than a week after Lee's surrender at Appomattox Court House. Blacks were particularly demoralized by his death and made up a huge swathe of the human beings lining the railway lines on his 1,654-mile funeral-train procession. In addition to his seminal Emancipation Proclamation, Lincoln had urged adoption of the Thirteenth Amendment—a provision that expressly called for the abolition of slavery and involuntary servitude. While the amendment passed the Senate decisively, it was initially crushed in the House of Representatives. But Lincoln's personal lobbying paved the way for the amendment's adoption in the House of Representatives four months before his death, in January 1865.

Lincoln's vice president, Andrew Johnson, assumed the presidency. Johnson's tenure as president was one of conciliation with the defeated South. Fending off the radical Republican congressional coalition, which demanded immediate civil rights action and Confederate acquiescence,

Johnson, a Republican at the start of his term, feared further fracturing of the delicate union. He feuded with his party and eventually switched allegiances to become a Democrat. But after the Republicans seized two-thirds of the seats in the Senate and House in 1866, his days veto-ing bills and kowtowing to Confederates were numbered. With the power to overcome Johnson's opposition to broad civil rights legislation, the Republicans took matters in their own hands, and the House of Representatives eventually impeached Johnson on a technicality. The Senate was one vote shy.

The Republicans successfully moved their agenda forward (inte-grating freed slaves into the fabric of society as quickly as possible) when they brought in the war hero Ulysses S. Grant as their 1868 presiden-tial candidate. He won in a landslide and ushered in an era of radical reconstruction that brought major congressional action. With the sup-port of President Grant, Congress passed a number of Reconstruction acts in 1867, the most effective being military occupation of ten Confed-erate states. Congress also oversaw all state and local elections in the South, the result of which brought more than 2,000 black men to elec-tive office to represent their constituents at the local, state, and federal level in just twelve years, from 1865 to 1877. Among these ranks in-cluded fifteen members of the House of Representatives, two members of the Senate, and even the governor of Louisiana. As the noted English scholar Thomas Paine remarked nearly one hundred years before, in 1791, in *The Rights of Man*: "all that extent of capacity" of ordinary people, in-visible in ordinary times, "never fails to appear in revolutions."[2]

Congress ratified the Fourteenth Amendment in 1868, which affords constitutional safeguards for equal protection under the law and ensured the rights of former slaves, and the Fifteenth Amendment in 1870, which assured freed slaves the right to vote. The confrontations and delibera-tions between black representatives who had been former slaves and white representatives who had once owned slaves were quite riveting.

One compelling (and it would prove prophetic) incident occurred in the House in 1874, during consideration of a civil rights bill to ban ra-cial discrimination in places of public accommodation. Representative

Alexander Stephens, from Georgia, was none other than the former vice president of the Confederacy. He argued the old states-rights platform: that states have the right to govern themselves—an argument that Thomas Jefferson and James Madison brilliantly made in the Kentucky and Virginia Resolutions of 1800. Representative Robert Elliott, a former slave from South Carolina, was quick to remind Mr. Stephens of the Fourteenth Amendment—a recently passed addition to the Constitution that asserted the supremacy of the federal government's interest to protect all its citizens against discrimination. Elliott then addressed his other colleagues in the House of Representatives: "It is scarcely twelve years since that gentleman [Stephens] shocked the civilized world by announcing the birth of a government which rested on human slavery as its cornerstone."[3] Elliott's argument carried the day, and President Ulysses S. Grant signed the bill into law the following year. For a time, it seemed that the inclusion of blacks in the political process could help sweep away the ghosts of slavery.

Another Republican triumph was their success lobbying for the establishment of universal public education in state constitutions. The legacy from Nat Turner's Revolt (a slave rebellion that took the lives of sixty white Virginian slaveholders in 1831) was finally being eradicated. Since Turner was a bright and thoughtful slave who taught himself to read and write, maintaining uneducated and ignorant slaves was thought to be crucial to secure slave owners security. Antiblack literacy laws were adopted throughout the South, making educating African-Americans a crime. Keeping the subjugated ignorant proved a crucial tool in maintaining white supremacy.

But as quickly as a new day dawned over the South, where blacks and whites could coexist in society, a political quagmire arose after the votes were counted in the 1876 presidential election. The end result was a betrayal by the very political stronghold that not only championed the abolitionist cause but also founded its core platform in 1854 as humanist and antislavery—the Republican Party.

The early civil rights victories advanced by a Republican executive-legislative coalition were short-lived. Ironically, if many of the federal statutes and constitutional amendments adopted during Reconstruction had been fully implemented, most of the landmark civil rights laws from the 1950s and 1960s would not have been necessary. And while President Grant would call Abraham Lincoln "incontestably the greatest man I ever knew," his devotion to Lincoln's memory would ultimately succumb to political pragmatism.[4] His office's widely documented corruption resulted in a Republican backlash, so much so that, by 1876, the Republican domination of Congress was at an end. What lay at stake at the end of the presidential election was nothing less than the executive office for Grant's party.

The presidential election of 1876 remains one of the most bitterly fought contests in American history. In the months following the election, but before the inauguration of the next president in 1877, Republicans and Democrats on Capitol Hill remained at odds as to who was the legitimate next chief executive. While Democrat Sam Tilden from New York had received 184 electoral votes to Republican Rutherford B. Hayes's 165 electoral votes, a dispute arose surrounding the twenty electoral votes from South Carolina, Louisiana, and Florida, where Reconstruction Republican governors still remained in power. As a practical matter, southern Democrats had chafed under the yoke and reins of Reconstruction, and they sought the removal of federal troops that protected the civil rights and liberties of blacks formerly under their control. Without an army standing behind them, black Americans would by necessity return to a secondary place in southern life.

As the conflict dragged on, racist southern Democrats were reluctant to undertake actions that could bring about another war, but they were also incapable of accepting blacks as equal citizens. A compromise was sought, and Grant capitulated. In exchange for the electoral votes from Louisiana, South Carolina, and Florida and the election of the Republican Rutherford B. Hayes as the eighteenth president of the United States, Grant would pull the troops out of the South. The removal of federal troops marked the end of Reconstruction. President Ulysses S. Grant, initially hailed as a hero by blacks following the enactment of the Civil Rights Act of 1866 (which legally bestowed the ability of blacks to vote at the federal level but was never formally enforced by Grant as president), was soon viewed as the great betrayer as a result of his decision to remove many federal troops in advance of Hayes's inauguration.

The removal of federal troops gave white Democrats the message that the executive branch would turn a blind eye to failures to enforce the new federal laws that safeguarded black citizens' rights in individual states. As a result, emboldened southern Democrats rapidly stamped out black advances through new voting laws, redistricting, and other punitive measures, which swept blacks from elective office as quickly as they had been voted in. Once the blacks were out of positions of voting power, other laws—discriminatory Jim Crow laws—were enacted.

Perhaps by living in an integrated neighborhood and working to reform education in New Orleans, Homer Plessy felt emboldened to seek justice and relief from the Louisiana brand of Jim Crow. He must have watched helplessly as federal troops departed Louisiana at the end of Reconstruction, ushering in wave after wave of laws passed to stifle the very ability of blacks to receive an education or even eat lunch at a place of their choosing. Long-fought freedoms vanished as quickly as they had come, and white oppression returned with a ferocity and vengeance that was largely ignored in the North. The reconstructed South was little better than the old South—changing nearly overnight from being an accommodating region in which blacks could live, work, and exercise political freedom to being one in which the approximately four million newly freed slaves found themselves looking down the barrel of a gun.

A particularly blatant Jim Crow law was Louisiana's Separate Car Act of 1890, which prohibited black and white train passengers from sitting in the same railcar on travel within the state of Louisiana. The act required railway companies to provide accommodations for whites and blacks. A group of concerned citizens, led by Louis Martinet (also founder of the newspaper *The Crusader*), formed the Citizens Committee to Test the Constitutionality of the Separate Car Law. Betrayed by the failure of the executive and legislative branches of government to stop the spread of Jim Crow laws—Hayes turned a deaf ear to black issues while Congress was dominated by southern Democrats—blacks, as the committee knew, had one last hope to protect federal enactments to provide equal protection under the law: the judicial branch. The scales of justice were said to be blind, and the time had come to test the adage. The committee found Albion W. Tourgée, a white Northerner who would work the pending case pro bono and who raised funds among sympathizers to hire another local white attorney, James C. Walker, as his co-counsel.

Politics makes strange bedfellows—even in the midst of nascent civil rights efforts to promote integration. As such, the committee found another ally, this one in the East Louisiana Railroad. The company supported the overthrow of the Separate Car Act, albeit for commercial rather than benevolent purposes: the rail carrier did not want to make the significant investment to procure additional passenger cars to accommodate blacks and whites traveling to the same destination. The railroad would play ball and help choreograph the challenge.

Now all they needed was a case. Tourgée argued that a man whose race was not easily identifiable would best serve the legal argument. By having a black man "act white," his legal arguments could attack the hypocrisy head-on. If there is no distinguishable physical difference between one human being and another, any outside categorization of one versus the other is by logical definition discriminatory. A citizen is a citizen, and legally separating one from the other is contradictory to the Constitution—a straightforward and reasonable argument for any court.

The committee searched for a black man who could act white. They found Homer Plessy, a man committed to making a better life for his children.

As the number 8 train departed from the Press Street Station on June 7, 1892, bound for Covington, Louisiana, Plessy hoped that his ultimate destination would take him far away from the Louisiana bayou to the chambers of the United States Supreme Court in Washington, D.C. Calmly sitting in his padded chair in the first-class section of the East Louisiana Railroad, Plessy carried out his plan when the conductor arrived to claim his ticket. As the train gathered momentum, Plessy announced that he was black and that he refused to sit in the car designated for use by blacks only. The train was brought to a halt at the corner of Royal and Press streets; a police detective informed by the East Louisiana Railroad company of the impending drama forcibly dragged Plessy from the train and charged him with violating the Separate Car Act. He was booked and processed at the Orleans Parish jail. The committee posted Plessy's bond, and the judicial process began in earnest.

As the ensuing litigation wound its way through the Louisiana state court system, Plessy challenged the constitutionality of separate but equal accommodations for black and white passengers. The newly restored social hierarchy in Louisiana ensured that Plessy would fail in the corrupt state legal system. Having exhausted his legal remedies in the state of Louisiana, there remained one last court in the land that could hear his case and judge whether separate but equal accommodations for blacks and whites offended the Constitution: the Supreme Court of the United States.

An appeal to the highest court in the land seeking to overturn separate but equal railway accommodations in Louisiana brought significant risks not only to Plessy but also to millions of blacks across the country. Both the executive and legislative branches of government had failed to carry out their responsibilities to enforce equal-protection rights enshrined in the Constitution. As the ultimate arbiter of justice, the Supreme Court's responsibility was to interpret the law through a prism that was color-blind. Could the Court dispense justice blindly, or would its judgment be clouded by the tenor of the times?

Ultimately, at issue before the Court as it heard Plessy's case on April 13, 1896, was not whether Plessy was black. He was an octoroon according to Louisiana law, a racial category used to describe the "mixed races." Octoroons had one great-grandparent of full African descent (seven-eighth white and one-eighth black). Polygenism (the theory that the different races evolved from different species of being), which had recently come under criticism by Charles Darwin in his seminal *Origin of the Species,* was the scientific gospel of the era and was very clear about race.

The dominant theory is best represented by Josiah Clark Nott and George Robins Gliddon's *Indigenous Races of the Earth* (1857), which posited a three-tiered hierarchy of evolution. Chimpanzees held the lowest rank, followed by Engross and "Greeks." White society was descendent from the Greeks and as such held the highest rank on the hierarchy. Thus, any dilution of the purity of any person's white blood would place that individual on the lower level of the evolutionary scale. As Plessy was one-eighth Negro, in the eyes of the law at the time he was black. Would the justices who would hear the case view Plessy blindly as a citizen seeking justice (the core character of the Fourteenth Amendment to the Constitution), or would they instead view him as an inferior being (the scientific "truth" of the era)?

Our founding fathers had the foresight to understand the difficulties people have maintaining perspective. As progressive humanists, they understood that the conventional wisdom of a particular era is suspect. One era's villain is another's hero. Thus, they limited each judicial court's role on ruling particular cases. The Supreme Court of the United States has "subject-matter jurisdiction," which limits the cases it can review. The primary subject matter that the Supreme Court is tasked with reviewing is any that challenges the Constitution of the United States, a document that can only be altered by special majority amendments.

The core issue of *Plessy v. Ferguson* is not Plessy's race designation but his unimpeachable rights as a United States citizen and whether or not his constitutional rights were violated by the Separate Car Act. Again, our founding fathers are clear about the rights of citizens, and they would not abide such inhuman treatment. In addition to the Fourteenth Amendment, the Ninth Amendment, one of the original amendments in the Bill of Rights, covers the unremunerated rights of every citizen. Essentially, the Ninth Amendment assigns the fundamental rights of humanity to any citizen of the United States. Certainly within that purview is the accordance to blacks of freedom from physical isolation and from being defined as "separate" by a powerful domineering class of people that formerly enslaved them.

Unfortunately for Plessy and millions of blacks for generations that followed, the Supreme Court's decision to deny his equal-protection claim institutionalized a uniquely American brand of corruption and hypocrisy. According to the justices in the 7–1 *Plessy* decision (Justice David Josiah Brewer abstained from the case), all is well on the American landscape so long as accommodations are provided for blacks and whites that are separate but equal—despite the fact that such a designation would span behavior that was inherently separate and unequal. As such, with dismal definitions of "equal" adopted throughout the South, the division between whites and blacks widened with the generations that followed the *Plessy v. Ferguson* decision in 1896.

For ambitious black Americans at the time, the only path left to advance through society was, ironically, the very behavior that Homer Plessy refused to condone—pretending that you are something that you are not. After the Supreme Court's decision, however, those who could "pass" as white were faced with a brutal dilemma—the American dream can be yours . . . all you have to do is deny your core being. As such, "acting white" became synonymous with betrayal.

The East Louisiana Railroad moved forward after dropping off Homer Plessy at the corner of Royal and Press Streets. But now it was wildly off course, destined for a half-century detour that alienated an inordinately talented and resourceful segment of the American population and tainted the core of humanity in American democracy.

4

W. E. B. Du Bois

The Souls of Black Folk *and the Roar*
of the Niagara Movement

July 6, 1903: Just across the way from the newly constructed Carnegie Library on the campus of the Tuskegee Institute stood The Oaks, the two-story brick home of its principal, Booker T. Washington. On this special evening, Washington would welcome into his home W. E. B. Du Bois, a one-time ally and now outspoken critic of Washington's belief that industrial education and accommodation with southern whites would lead blacks on a more equal path and stature with their white counterparts. Du Bois and his ever-expanding followers had different ideas and chose to follow a different path—a path that called on blacks to advance through the power of a well-balanced education with arts and letters rather than through the pull of the plough and an agrarian-industrial curriculum. Or, Du Bois and his followers averred, blacks would gain intellectual, economic, and political power by demanding to be treated as equals of whites—a viewpoint resisted by Washington and his wealthy white benefactors, who believed in the subservience and obedience of blacks at the turn of the twentieth century in America. In their view, blacks acting as whites were socially and morally repugnant.

Unfortunately, history does not provide us an accounting of the dinner conversation between Booker T. Washington and W. E. B. Du Bois that July evening in 1903. As Du Bois's Pulitzer Prize–winning biographer, David Levering Lewis, notes of the historic gathering: "What was discussed between Dr. and Mrs. Washington and their distinguished dinner guest on the evening of July 6, 1903, as white-jacketed students served choice cuts of poultry and meat is unrecorded."[1]

And yet the conversation that night must have been tense—beyond discussing the platitudes and areas of mutual agreement, the two leaders must also have discussed areas of disagreement about how best to advance the lives of black Americans: Du Bois had recently launched a historic broadside against Washington and his accommodating apologists just three months before with the publication of *The Souls of Black Folk*.

While the two men were originally allies in their shared goal to ameliorate social and educational opportunities for blacks at the dawn of the twentieth century, Du Bois eventually sought to break free from the monolithic stranglehold that placed the hopes, dreams, and aspirations of one race in the hands of one man who purported to speak for and on behalf of blacks.

One can only imagine that a clash of the titans took place that evening—a clash that would eventually bring about a dramatic change in the condition of blacks in America. For W. E. B. Du Bois and his "Talented Tenth"—leaders of the Niagara Movement that would challenge and forever change the manner in which blacks would receive an education, wield political power, and enter professional (rather than menial) occupations—laid the groundwork for blacks to act and live as equals to whites under the law later in the twentieth century.

William Edward Burghardt Du Bois was born in February 23, 1868, in Great Barrington, Massachusetts. Adroit and comfortable with academics at a young age, Du Bois earned a degree from Fisk University in 1888, followed by a bachelor's degree cum laude from Harvard University in 1890.

Moreover, Du Bois would go on to become the first African-American to earn a Ph.D. from Harvard University in 1895. Eventually, Du Bois would settle at Atlanta University, where he would establish the Department of Social Work (presently Clark Atlanta University's Whitney M. Young School of Social Work).

A prolific writer, Du Bois had published two critically acclaimed monographs by his thirty-first birthday, and by age thirty-seven he had published a major essay in Max Weber's *Archiv fur Sozialwissenschaft und Sozialpolitik*.[2] Soon, Du Bois's office at Atlanta University became a hub for visiting academics, scholars, and the intellectually curious. According to Lewis, Du Bois was deeply shaken following the lynching and killing of Sam Hose in April 1899.

Hose, a black farmer living on the outskirts of Atlanta, had been involved in an altercation with a white farmer over a debt and shot the farmer dead. Hose was summarily captured, lynched, and burned to death. A throng of two thousand white men, women, and children fought over pieces of Hose's flesh for souvenirs—his charred knuckles were later on display in the window of a white shop owner's on Mitchell Street in Atlanta. As Lewis notes in his biography of Du Bois, "From that moment forward [Du Bois] recognized that 'one could not be a calm, cool, and detached scientist while Negroes were lynched, murdered and starved.'"[3] This event, coupled with the loss of his two-year-old son to diphtheria the following month, made Du Bois feel he needed to escape from Atlanta, and Booker T. Washington offered him an academic appointment to teach at Tuskegee during the academic year 1900–01 at the salary of $1,400—$200 more than his current appointment at Atlanta University.

While much has been written about the competition and eventual confrontation of outlook and ideology between Washington and Du Bois, the eventual rivals began their relationship on a foundation of mutual respect if not grudging admiration for each other. For a time following Washington's infamous Atlanta Compromise speech in 1895, Du Bois was even complimentary of the remarks.

Eventually, Du Bois chafed against the artificial ceiling imposed by manual and agrarian occupations for blacks and instead looked to a three-pronged platform designed to elevate the political and social advancement of blacks: the power of politics through access to the ballot box, insistence on civil rights, and higher education for young blacks—the tools that would shatter black inequality in America at the dawn of the twentieth century.[4]

The five-year period from 1895 to 1900 was particularly dispositive in the evolution of the relationship between Washington and Du Bois from cordial colleagues to direct competitors over the future well-being of blacks in America. For one, the end of Reconstruction saw a dramatic decline in the ability of blacks to exercise political power through access to the ballot box. In *Biography of a Race* Lewis reveals that

> [T]en years after Booker Washington famously spoke in Atlanta, the nightmare and the specter was fast receding from the southern white consciousness. Where 130,344 African-Americans had been registered to vote in Louisiana in 1896, 5,320 remained on the rolls four years later. After 1900, there were some 3,000 registered voters in Alabama out of a black male voting-age population of 181,471.[5]

Blacks were not permitted to act as equal political partners to whites at the ballot box: Literacy tests, poll taxes, and other inequitable tactics were used to dilute the power of blacks to enact meaningful political and societal change. Du Bois bristled at Washington's apparent acquiescence to white efforts to disenfranchise blacks: political power was to be cherished and preserved rather than given away—the power of one black man rose while the lot of millions of blacks living in the South fell with the dissolution of their suffrage.

The rift between the two men would grow wider in 1900 when Du Bois fell victim to the deceptive and manipulative behavior exhibited by Washington, who steered a key political appointment away from Du Bois to an ally who shared his own philosophy that blacks should be subservient rather than equal to whites. At issue were the two men's competing visions and ideology regarding the power and importance of a liberal arts–based education. Du Bois became further disillusioned by Washington's rejection of the power of education to lift blacks to a stature more equal to whites and to enable blacks to lead more productive and rewarding lives.

The impetus for the rift was new legislation enacted by Congress that restructured the governance of public schools in the District of Columbia. Under the direction of a superintendant of schools, Congress mandated the establishment by July 1, 1900, of two new assistant superintendant positions—one for white schools and the other for "colored" schools.

According to his biographer, Du Bois was excited by the prospect of obtaining the new appointment to become the assistant superintendant of black schools in Washington, D.C.—unlike much of the American South, the public parks, libraries, train station, and other public facilities were not segregated by color in the nation's capital. Lewis notes:

> The D.C. assistant superintendency of schools was one of the most estimable and quietly influential positions available anywhere to an African-American, a plum. Anchored to the flagship M Street High School (the future Dunbar) with its classical curriculum, the city's segregated black public school system was said to provide one of the best educations in America.[6]

Du Bois was very desirous to receive the coveted appointment, and he solicited Washington for his advice and leadership about how to best secure it.

For his part, Washington was initially solicitous of Du Bois's entreaties for assistance in obtaining the assistant superintendant position for colored students in the District of Columbia. To this end, Washington wrote a letter of recommendation on behalf of Du Bois and appeared willing to advocate for Du Bois's appointment. But then the political winds that blow through the nation's capital, then as now, have an interesting propensity to change direction without notice. To this end, Du Bois's apparent edge to receive the assistant superintendency was severely damaged when Washington ultimately decided that the position would be best held by one who subscribed to his belief that blacks should receive an agrarian-mechanical education that would not threaten whites rather than study a curriculum based in the arts and sciences that could place blacks on an equal intellectual footing as whites—a position openly advocated by Du Bois.

A leading critic of Washington's apparent endorsement of Du Bois's appointment was William A. Pledger. Pledger was a self-made black lawyer, the former head of the Georgia Republican Party, and a graduate of Atlanta University—the same institution where Du Bois taught.

In a communication warning against Du Bois's appointment, Pledger lamented to Washington that "I am so sorry that you endorsed Du Bois. . . . He is not of your people."[7] How does one interpret Pledger's comment that Du Bois was not "one of your people" when comparing the substance and style of the two black leaders? Could it be that Washington and his followers thought that Du Bois and his ilk were too "uppity" and needed to learn that the place for blacks was in the fields rather than in the classroom? Was Du Bois trying too hard to act white by excelling in the classroom and encouraging other blacks to do the same rather than endeavoring to keep his place among lesser-educated blacks?

Interestingly, if not surprisingly, the historical record reveals that Washington and his followers—black and white—often denigrated those blacks that dared or deemed themselves worthy of a liberal arts education. Incredibly, for his part, Washington enjoyed offering "darky" jokes to white audiences, where blacks were made the scapegoats of his off-color remarks.

On one occasion where Washington was on hand to receive an honorary degree from Harvard University (where Du Bois was the first African-American to receive a Ph.D.), Washington referred to himself as a huckleberry in a bowl of milk.[8] Or Washington would regale white audiences with a "joke" about a black laborer who was tasked with cleaning out a henhouse that was to serve as the future home of the first classroom at the Tuskegee Institute; the laborer was said to ask in astonishment: "What you mean, boss? You sholy ain't gwine clean out de henhouse in de *day*-time?"[9]

Washington did not just denigrate blacks who sought to improve their condition through knowledge gained through study in higher education, he did little to stop his white supporters from doing the same—a practice that offended Du Bois and his followers. For example, an ardent and early white supporter of Washington's ideological and philosophical belief of the inferiority of blacks was William Baldwin, a railroad baron and the eventual president of the Long Island Railroad. In Baldwin's view, the manner to best smooth over relations between the races in the South at the turn of the twentieth century was for blacks to be subservient and obedient toward whites. Baldwin further believed that black intellectuals posed the greatest threat to the evolution of the South following Reconstruction—a view that he frequently communicated to his friend, Booker T. Washington.[10]

To this end, Baldwin wrote to Washington in February 1900, just as Washington and Du Bois were corresponding regarding the assistant superintendant position in the nation's capital. Baldwin, a Harvard University graduate, warned Washington that Du Bois and his fellow blacks who sought to reap the benefits gained through advanced educational training were acting in a manner that was "purely an attempt on their part to be white people."[11] Blacks acting white by broadening their intellectual horizons offended Baldwin, and he made sure to communicate his views to Washington before a final decision had been reached regarding the appointment of the new Assistant Superintendant of Schools. Whether Washington heeded Baldwin's advice is unknown—what is known is the contents of a letter Washington mailed to Du Bois on March 11, 1900, regarding the appointment for the superintendant position, in which Washington abruptly withdrew his support of Du Bois's candidacy:

Dear Dr. Du Bois:

Please consider the contents of this letter strictly private. If you have not done so, I think it not best for you to use the letter of recommendation which I have sent you. I have just received a letter direct from one of the Commissioners in the District asking me to recommend someone for the vacancy there and I have recommended you as strongly as I could. Under the circumstances it would make your case stronger not to present the letter which I have given you for the reason that it would tend to put you in the position of seeking the position. It is pretty well settled, judging by the Commissioner's letter, that some one outside the District is going to be appointed.

> Yours truly,
> Booker T. Washington[12]

Du Bois would later discover that an African-American member of the District of Columbia school board would warn President Roosevelt about the "danger" of his appointment—regardless, the position sought by Du Bois was awarded to another candidate, and Du Bois was convinced that the so-called Tuskegee machine was behind his rejection.[13] If Washington and his supporters believed that blacks were acting white by seeking emancipation through higher education, Du Bois was about to challenge this status quo through the rise of his Talented Tenth and the roar of the Niagara Movement.

Despite his disappointment in failing to receive the appointment as assistant of schools in the District of Columbia, Du Bois redoubled his efforts to give blacks an alternative to the monolithic vision and leadership offered by Washington. To this end, Du Bois steadily ratcheted up his critiques in print toward those who dismissed the importance of African-Americans to receive a well-rounded rather than industrial education. President Theodore Roosevelt perhaps best summarized the thinking of many whites in America at the turn of the century when he offered the following observation just before his infamous dinner with Booker T. Washington in the White House and shortly following his inauguration: "A perfectly stupid race can never rise to a very high plane; the Negro, for instance, has been kept down as much by lack of intellectual development as by anything else."[14]

Not content to suffer the views of President Theodore Roosevelt (and the acquiescence to such views by so-called black leaders such as Booker T. Washington), Du Bois sought to challenge both the status quo and the belief that because blacks were inferior they should not seek social and intellectual advancement with the publication of *The Souls of Black Folk* in 1903. Du Bois opened *The Souls of Black Folk* with a searing assessment of what it meant to be a black American living in a world dominated by whites. In the thought-provoking essay "Of Our Spiritual Strivings" Du Bois confronted head-on the notion that blacks derived their identify and self-worth only as a reflection of how whites allowed them to be perceived:

> After the Egyptian and Indian, the Greek and Roman, the Teuton and Mongolian, the Negro is a sort of seventh son, born with a veil, and gifted with second-sight in this American world,—a world which yields him no true self-consciousness, but only lets him see himself through the revelation of the other world. It is a peculiar sensation, this double-consciousness, this sense of always looking at one's self through the eyes of others, of measuring one's soul by the tape of a world that looks on in amused contempt and pity. One ever feels his twoness,—an American, a Negro; two warring souls, two thoughts, two unreconciled strivings; two warring ideals in one dark body, whose dogged strength alone keeps it from being torn asunder. The history of the American Negro is the history of this strife,—this longing to attain self-conscious manhood, to merge his double self into a better and truer self.[15]

The "twoness" doctrine Du Bois unveiled in "Of Our Spiritual Strivings"—the warring ideals within a black body exposing a duality of consciousness—is a concept that has poignantly captured the feelings of isolation and exclusion felt by many African-Americans for more than one hundred years. Ralph Ellison, for one, would draw upon Du Bois's quest for African-Americans to seek identity and self-consciousness from their own accomplishments and achievements rather than through the distorted prism of their self-worth offered by whites—an effort that led Ellison to publish *Invisible Man* in 1953, to critical success. The novel documents the struggles for identity encountered by African-Americans in the early twentieth century.*

The concept of racial twoness put forth by Du Bois was both radical and transformative because of the manner in which he sought to unshackle the perceptions of both blacks and whites as they confronted issues of race. For whites, he fought to dispel the notion that blacks were racially inferior and could only derive validation in life through what whites sanctioned were proper activities and vocations for blacks to pursue. For blacks, Du Bois's message was equally revolutionary: draw self-worth from your own accomplishments and actions without looking to whites or others for validation. The color of black accomplishment for Du Bois did not require a reflection of worthiness first reflected from a white image of success. Taking steps to enrich one's life through education and hard work, Du Bois would undoubtedly agree, wasn't acting white—instead it was acting properly to step farther away from the bonds of slavery toward a world of equality and personal fulfillment.

If Du Bois used allegorical references and imagery to argue for racial equality in "Of Our Spiritual Strivings," he also systematically dissected and debunked much of the conventional wisdom held about blacks and their station in American society in the early twentieth century in another essay from *The Souls of Black Folk,* "Of Mr. Booker T. Washington and Others."

---

* Several of the characters in *Invisible Man* are based upon many of the black leaders at the dawn of the twentieth century. Dr. Bledsoe, the principal of a school that is clearly the Tuskegee Institute, is a thinly disguised Booker T. Washington, while the narrator's quest for education and equality echoes the sentiments expressed by W. E. B. Du Bois.

Finally, in the aftermath of his rejection for the educational position in Washington, D.C., Du Bois publicly broke with the man who was once his colleague in the quest for blacks to assimilate more freely in American society. Rather than accept the prevailing wisdom that Booker T. Washington spoke for all black people, W.E.B. Du Bois instead chose to directly—and publicly—challenge the racist assertion that blacks were intellectually incapable and inferior to whites in American society.

Moreover, the essay was the most prominent and pointed rebuttal in the public domain challenging the notion that blacks who sought a higher education to move them away from the fields and into the cities and a better life were doing nothing more than acting white. That Du Bois would confront Washington and his supporters in such a direct and public manner is not to be overlooked or considered trivial or insignificant. Many members of the leading white establishment—politicians, newspapermen, philanthropists, and corporate titans—viewed Washington as the titular head of black America.

As such, Du Bois's essay criticizing Washington's policies of accommodation would be the modern-day equivalent of a young up-and-coming black intellectual castigating either Jesse Jackson or Al Sharpton for daring to allegedly speak on behalf of all black people at the dawn of the twenty-first century. Not only would either reverend take public (rather than private) exception to that remark, many in the contemporary American media and in corporate boardrooms would shake their heads at the audacity of articulating a broadside against the conventional wisdom that Sharpton or Jackson *didn't* speak for all black Americans—a myth that they themselves have not only bought into but have perpetuated and one that is nothing short of fraudulent.

Recognizing the daunting nature of his task, Du Bois first observed that

> Mr. Washington's cult has gained unquestioning followers, his work has wonderfully prospered, his friends are legion, and his enemies are confounded. To-day he stands as the one recog-

nized spokesman of his ten million fellows, and one of the most notable figures in a nation of seventy million. One hesitates, therefore, to criticize a life which, beginning with so little, has done so much.[16]

This hesitation was momentary, and Du Bois immediately delved into the heart of his critique of Washington's philosophy that accommodation was the best path forward to eradicate the stain of slavery that had darkened the American consciousness and strained relations between her black and white citizens. Of Washington, Du Bois wrote, "[He] represents in Negro thought the old attitude of adjustment and submission; but adjustment at such a peculiar time as to make his programme unique."[17] And Du Bois does not only criticize Washington for serving as the perceived leader of blacks in the minds of white establishment but for being

> The leader not of one race but of two—a compromiser between the South, the North and the Negro. Naturally, the Negroes resented, at first, bitterly, signs of compromise which surrendered their civil and political rights, even though this was to be exchanged for larger chances of economic development.[18]

This passage is particularly bold in its pronouncements about Washington's leadership on two distinct levels. First, media accounts surrounding Washington's Atlanta Compromise speech had been nearly universal in their praise for his position of black accommodation and submission toward whites; Du Bois overtly and systematically rejected this philosophy on its face. Perhaps more revealing, Du Bois articulated in a very public forum resentment felt by many blacks against Washington's leadership and bitterness toward his unilateral decision to reject black advancement and civil rights in favor of Washington's personal elevation in status. There was an alternative path forward in Du Bois's view, a path that would lead to greater freedom and assimilation for blacks in twentieth-century society through a demand for political power, insistence on civil rights, and a push for black children to reap the benefits provided through higher education.

This three-pronged assault on Washington's acquiescent and accommodating leadership, which placed blacks as the subservient inferiors of whites, would serve as a rallying call for Du Bois and his supporters to forge a new direction for African-American success. Closing out "Of Mr. Booker T. Washington and Others," Du Bois issued the following clarion call to supporters and detractors of the Tuskegee wizard:

> But so far as Mr. Washington apologizes for injustice, North or South, does not rightly value the privilege and duty of voting, belittles the emasculating effects of caste distinctions, and opposes the higher training and ambition of our brighter minds—so far as he, the South, or the Nation, does this—we must unceasingly and firmly oppose them. By every civilized and peaceful method we must strive for the rights which the world accords to men, clinging unwaveringly to those great words which the sons of the Founders would fain forget: "We hold these truths to be self evident: That all men are created equal; that they are endowed by their Creator with certain unalienable rights; that among these are life, liberty and the pursuit of happiness.[19]

That Washington was the most prominent and well-known black man in America in 1903 was unquestioned. That Du Bois would elect to publicly and forcefully break ranks with the ideological and political leadership of Booker T. Washington would reverberate in black and white communities across the country. The punishment against Du Bois for seeking to change the status quo of Washington's belief of black inferiority—believed by many whites in the North and South alike—was swift. While Washington's heroic autobiography *Up from Slavery* had received lavish attention in the press just two years before, many in the white political and academic elite circles sought to dismiss or ignore Du Bois's publication of *The Souls of Black Folk* in 1903. Du Bois's alleged transgression? Daring to eradicate the stigma, perpetuated by Washington and his supporters, that a black person seeking equality through access to the ballot box, civil rights, and a quality education was nothing more than a black person acting white.

Many in the media who upheld Washington's model of black subservience and accommodation toward whites met *The Souls of Black Folk* with indifference, if not outright hostility. The *Nashville American* claimed in a review: "This book is indeed dangerous for the Negro to read," while a reviewer from the *Houston Chronicle* urged authorities to indict Du Bois for "inciting rape."[20] Even *The New York Times* criticized Du Bois for his work and accused him of undertaking a pursuit that would allow him to "smoke a cigar and drink a cup of tea with the white man in the South."[21] Once again, Du Bois's efforts were summarily dismissed as those of a black man seeking to act white rather than seen as those of a man pursuing an effort to transform the dream of blacks to act as equal and free participants in American society into reality.

A new day had dawned, a new line had been drawn in the sand, and no longer would America have one voice that spoke on behalf of the political and social direction blacks would pursue in the days to follow. Despite the widespread denunciation of *The Souls of Black Folk* in white media outlets, Du Bois had lent voice and strength to the views held by many African-Americans across the country. The AME (African Methodist Episcopal Church) *Christian Recorder,* an African-American publication in Philadelphia, hailed Du Bois's effort as possessing "penetration of thought and a glow of eloquence that is almost unexampled in the literature of the Negro question," while Cincinnati's black publication *Ohio Enterprise* commented that *The Souls of Black Folk* "should be read and studied by every person, white and black."[22]

Perhaps the most touching tribute to Du Bois's work would come from Jessie Fauset, a black Cornell University English major who proclaimed that "[w]e have needed someone to voice the intricacies of the blind maze of thought and action along which the modern educated colored man or woman struggles."[23] Or, perhaps more prophetically, blacks needed a strong black leader to challenge them by declaring that applied study in pursuit of a higher education wasn't acting white, it was acting properly to advance in an evolving American society.

July 30, 1903, AME Zion Church, Boston, Massachusetts: a mere three weeks had passed since Booker T. Washington had hosted W. E. B. Du Bois in his home for dinner in Tuskegee, and it was only months following the publication of *The Souls of Black Folk,* where Du Bois publicly broke ranks with Washington. Now, thousands of miles away from home, Washington, the great orator, strode slowly to the stage, standing amid the throngs who had gathered that sweltering evening to hear him speak. The evening started off like so many others for Washington as he stood before his people to preach the gospel of industrial education and accommodation that had catapulted him to prominence and fortune.

Several thousand people—both black and white—packed the pews to hear Washington that evening, including prominent politicians, university presidents, and other civic leaders. Rather than observe a vintage performance from the wizard of Tuskegee, members of the audience instead witnessed the first cracks in the glass ceiling—a ceiling constructed by Washington and his followers—that allowed him and him alone to represent black America to whites and members of his race. Before Washington could take the stage, a fight broke out, chairs were hurled about, and jeers and catcalls cascaded upon Booker T. Washington rather than the praise to which he was well accustomed.

An astonished white reporter covering the event heard words such as, "We don't like you" and "Your views and aims are not what we sympathize with or think best for our race."[24] The event, later described as the "Boston riot," was a pivotal moment in the newly emerging civil rights movement for blacks. As described by the Du Bois biographer Lewis: "[When] the scrimmaging finally stopped, and when the savior of his people was able to speak, it was clear that he had nothing new to say."[25] Publication of *The Souls of Black Folk* sparked new discussion and fueled new debates about how black people could conduct themselves in society while maintaining their dignity and fighting for political power, civil rights, and a quality education. The impact of the battle at Old

North Bridge in Concord, Massachusetts, on April 19, 1775, was a key turning point in the American Revolutionary War, about which Ralph Waldo Emerson famously wrote,

> *Here once the embattled farmers stood,*
> *And fired the shot heard 'round the world.*[26]

But the new shot heard round the world was from the AME Zion Church in Boston, Massachusetts, and on the evening of July 30, 1903, announced a turning point not just in the style and substance of how blacks would advocate for equality in American society. No longer would blacks be content to uniformly follow the vision of one man, however great, especially one who called for blacks to be subservient and accommodating members of society rather than equal participants in it.

Even Washington recognized that the strong gravitational pull of his leadership and alleged representation of black people in America was warning quickly and significantly following publication of *The Souls of Black Folk*. Eager to mend any perceived rift in his power, Washington reached out in September 1903 to his patron, President Theodore Roosevelt, to dispel any notion of unrest or erosion of his leadership. Of the Boston riot, Washington would famously tell the president that he

> was "sorry that the matter had caused [Roosevelt] any concern"; reports were "very much exaggerated"; his attackers were "artificial" men "graduates of New England colleges." But the president should know that the "rank and file" colored people loved and supported them both.[27]

This is rather revealing in two distinct ways. First, Washington sought to calm any fears the president may have had about their singular and collective standing within the black community. Here Washington assures the president that the "rank and file" of colored people loved and supported them both. Was public support and standing more important to Washington than constructive criticism on how best to move black people forward at the dawn of the twentieth century?

Second, unlike Washington's rather flip assertion that *Souls* represented the interest of a few misguided souls from New England academia, *The Souls of Black Folk* breathed new life, fire, and determination into a people that had known hostility and oppression for so long and that had been "represented" by one thinker who did not have their full economic, social, and political views in mind. Civic and academic leaders, fearful of advocating an ideological and philosophical path by which blacks could attain success that differed from that dictated from Tuskegee, now found support and strength to discuss new alternatives for gaining black equality in American society.

As a result, the first significant black organized protest movement of the twentieth century in the United States was formed to combat racism and discrimination in a more confrontational manner. The movement would stake its claim for black advancement in the classroom and reject the ceding of the "ivory tower" to the white world.

Emboldened by the reception of *The Souls of Black Folk* by black and white audiences alike, Du Bois would continue to press for black equality and opportunity for success through social, political, and educational advancement. Many Americans could well articulate the beliefs of Booker T. Washington, but W. E. B. Du Bois's name was slowly gaining stature and recognition among members of its broad audience.

Du Bois followed up on *The Souls of Black Folk* with *Credo* in 1904, published in the periodical *The Independent. Credo* offered a shorter yet more crystallized notion of what it meant to be a man, either white or black, at the beginning of the twentieth century. The seventh and most-well-known paragraph of his short manifesto reads in part:

I believe in Liberty, for all men; the space to stretch their arms and their souls; the right to breathe and the right to vote, the freedom to choose their friends, enjoy the sunshine and ride on the railroads, uncursed by color; thinking, dreaming, working as they will in a kingdom of God and love.

I believe in the training of children, black even as white; the leading out of little souls into the green pastures and beside the still waters, not for self of peace, but for Life . . . [28]

In clear, precise language Du Bois asserted—to the consternation of Washington and his supporters—that the right to vote, travel unencumbered, and receive a quality education were not the attributes of acting white but the trademarks of acting in harmony and equality with fellow Americans regardless of the color of one's skin.

Over time, with the republication of *Credo*, the manifesto gained acceptance, as Lewis notes: "They would hang 'Credo' on their living room walls after Du Bois included it in *Darkwater* sixteen years later, just as their grandchildren would mount 'I Have a Dream' on theirs."[29] The notoriety garnered by the publication of *The Souls of Black Folk* and *Credo* in 1903 and 1904 laid the groundwork for a revolutionary gathering of twenty-nine men and one teenage boy with Du Bois shortly thereafter that would forever change the civil rights landscape of America.

July 11, 1905: Two years following the publication of *The Souls of Black Folk*, W. E. B. Du Bois assembled a group of twenty-nine well-known anti-Washington leaders on the Canadian side of the Niagara Falls to form the Niagara Movement, dedicated to the location and the "mighty current" of protest they sought to unleash. Rather than remain content with the status quo of blacks remaining separate and unequal, the Niagara Movement sought to bring about momentous social and cultural change by lobbying against Jim Crow while encouraging young blacks to aspire to form a Talented Tenth of educated elders to lead the march toward equality.

The irony that the first significant civil rights gathering took place on the Ontario (Canada) side of the Niagara Falls at Fort Erie was not lost on Du Bois and his pioneers. The fact that an American hotel refused them accommodations for what would prove to be a historic meeting was significant in and of itself. The notion that Booker T. Washington could exert significant influence with the publishers of African-American newspapers and periodicals to stifle reportage of the first gathering of the

Niagara Movement spoke volumes about the security of the Tuskegee wizard's monolithic grasp on the mantle of black leadership in America.

A new day had dawned in America on July 12, 1905—a day following a series of meetings between African-American leaders convening outside their country, where they had declared war on the notion that exercising political power through the ballot box, pushing for equality through nascent civil rights efforts, and ensuring the highest quality of education for black children was acting white. Instead, the day had come when the rights enshrined within the Bill of Rights of the Constitution applied to all Americans, regardless of the color of their skin.

The roar of the Niagara Movement led to the formation of the National Association for the Advancement of Colored People, which provided leadership to attain the goals sought and articulated by Du Bois. The very group Du Bois helped found in the 1909 Conference on the Status of the Negro would work tirelessly to overturn the onerous separate but equal doctrine established by *Plessy v. Ferguson* in 1896, chiefly through the efforts of a young lawyer hired some fifty years later. That the lawyer in question would go on to become the first African-American elevated to the United States Supreme Court is impressive in and of itself. That a group of pioneers fought against the ironclad strength and influence of one black man who proclaimed to speak for millions at the turn of the twentieth century and laid the groundwork for generations of black Americans to exercise the right to vote and unleash their intellectual prowess to achieve their dreams through a quality education is one of the most resonant legacies W. E. B. Du Bois has given his country. That the roar of the Niagara Movement is still heard today to remind black students that it is not acting white but acting right to take affirmative steps to fulfill their dreams at the dawn of the twenty-first century is nothing short of remarkable.

5

The Rise of Marcus Garvey versus the Roar of the Niagara Movement

Who Best to Lead Blacks Forward at the Dawn of the Harlem Renaissance?

. . .

Marcus Garvey was the first man of color in the history of the United States to lead and develop a mass movement. He was the first man, on a mass scale, and level, to give millions of Negroes a sense of dignity and destiny, and make the Negro feel that he was somebody.

DR. MARTIN LUTHER KING JR., *Kingston, Jamaica, 1965*[1]

The roar of the Niagara Movement, led by W. E. B. Du Bois, would soon make way for the new social and cultural transformation of the roaring twenties in the United States. Before America would celebrate the end of World War I with dance, jazz music, and the proliferation of new technology such as automobiles and radio, an important battle was yet to take place over the manner in which blacks would seek to achieve freedom and equality and the direction they would take to do so.

Just prior to the Harlem Renaissance—a cultural revolution that challenged white paternalism and racism while celebrating black dignity and creativity in literature, music, philosophy, and intellectual pursuits—a new revolution unfolded that pitted the established black leadership and goals articulated by Du Bois against the fiery rhetoric of the immigrant Marcus Garvey, who came to the United States from Jamaica. Amid the backdrop of a Harlem that found new strength celebrating black culture and that distinguished black accomplishments as separate and distinct from those of whites in their intellectual achievements, Garvey and Du Bois would engage in an increasingly divisive campaign to set the compass and steer the moral, cultural, and political path blacks would follow at this pivotal point in American history. At the same time, the initial professional respect established between the two leaders would eventually devolve along racial lines in a discord not dissimilar to the conflicting viewpoints held between Du Bois and Booker T. Washington over a decade earlier. Once again, one man would extol the virtues of blacks having an equal opportunity to receive a proper education as a tool to success in America while his adversary would essentially decry such intellectual advancement as the province of whites and denigrate blacks who sought such an opportunity for acting white.

We begin our inquiry into two strong black leaders who grappled for the mantle of leadership in the late teens and early 1920s in America with the contrast between Du Bois's call for education and his Talented Tenth movement and Marcus Garvey's call for the self-segregation and unity of all blacks of African descent that would culminate in the return of these descendents to the African continent, where they would resettle separate from the evils and prejudices inflicted upon blacks by whites. As for Du Bois and his belief that education and activism would ameliorate the conditions of blacks, Garvey would ultimately refer to Du Bois as "purely and simply a white man's nigger."[2]

Malcus Mosiah "Marcus" Garvey Jr. was born at Saint Ann's Bay, Jamaica, on August 17, 1887. Born into poverty, Garvey received little formal educational training. As a young man, Garvey began work as a printer's apprentice, a training and skill set that eventually placed Garvey in the printing department of P.A. Benjamin Manufacturing Company in Kingston, Jamaica.

In 1910, Garvey was elected assistant secretary of the National Club of Jamaica—the same year in which he would publish a pamphlet called *The Struggling Masses.* After several years abroad traveling throughout Central America and England, Garvey became convinced that the only way for blacks to ameliorate their condition and break free of the chains of oppression brought forth by discrimination was for blacks around the world to unite.

To help accomplish this goal, Garvey would create the Universal Negro Improvement Association (UNIA) and the African Communities League (ACL) in August 1914. The mission of the group, soon to be known simply as UNIA, was to unify all blacks from around the world by expelling whites from territories to be determined in Africa, where blacks could form their own society. Ironically, Garvey was very much inspired by the work of Booker T. Washington, an inspiration that led Garvey to write Washington seeking his assistance in establishing an industrial institute in Jamaica modeled on the Tuskegee Institute, where blacks of African descent could be taught the skills necessary to support themselves.

Later that year (1914), Washington extended Garvey an invitation to visit him in Tuskegee—an invitation that was never accepted because of Washington's death in 1915. Undeterred by Washington's death, Garvey set his sights on the United States and set sail from Jamaica, arriving in New York City in March of 1916. Working as a printer by day, Garvey would deliver his first public lecture about his new vision and direction for blacks at Saint Mark's Church in lower Manhattan on May 9, 1916. Shortly thereafter, Garvey embarked on a yearlong, thirty-eight state tour, where he sought to galvanize money and support for his mission.

To this point, Garvey's speaking tour of the United States had generated relatively little publicity and interest. With the death of Washington, Du Bois was arguably the best-known black man in America, and his Talented Tenth movement and call for education as a path to emancipation through voting rights and political power was widely accepted as the path forward for many blacks to achieve success in America. To this end, as Robert A. Hill and Barbara Bair would note in *Marcus Garvey, Life and Lessons:*

When the UNIA was organized in Harlem in February 1918, its Jamaican leader merged not only with representatives from the New Negro, but with another minority: from the perspective of America's polyglot of ethnic groups, Garvey was simply one more immigrant voice.[3]

Garvey's voice would not be lost in the din and clamor for long; Garvey would launch the *Negro World* newspaper in January 1918, a periodical that served both as the voice for the UNIA and Marcus Garvey himself. By mid-1919, *Negro World* was widely distributed, and the UNIA had established more than thirty chapters across the United States and abroad and had an estimated membership of two million people. Suddenly the immigrant from Jamaica was beginning to gain traction with his message of self-segregation and of a return to the African continent. As money flowed into the UNIA's coffers from blacks living in America and abroad, Garvey's voice and vision were becoming entities to be reckoned with.

In 1919, Garvey decided to found the Black Star Line, a shipping company he hoped would transport black passengers and cargo throughout the Caribbean to the African continent. The name of the shipping company was deliberate: the White Star Line, was the owner of the famous R.M.S. *Titanic* that had catered to an exclusively white, privileged clientele—the "unsinkable ship" that had had only one black family aboard for its maiden and final voyage. The Black Star Line, by contrast, would cater to black business and be manned by a black crew. In an autobiographical essay, Garvey would reveal the following:

The Black Star Steamship Corporation that I organized in 1919 . . . was the great attraction that brought to the Universal Negro Improvement Association millions of supporters from Central America, South America, Africa and the West Indies.

The idea became immediately popular—that of having ships. The Negroes of the West Indies, Central America and Africa could better appreciate the scheme of steamships than the Negroes of America. . . . It was not until after the first ship, the S.S. Yarmouth, afterwards christened "Frederick Douglass," was launched in New York that the American Negroes got to know what it was all about, and subscribed speedily their quota to help purchase the other ships.[4]

Black ships, black commerce, black communion, and black exclusion of whites from their enterprise were the essence of the commercial and political empire Garvey sought to build. Instead of seeking to act as equals of whites in American society, Garvey and his growing supporters sought racial parity and racial exclusion simultaneously. With more than two million members as part of the UNIA and millions of dollars at Garvey's disposal, many of America's elite—both black and white—began to follow Garvey and his activities more closely.

In 1920, Garvey would be at the apex of his rapid trajectory of power and influence in black America. With Du Bois and his NAACP watching carefully, Garvey would famously take to the streets of Harlem on August 1, 1920, to participate in an event where he gathered more than 25,000 blacks of African descent from around the world to march, congregate, and wind their way to Madison Square Garden, where Garvey would unveil his famous call to action for the UNIA.

The events leading up to the UNIA convention would reveal a perceived slight from Du Bois toward Garvey that would forever poison their relationship. For his part, Garvey invited Du Bois to participate in the gathering and expected that Du Bois would attend. From his autobiographical essay, Garvey would note in regard to Du Bois's demurring to attend that "Dr. Du Bois in his reply suggested contempt more than anything else. . . . This, in my mind, eliminated [him] . . . from serious race leadership in America."[5] As we shall see, the comity that existed between the two men later erupted into a very nasty and public dispute. At this point in time, however, Garvey's UNIA convention and the actions taken there transformed him from a charismatic and emerging leader of blacks in America to a figure regarded suspiciously by whites and blacks around the world who held a strong degree of mistrust about his true intentions.

At approximately eleven o'clock on the evening of August 1, 1920, Garvey opened the UNIA convention by infamously proclaiming: "Four hundred million Negroes were sharpening their swords for the next world war."[6] Even far from Madison Square Garden Garvey's words were electrifying both for whites weary from the impact of World War I that had just concluded and for blacks in America seeking racial equality with whites rather than armed conflict. Later reflecting on his ill choice of words, Garvey would observe:

> Among all the things I said these words were taken out and cabled to every capital in Europe and throughout the world. The next morning every first class newspaper proclaimed me as the new leader of the Negro race and featured the unfortunate words I used. Words which have been making trouble for me since 1920.[7]

While Garvey's call to arms for 400 million blacks was controversial, the UNIA bill of rights adopted during the ten-day convention would create a level of consternation and concern for black and white leaders in America.

The following four items are merely an illustrative representation of the more than forty rights and entitlements Garvey sought for all blacks of African descent, which alarmed black and white leaders in America about his true aims and intentions:

> That we believe in the supreme authority of our race in all things racial; that all things are created and given to man as a common possession . . . and in consideration of the [fact] that as a race we are now deprived of those things that are morally and legally ours, we believe it is right that all such things should be acquired and held by whatever means possible . . .

We declare that Negroes, [wherever] they found a community among themselves, should be given the right to elect their own representatives to represent them in legislatures, courts of law, or such institutions as may exercise control over that particular community . . .

We believe in the freedom of Africa for the Negro people of the world, and by the principle of Europe for the Europeans, and Asia for the Asiatics, we also demand Africa for the Africans at home and abroad . . .

We declare that the teaching in any school by alien teachers to our boys and girls, that the alien race is superior to the Negro race, is an insult to the Negro people of the world.[8]

Suddenly the eloquent yet self-proclaimed leader of blacks around the world had taken a more militant, aggressive, and even sinister tone in his demands for equality. Africa for Africans—with Ethiopia serving as the ancestral homeland—separate elective representation, and the declaration of white teachers as aliens were just the tip of the iceberg of policies advocated by Garvey and his now infamous UNIA that caused black and white leaders to have reservations.

For its part, the Department of Justice would quietly initiate an investigation into Garvey's activities, led by a young but aggressive agent within the United States Bureau of Investigation—a precursor to the modern FBI—by the name of J. Edgar Hoover. Hoover's infiltration of the UNIA would lead to a controversial investigation and prosecution that would eventually lead to Garvey's imprisonment and deportation from the United States years later. For now, however, the overt neutrality and benign treatment of Garvey by those within the NAACP and Du Bois would end—the last thing the leaders of the nascent Niagara Movement wanted was an overt battle with white America for equal rights through self-segregation.

Instead, Du Bois and his followers sought the freedom to act equally as whites through the strength derived through education, civil rights, and political power. Garvey's militant call to action by 400 million Negroes to begin the next world war coupled with his views on segregation and assimilation in a society free from rather than inclusive of whites was too much for the more moderate black leaders to tolerate. The gloves were about to come off, and the fight for the fulcrum of power for black leadership and direction was about to begin in the shadows of Harlem, just before her celebrated renaissance of black intellectual, cultural, and political power.

Despite Garvey's assertions that Du Bois had been contemptuous and dismissive of him, there is little in the record to indicate that Du Bois had publicly or privately disagreed with Garvey over the creation of UNIA. In an essay published in his periodical *The Crisis* from February 1928, Du Bois observed that five articles had been written that featured Marcus Garvey and that the first two were written in March 1920 (before the Africa for Africans speech) and the second was written in January 1921. Contrary to Garvey's assertions that Du Bois had denigrated his work early on, Du Bois points to the summation of the article written in 1921, where he offered the following thoughts and words of advice to Garvey—some six months following Garvey's convention in New York City:

> To sum up, Garvey is a sincere, hard-working idealist; he is also a stubborn, domineering leader of the mass; he has worthy industrial and commercial schemes but he is an inexperienced business man. His dreams of Negro industry, commerce and the ultimate freedom of Africa are feasible; but his methods are bombastic, wasteful, illogical and ineffective and almost illegal. If he learns by experience, attracts strong and capable friends and helpers instead of making needless enemies; if he gives up secrecy and suspicion and substitutes open and frank reports as to his income and expenses, and above all if he is willing to be a

co-worker and not a czar he may yet in time succeed in at least starting some of his schemes toward accomplishment. But unless he does these things and does them quickly he cannot escape failure.[9]

While objectively critical, Du Bois's assessment offers praise and constructive advice as to how the inexperienced young leader could take the necessary steps to achieve his stated goals.

Du Bois's assessment of Garvey from 1921 stands in stark contrast to the feelings held by Garvey toward the NAACP leader at the time of his UNIA convention in 1920, where his bill of rights were unveiled. In his biographical essay regarding his relationship with Du Bois, it is clear that Garvey believed Du Bois viewed him as a threat to the tenure and legitimacy of the NAACP:

> . . . But the hypocrisy of Dr. Du Bois was made manifest in that he no doubt under-rated the success of the Universal Negro Improvement Association at the time when he answered the invitation of the First Convention, but after the movement became established and regarded as more than a serious competitor of the N.A.A.C.P he started to oppose the movement with might and main. We are able to get on without the aid of Dr. Du Bois and the leaders of his stamp.[10]

The competing visions and leadership of the men would not turn publicly acrimonious until the following year, after Garvey's overt solicitousness toward the Ku Klux Klan. Garvey maintained that the Klan was overt about their true intentions whereas many white Americans purported to be favorably inclined toward blacks, but their words were betrayed by their deeds. In the September 1922 issue of *The Crisis*, Du Bois took exception to Garvey's embrace of the KKK and publicly denounced the leader of the UNIA by first reprinting Garvey's words and then criticizing them in the following editorial:

"The white race can best help the Negro by telling him the truth, and not by flattering him into believing that he is as good as any white man."

Concerning this we said:

Not even Tom Dixon or Ben Tillman* or the hatefullest enemies of the Negro has ever stooped to a more vicious campaign than Marcus Garvey, sane or insane, is carrying on. He is not attacking white prejudice, he is groveling before it and applauding it; his only attack is on men of his own race who are striving for freedom; his only contempt is for Negroes; his only threats are for black blood.[11]

Thus the two men were a competing set of leaders with contrasting ideological views on the present and future equality of blacks in America. Marcus Garvey believed in the industrious nature of blacks, but not their equality. W. E. B. Du Bois, on the other hand, believed that black integration and equality with whites would occur once blacks had established a strong baseline of knowledge through education. With the rhetorical gloves dropped, the conflict between Garvey and Du Bois would publicly escalate over the years, until Garvey's imprisonment and ultimate deportation from the United States to Jamaica by President Calvin Coolidge in 1928.

Whether conscious of it or not, Du Bois must have taken exception to the manner in which Garvey essentially accused him of seeking to act or become white. In *Sellout: The Politics of Racial Betrayal* Randall Kennedy discusses the conflict between the two men in strictly racial terms.

---

* Thomas Dixon Jr. was a North Carolina politician and author who held blacks in contempt during Reconstruction and afterward. He wrote a popular novel called *The Clansman*, which served as the inspiration for the 1915 film *The Birth of a Nation*. Ben Tillman was a segregationist senator and governor from South Carolina who famously stated: "We of the South have never recognized the right of the Negro to govern white men, and we never will. We have never believed him to be the equal of the white man, and we will not submit to his gratifying his lust on our wives and daughters without lynching him."

For one, he asserts, Garvey was quick to frame issues and perceived conflicts in terms of racial treachery and/or betrayal. In a direct affront to Du Bois's call for education as a means of empowerment, Kennedy points out that Garvey distrusted those blacks who had been educated or sought to do so. Garvey lamented the role of black intellectuals:

> Garvey maintained, "The traitors among the Negro race are generally to be found among the men highest placed in education and society, the fellows who call themselves leaders." . . . The purpose of most Negro intellectuals, he scoffed, "is to deceive the less fortunate of his race, and, by his wiles ride easily into position and wealth at their expense."[12]

That Garvey, who had little formal educational training, would consider those of the highest education and stature in society traitors must not have been well received by the first black man to earn a Ph.D. from Harvard University and believed that black emancipation and equality would occur through a dedicated study of arts and letters.

Garvey escalated his rhetoric against Du Bois by asserting that Du Bois disliked black people, was inauthentically black, and in fact sought to be white in a scathing editorial published in New York City on February 13, 1923, entitled "W.E. Burghardt Du Bois as a Hater of Dark People"—"Calls Own Race 'Black and Ugly,' Judging from White Man's Standard of Beauty: Trick of National Association for the Advancement of Colored People to Solve Problem by Assimilation and Color Distinction."[13]

Any pretext that Garvey viewed Du Bois as being authentically black is dashed by the repeated assertions that Du Bois acted white to curry favor with and for his benefactors while turning his back on fellow blacks. While the notion of being authentically black is a topic and concept we shall discuss in greater length in chapters to follow, for the present we shall confine our examination to the manner in which Garvey repeatedly accuses Du Bois of seeking to act and be white as his ultimate aspiration instead of seeking to elevate the black people he ostensibly led.

To this end, Garvey launched his attacks on Du Bois in the opening paragraph of an editorial where he lambasted the NAACP head:

> This "unfortunate mulatto," who bewails every day the drop of Negro blood in his veins, being sorry that he is not Dutch or French, has taken upon himself the responsibility of criticizing and condemning other people while holding himself up as the social "unapproachable" and the great "I AM" of the Negro race.[14]

Garvey's fury was sparked by an article Du Bois published in *Century* magazine entitled "Back to Africa" that was published the same month as Garvey's fierce retort, February 1923. Garvey had taken particular exception to Du Bois's description of him as a "little, fat black man, ugly, but with intelligent eyes and a big head."[15] The remainder of Du Bois's piece is a systematic refutation to Garvey's arrival in America, his work in establishing the UNIA, and Du Bois's disdain for the effort to solve America's race problems by retreating to Africa to establish a new homeland. Du Bois continued his missive by condemning Garvey for seeking to address black advancement through self-segregation, for the ultimate failure of the Black Star Line, and for Garvey's failed attempt to establish a homeland for the UNIA in Liberia.

While the tone of Du Bois's "Back to Africa" article is dismissive and belittling of Garvey, Garvey's response in "W.E. Burghardt Du Bois as a Hater of Dark People" is an attack concentrated almost solely on Du Bois and based strictly on race; it asserts that one man seeks to act white while the other is authentically black.

For one, note the manner in which Garvey manipulates the title of his editorial to extrapolate that since Du Bois had referred to him as being dark and ugly, then Du Bois, in turn, viewed the entire black race as being such. Moving forward from this extrapolation, Garvey alleged:

So if there is any ugliness it is on the part of Du Bois and not on the part of the "little fat, black man with the big head," because all this description is typical of the African. But this only goes to show how much hate Du Bois has for the black blood in his veins. Anything that is black to him is ugly, is hideous, is monstrous, and this is why in 1917 he had but the lightest of colored people in his office, where one could hardly tell whether it was a white show or a colored vaudeville he was running on Fifth Avenue.

Escalating his rhetoric one step further, Garvey continued:

It is no wonder that Du Bois seeks the company of white people, because he hates blacks as being ugly. That is why he likes to dance with white people, and dine with them, and sometimes sleep with them, because from his way of seeing things all black is ugly, and all that is white is beautiful.[16]

For such words to be uttered during the height of the Black Power movement during the late 1960s and into the 1970s would have been controversial in and of itself. For such heated rhetoric as Garvey charges that Du Bois seeks to act, assimilate, and congregate with white people to be used during the early 1920s in America, where a black man's looking at a woman could lead to a lynching, is particularly explosive. At the same time, the insinuation that Garvey made about Du Bois in 1923 is as contentious then as it is today: a black man finding comfort in the company of whites is accused of loathing his own race while seeking to act and become white at the expense of the black race.

Further still, Garvey accused the head of the NAACP of using the nascent civil rights organization to cloak his hatred of blacks, allowing him to congregate in the company of whites. Garvey charged:

Yet this professor, who sees ugliness in being black, essays to be a leader of the Negro people and has been trying for over fourteen years to deceive them through his connection with the National

Association for the Advancement of Colored People. Now what does he mean by advancing colored people if he hates black so much? We can conclude in no other way than that it is in the direction of losing our black identity and becoming, as nearly as possible, the lowest whites by assimilation and miscegenation.[17]

Before we conclude our examination of Garvey's repeated charges that Du Bois had advanced his career by acting white while trying to gain favor with whites, it is important that we distinguish Garvey's comments above, which assert that Du Bois sought to dilute the black identity and persona in order to literally become white and that he accomplished this by equating education as the province of whites rather than blacks. Thus to be educated, like Du Bois, was to be white.

Late in his editorial, Garvey downplays the academic accomplishments of Du Bois and belittles the professor's formal training by comparing it to his own education derived from his impoverished upbringing. Garvey was prescient in his criticism of Du Bois for similar charges that would be leveled against black schoolchildren, particularly during the civil rights movement, but also in the present day: to excel in school and academic pursuits while black is to be accused of acting white. Consider Garvey's challenge:

Du Bois says that "Garvey has had no thorough education and a very hazy idea of the technique of civilization." Du Bois forgets that Garvey has challenged him over a dozen times to intellectual combat, and he has for as many times failed to appear. Garvey will back his education against that of Du Bois at any time in the day from early morning to midnight, and whether it be in the classroom or on the public platform will make him look like a dead duck on a frozen lake.[18]

The election to defer academic success with accomplishment while challenging an opponent to compete in a public forum is a recurrent theme that has hampered black academic progress to this day: black success in school is somehow inauthentic and only the province of whites. A true black could measure their value by overcoming adversity on the streets while demonstrating their authenticity away from the classroom rather than in it.

Garvey cemented his disdain for formal education as a method of advancement in society by stating:

> If Du Bois' education fits him for no better service than being a lackey for good white people, then it were better that Negroes were not educated. Du Bois forgets that the reason so much noise was made over him and his education was because he was among the first "experiments" made by white people on colored men along the lines of higher education. No one experimented with Marcus Garvey, so no one has to look upon him with surprise that he was able to master the classics and graduate from a university.[19]

Garvey's notion that receiving an education makes blacks the lackeys of whites and therefore is a worthless pursuit is an unfortunate and recurrent theme we shall encounter repeatedly in the pages that follow: learning in and succeeding at school is a practice that makes one inauthentically black and, worse, learning in school while black is trying to succeed by acting white.

For his part, Du Bois responded to the threat he perceived Garvey posed to the future direction of black leadership in America in an incisive article from *The Crisis* entitled "A Lunatic or a Traitor." From the opening lines of his editorial, Du Bois attacked Garvey:

> In the face, however, of the unbelievable depths of debasement and humiliation to which this demagog has descended in order to keep himself out of jail, it is our duty to say openly and clearly:
>
> Marcus Garvey is, without doubt, the most dangerous enemy of the Negro race in America and in the world. He is either a lunatic or a traitor.[20]

Du Bois based this assessment not only on the manner in which he felt Garvey had squandered hundreds of thousands of dollars for the failed Black Star Line but also on Garvey's insinuation that blacks would never be as good as or equal to whites. Here, Du Bois cited as evidence one line from a Garvey pamphlet that proclaimed: "The White Race Can Best Help the Negro by Telling Him the Truth, and Not by Flattering Him into Believing That He Is as Good as Any White Man."[21]

The NAACP and Du Bois sought an integrated society where blacks could assimilate as freely as whites through education, political power, and civil rights; Garvey openly advocated racial segregation and a return to Africa as the way for blacks to resolve the racial impasse in America. Du Bois believed in the power of an education as a way to free blacks from the oppressive constraints of segregation; Garvey believed that blacks receiving a formal education were serving as lackeys of whites—in essence, acting white. For these transgressions and the sense that Garvey was a threat to the American black during the Harlem Renaissance and resurgence of black academic, cultural, and political pride, Du Bois offered a damning pronouncement:

> I have been exposing white traitors for a quarter century. If the day has come when I cannot tell the truth about black traitors it is high time that I died.
>
> The American Negroes have endured this wretch all too long with fine restraint and every effort at cooperation and understanding. But the end has come. Every man who apologizes for or defends Marcus Garvey from this day forth writes himself down as unworthy of the countenance of decent Americans. As for Garvey himself, this open ally of the Ku Klux Klan should be locked up or sent home.[22]

Both of Du Bois's wishes regarding Marcus Garvey would soon come true: led by evidence collected by J. Edgar Hoover, Garvey was tried and convicted of mail fraud in connection with his stewardship of the Black

Star Line. Imprisoned in the Atlanta Federal Penitentiary in February 1925, he would remain in jail until President Calvin Coolidge pardoned Garvey in order to deport him back to Jamaica in November 1927. Marcus Garvey would never set foot in the United States again, but his legacy has permeated the black cultural consciousness to the present day. From *Invisible Man*'s enunciation of Garvey's Africa for Africans crusade and the adoption of black nationalism and Afrocentric ideology expressed by the novel's character Ras the Exhorter in Harlem to the invocation of Garvey's name by Dr. Martin Luther King Jr. to current hip-hop artists, Marcus Garvey's legacy remains.

Fortunately, the early efforts of W. E. B. Du Bois and the NAACP have had a more lasting impact on American culture—in particular the belief that blacks who seek to become equal participants in American society, armed with the knowledge gained through education, were acting responsibly. This stands in contrast to the belief of Marcus Garvey that such behavior made blacks the lackeys of whites—a belief in which blacks seeking to learn were accused of acting white.

6

Brown v. Board of Education

A Milestone to Equality

From the dark days of reconstruction to the midpoint of the twentieth century, the road to equality for blacks in America was marked with many detours on a steep climb to freedom. Once the Supreme Court codified the de jure discrimination faced by blacks into law in the *Plessy v. Ferguson* case, separate and inherently unequal accommodations for blacks became an accepted facet of life—accepted by both blacks and whites.

For some fifty-eight years following the *Plessy* decision, blacks could not legally enjoy a meal at the same lunch counters, attend class in the same schoolrooms across America, or even enjoy a drink of water from the same water fountain as whites. With the legal justification of separate and inherently unequal conditions set into place by the Supreme Court of the United States, blacks who sought to act as freely as whites in a society marked by discriminatory Jim Crow laws were often cruelly reprimanded . . . or worse.

The NAACP—the very group W. E. B. Du Bois helped establish in the 1909 Conference on the Status of the Negro—would work tirelessly to overturn the onerous separate but equal doctrine established by *Plessy v. Ferguson* in 1896. While the stalwart civil rights organization originally set its sights on forcing southern states to provide black children with schools and facilities that were comparably equal to whites, the group would not tackle the larger issues presented by *Plessy* until the 1930s.

Charles Hamilton Houston would emerge as one of the many heroes of the civil rights movement who was instrumental to the NAACP's fight to overturn the separate but equal doctrine. Interestingly, Houston had been born in 1895 just blocks away from the Supreme Court building where *Plessy v. Ferguson* would be argued before the high court the following year. Later Houston would earn his undergraduate degree from Amherst College and his law degree from Harvard University. Houston subsequently served as an artillery officer for the United States Army during World War I and the racial injustice he would witness toward black soldiers in France would fuel his desire to use the law to bring about societal change.[1]

Houston returned to Washington, D.C., following his educational training and military service to eventually become the vice dean of the Howard University School of Law in 1929. Beyond his work at Howard University, Houston would also serve as the head of the NAACP legal team, where he would challenge the validity of the separate but equal doctrine.

Known as "the man who killed Jim Crow," Houston was a skilled litigant and argued many of the significant civil rights cases before the Supreme Court between 1930 and his death in 1950. Houston's work would lay the cornerstone that would forever change the manner in which blacks and whites would interact with one another in American society. To this end, he undertook two significant steps to achieve an unthinkable result toward equality.

First, Houston left Howard University in 1934 to become the head of the NAACP Legal Defense Committee in New York City. In this capacity, Houston would travel throughout the South with a portable typewriter and a camera to document instances of discrimination and accommodations that were decidedly separate and inherently unequal toward blacks. These heroic efforts of documenting the discrimination and oppression facing blacks in the South were not without peril: a black man armed with a camera would prove no match to roving Klansmen intent on inflicting fear or far worse upon those who dared to challenge discriminatory Jim Crow policies. Fortunately, Houston was able to chronicle much of his travels through the South free from harm and to use the materials collected in subsequent court trials to dismantle segregation.

Perhaps most famously, Houston also recruited his star pupil from the Howard University School of Law, Thurgood Marshall, to join the Legal Defense Committee and assist the NAACP in their daunting mission to challenge the constitutionality of legalized discrimination. By 1939 Houston's protégé had taken over the reins as head of the legal team for the NAACP, and he began to challenge the legality of segregation in higher education. A decade later, in 1949, Marshall would accept five grade-school cases that directly challenged the legality of separate accommodations for black schoolchildren in a consolidated case that would become *Brown v. Board of Education*.[2]

While there are numerous individuals who worked tirelessly to bring the consolidated cases that became *Brown v. Board of Education* to the chambers of the Supreme Court, often forgotten in the historical record is the strength of the well-nuanced briefs filed and the fiery oratory of Thurgood Marshall and Robert Carter during oral arguments before the Court, which proved convincing. Moreover, the pair of litigants would receive critical assistance in their heroic efforts from a most unlikely pair of relatively obscure psychologists and from the daunting findings presented from their "doll test," which would ultimately sway the Court to overturn government-sanctioned discrimination in the form of separate but equal educational accommodations for blacks in the United States.

Much has been written about the courageous efforts of the NAACP and the many brave citizens who never relented in their ultimate goal of having the Supreme Court overturn the state-sanctioned discrimination brought about by the *Plessy* decision. We need not replicate much of that discussion here; much of our focus in *Acting White* thus far has examined the impact of the slur upon blacks in general and often the detrimental impact such discrimination has had upon children in particular. It is within this context and framework that we shall examine the desire of blacks to act freely in American society in late 1953 and early 1954 as the Supreme Court deliberated the facts and evidence presented them in *Brown v. Board of Education*.

Thus in both his written briefs and presentations before the Supreme Court, Thurgood Marshall powerfully and illustratively described the harm and devastating impact separate but equal was having upon black children seeking an equal opportunity to receive instruction in the classroom. Consider, for example, the following passionate exchange between Thurgood Marshall and Justices Felix Frankfurter and Stanley Reed during the oral arguments of *Brown*:

JUSTICE FRANKFURTER: I did not suppose that you would say that we had to open this case, that they were not equal, whether psychologically, whether buildings, whether they spent X million dollars for white, or X minus Y for the black, that that does not open any doctrine?

MR. MARSHALL: No, sir; and the Delaware case, if I can go to that without going outside of the record, demonstrates a situation more so than it does in South Carolina, because in Delaware so long as the schools are unequal, okay. And then the schools are made equal, and if I understand the procedure, you move the Negroes back to the colored school, and then next year you put ten more books in the white school, and the colored school is unequal, and I do not see how that point would ever be adequately decided, and in truth and in fact, there are no two equal schools, because there are not two equal faculties in the world in any schools.

They are good as individuals, and one is better than the other, but to just—that is the trouble with the doctrine of "separate but equal" assumes the two things can be equal. . . .

JUSTICE REED: There is not absolute equality, but substantially equal, in the terms of our cases.

MR. MARSHALL: Yes, sir; starting with Plessy the word "substantial" and we say in our brief—I mean we are absolutely serious about it—that the use of the word "substantial" emphasizes that those cases in truth and in fact amend the Fourteenth Amendment by saying that equal protection can be obtained in a substantially equal fashion, and there is nothing in the debates that will hint in the slightest that they did not mean complete equality—they said so—to raise the Negro up into the status of complete equality with the other people. That is language they used.

"Substantial" is a word that was put into the Fourteenth Amendment by Plessy v. Ferguson, and I cannot find it, and it cannot be found in any place in debates . . . [3]

While Marshall's brilliant written and oral presentations before the Court were instrumental in overturning the *Plessy* decision, the work of a relatively obscure husband-and-wife team of psychologists would also dramatically sway the Court regarding the negative impact segregation had upon black schoolchildren. The pair, Kenneth B. Clark and Mamie Clark, had created a self-awareness test they used to gauge the self-awareness and perception of young black schoolchildren.

The test was first used in the 1940s, and Kenneth Clark wrote a report in 1950 summarizing the results of the Clarks' findings for the White House Mid-Century Conference on Children and Youth. This is how the Library of Congress described the doll test in their online exhibition to commemorate the fiftieth anniversary of the *Brown* decision in 2004:

In the "doll test," psychologists Kenneth and Mamie Clark used four plastic, diaper-clad dolls, identical except for color. They showed the dolls to black children between the ages of three and seven and asked them questions to determine racial perception and preference. Almost all of the children readily identified the race of the dolls. However, when asked which they preferred, the majority selected the white doll and attributed positive characteristics to it. The Clarks also gave the children outline drawings of a boy and girl and asked them to color the figures the same color as themselves. Many of the children with dark complexions colored the figures with a white or yellow crayon. The Clarks concluded that "prejudice, discrimination, and segregation" caused black children to develop a sense of inferiority and self-hatred.[4]

As word of the doll test and the impact of its devastating psychological discovery that black children were being taught by society to loathe themselves reached the NAACP, three key members were quick to act to see and gauge the results of the test for themselves.

Accordingly, Thurgood Marshall and Robert Carter soon traveled with Kenneth Clark from New York City to Clarendon County, South Carolina, to assess whether the doll test could prove black children were being embedded with feelings of inferiority and self-hatred at the hands of the separate but equal doctrine that had been the law of the land for nearly sixty years.

For this particular investigation, Clark would test sixteen children, aged six to nine, at Scott's Branch, a joint elementary and high school for black children located within Clarendon County.[5] Sadly, Clarendon County would prove an ideal testing ground for Clark to conduct his experiment to demonstrate the psychological inferiority of black children with Marshall and Carter beside him: while there were nearly three times as many black students as whites in the county, spending for the education of whites accounted for nearly sixty percent of the available funds. Or, per capita spending for white children was $179 per year, while blacks received a paltry $43 per capita each year.[6]

In his award-winning account of the civil rights movement, *Eyes on the Prize,* the journalist and social commentator Juan Williams movingly describes the findings of this particular application of the doll test witnessed by Marshall and Carter:

> Clark tested sixteen black children, aged six to nine. Ten of the children looked at the black and white dolls Clark showed them and said they liked the white doll better. Eleven of them added that the black doll looked "bad." Nine of the youngsters said that the white doll looked "nice." While all the children stated correctly which doll was black and which was white, seven of the sixteen children said they saw themselves as the white doll.
>
> Clark recalls, "The most disturbing question—and the one that really made me, even as a scientist, upset—was the final question: 'Now show me the doll that's most like you.' Many of the children became emotionally upset when they had to identify with the doll that they had rejected. These children saw themselves as inferior and they accepted the inferiority as part of reality."[7]

Sadly, perhaps even the children themselves did not realize the depths of their perceived inferiority; how else to explain why they self-identified with being white as a *positive* development while they viewed themselves and blacks as being negative? Even more poignant is the manner in which the darker-complexion black children, when asked to shade in drawings the color closest to themselves, chose a white or yellow crayon rather than a brown or black color. It is striking that the children apparently didn't want only to act as freely as whites could by attending the same schools or engaging in society at large, they also wanted to be white, because being white had positive attributes and characteristics associated with it that being black in the 1950s did not.

Stunned by what they had seen, the NAACP lawyers knew that the Clark study could provide tangible and substantial evidence that separate could never be equal when it came to the manner in which black and white children were educated. The NAACP asked the Clarks to testify about their findings in several desegregation cases to highlight the psychological harm suffered by black children—including the *Briggs v. Elliott* and *Davis v. County School Board* cases, which were later consolidated as part of the *Brown v. Board of Education* case the Court would hear to determine whether *Plessy v. Ferguson* should be overruled. Would the combination of the lawyers' empirical evidence and the psychological damage the separate but equal doctrine had wrought upon black children sway the high court to overrule their previous decision in *Plessy v. Ferguson?*

On the momentous day, May 17, 1954, when the Supreme Court announced its unanimous decision regarding *Brown v. Board of Education,* there is little question that the Court had been moved not only by the persuasive nature of Marshall's and Carter's oral presentations but also by the devastating psychological impact the government-sanctioned separate but equal policy had wrought upon the development of black children at the midpoint of the twentieth century in America. Why?

Beyond the legal rationale adopted by the Court in its legal opinion overturning the separate but equal doctrine, there is little question the justices also weighed the devastating cultural and societal impact the practice must have had to lead many black children to believe they were inferior to whites. Writing for the unanimous majority, Chief Justice Earl Warren's opinion actually cited (in the opinion's footnote section) the paper Clark had presented to the White House Mid-Century Conference on Children and Youth. There is no question of its impact upon the Court when one considers the language used to discuss the detrimental effect separate but equal had upon the development of black children:

> We must consider public education in light of its full development and its present place in American life throughout the Nation. Only in this way can it be determined if segregation in public schools deprives these plaintiffs of the equal protection

of the laws. Today education is perhaps the most important function of state and local governments . . . Today it is a principal instrument in awakening the child to cultural values, in preparing him for later professional training, and in helping him adjust normally to his environment. In these days, it is doubtful that any child may reasonably be expected to succeed in life if he is denied the opportunity of an education.

Going on to cite a previous desegregation case, Chief Justice Warren would then quote in language that mirrors the Clarks' findings by arguing:

Segregation of white and colored children in public schools has a detrimental effect upon the colored children. The impact is greater when it has the sanction of law; for the policy of separating the races is usually interpreted as denoting the inferiority of the Negro group. A sense of inferiority affects the motivation of a child to learn. Segregation with the sanction of law, therefore, has a tendency to retard the educational and mental development of Negro children and to deprive them of some of the benefits they would receive in a racially integrated school system.

Whatever may have been the extent of psychological knowledge at the time of *Plessy v. Ferguson,* this finding is amply supported by modern authority. Any language in *Plessy v. Ferguson* contrary to this finding is rejected.

We conclude that in the field of public education the doctrine of "separate but equal" has no place. Separate educational facilities are inherently unequal.[8]

While the Court was unanimous in the *Brown* opinion to declare separate but equal offensive to the equal protection clause of the Fourteenth Amendment, there were many detractors who questioned whether the case had actually overturned *Plessy* or had instead tried to walk a thin legal tightrope open to interpretation as to what the Court had actually decided.

Recognizing the historical importance of its first decision, the Supreme Court issued a second opinion—the so-called *Brown II* decision—on May 31, 1955, to emphatically declare racially based segregation in schools unconstitutional while providing a more nuanced legal framework to ensure compliance and implementation with its earlier decision in states and localities across the United States. In this second unanimous opinion by the Court on the question of separate but equal accommodations for black and white schoolchildren, the Court declared that racial discrimination in regard to education was unconstitutional but provided segregationists with a key tool to delay implementation of the decision by stating that steps must be taken consistent with the Court's new opinion to implement racially desegregated schools "with all deliberate speed."[9]

The question of what the Court meant by the phrase "all deliberate speed" has been hotly contested ever since: how would the Court implement and enforce the integration it sought? Many believed that the Court, while seeking to eliminate racially based discrimination in the schools, did not want to anger many across the South by providing an implementation plan based on the Court's opinion about how to integrate the schools. When asked for his thoughts on what the Court meant by "all deliberate speed," "Thurgood Marshall frequently told anyone who would listen that the term meant S-L-O-W."[10] Indeed, it would take decades for the full effect of *Brown* to be fully implemented across America.

An early critical challenge to the authority of *Brown* to require integration in the schools occurred after a federal district court had ordered nine black students to be admitted to Central High School in Little Rock, Arkansas, in 1957. The students were famously barred admission by the Arkansas National Guard on September 23, 1957, before an unruly crowd of 1,000 protestors who objected to their enrollment.

Not to be deterred by the decision of the governor of Arkansas to mobilize the National Guard to block the students' admission, the following day President Dwight D. Eisenhower ordered the 1,200-man 327th Airborne Battle Group of the U.S. Army's 101st Airborne Division from Fort Campbell, Kentucky, to escort the nine students into the school to assert federal supremacy to integrate the schools and eradicate separate but equal facilities.

Following the historic victory achieved through the *Brown* decision, the leaders of the NAACP remained undaunted in their mission to eliminate all forms of segregation in American life so blacks could act as freely as whites to register to vote, purchase a home, or elect to travel the interstate highway system free from harm due merely to the color of their skin. While the road to full racial equality and integration proved a steep climb for these pioneers, they first recognized the importance for black children to receive the benefits provided by a strong grounding in education to emancipate future generations from the tentacles of segregation and oppression.

Nearly six years following the historic victory in *Brown,* President John F. Kennedy would appoint Thurgood Marshall to become a judge on the United States Court of Appeals for the Second Circuit, a position that he held until President Lyndon Johnson named him solicitor general—the chief advocate of the United States before the Supreme Court—in 1965. Just two years later President Johnson appointed Marshall to the Supreme Court, making him the first black to sit on the high court. It was a position from which he would burnish his reputation as one of the greatest defenders of equality and justice for all for the next twenty-four years.

While it would ultimately take decades of legal action and civil activism to integrate much of American society in the wake of *Brown,* progress was relatively overt and easy to discern over the decades: blacks were either able to live, drive, and vote in particular neighborhoods—or they were not. With the doors *Brown* would eventually open to the classrooms for millions of black children, the question remained whether the students would avail themselves of the opportunity to learn beside students of all races and not ascribe participating in educational endeavors as acting white. Rather than seek an immediate response to the question posed above, the reflection of time would allow a more accurate gauge to ascertain whether the work of NAACP pioneers such as Thurgood Marshall, Robert Carter, and many, many others had allowed black children to thrive in school and to achieve the American dream without feeling inferior. Had blacks used the key to unlock the door to the barriers that had been placed before them? Could they slowly but surely over time act as freely as whites to pursue their dreams, powered with the strength derived through education?

Fifty years following the work of Justice Thurgood Marshall and the numerous pioneers of the civil rights movement, leaders of the NAACP, past and present, gathered in Washington, D.C., to mark the anniversary of the momentous event at a gala. By many measures, schools in America had been integrated, and black children had been given an opportunity unlike generations before them to learn in the classroom free from intimidation and derision from whites seeking to block their educational advancement. Had the lessons learned from the Clarks' doll test changed such that black children took pride in their own racial identity rather than seeking to act or be perceived as being white in order to be positive and/or successful?

A new doll test would take place more than half a century after the Clarks' famous survey. In late 2009 Mattel Inc. sought to fill the void of black dolls for children to play with when they released their So in Style doll line—dolls with darker skin, wider noses, and fuller lips catered specifically for black parents and their children. And yet, despite praise from many for the efforts of Mattel to launch a new line aimed specifically at black children, the criticism of the new dolls is perhaps best encapsulated in an article from *The Wall Street Journal* published on December 3, 2009, entitled: "Are Mattel's New Dolls Black Enough?"

Some parents felt that despite the efforts to create dolls with darker complexions and certain physical attributes associated with blacks, the dolls weren't "black enough." Critics would

[C]omplain that five of the six dolls feature fine-textured, waist-length hair; half of them have blue or green eyes. Moreover, all have the freakishly skinny body of a Barbie (something that irks some white parents as well).[11]

We shall examine the legacy and perceived success or failure of the *Brown* decision in greater detail in chapter 10. But with the introduction of dolls specifically geared to black children and the release of Walt Disney's *The Princess and the Frog*, the first animated film featuring a black heroine, two significant steps were taken in 2009 to create characters that looked more like black children. These steps would help them draw pride and inspiration rather than encourage poor self-esteem or allegations that admiring white dolls was tantamount to seeking to act white.

7

Hawk v. Dove?

Malcolm X v. Martin Luther King and the Struggle for New Black Leadership

In the aftermath of the *Brown* decision, black and white Americans alike struggled to find ways to live, learn, and interact with each other in a turbulent new world. Blacks marching for peace and equality were met with rocks, bottles, water cannon, and dogs as they sought to bring the eyes of the world upon their unequal treatment before the law in America—the supposed beacon of freedom and equality.

Many of the prominent black leaders from the nineteenth and twentieth centuries built upon the foundations of success established by their predecessors. Booker T. Washington and W. E. B. Du Bois benefited from the steps and sacrifices of Frederick Douglass, while Marcus Garvey was strongly influenced by the notion of self-reliance and sufficiency set forth by Booker T. Washington.

Similarly, the pioneers who had come before them influenced two of the most significant black leaders from the 1960s—Dr. Martin Luther King Jr. and Malcolm X. First, both drew inspiration from the lessons of Du Bois, who stressed the importance of education as a manner in which blacks could arm themselves with the power of knowledge, but they diverged in their interpretations of the message set forth by Marcus Garvey. Next, while Dr. King was appreciative of Garvey's attempts to unite people of color through the development of a mass movement, he believed that integrating Americans and judging people by their character rather than the color of their skin were the best ways for America to address matters of race.

For his part, Malcolm X not only embraced Garvey's belief that the races should remain segregated rather than integrated, he further believed that racial, social, and political change must be brought about through violence rather than peaceful negotiation. Conversely, Dr. King advocated a path forward that stressed the embrace of rather than an attack upon his fellow man. Unlike Garvey's belief that blacks seeking an education were acting white by becoming the lackeys of whites, both King and Malcolm X believed that education provided a clear path forward to achieve power that would lead to societal change. Moreover, both men considered dressing well and speaking properly not acting white but the stamp of a sophisticated individual—a position that would be discarded by those who gave rise to the Black Power movement following the deaths of these two transformative leaders.

It is here that we begin our examination of the competing philosophies of these two emerging leaders who sought to change America at a pivotal point in history—the civil rights era of the early to mid 1960s, a period marked by violence and attempts to achieve social change. The commonality between the two radically different movements and those who followed them was a vehement advocacy of intellectualism and achievement; their divergence was marked by one's vision of a world in which blacks and whites could live together in a harmonious existence and the other's vision of a world in which the two races were segregated and where blacks were superior to, rather than inferior to, whites.

One of these competing ideological philosophies advocated violence as a means to achieve social equality, and the other saw nonviolence as a powerful means to achieve the same objective. One unfortunate theme resonated throughout the 1960s, before the rise of the Black Power movement: those who believed in nonviolence and integration with whites were often labeled as being an Uncle Tom or seeking to act white and were not considered to be in solidarity with blacks who pursued violent means to achieve their desired outcome.

Martin Luther King Jr. was born on January 15, 1929, in Atlanta, Georgia, the son to Reverend Martin Luther King Sr. and Alberta Williams King. Growing up in Atlanta, King attended the Booker T. Washington High School before skipping both ninth and twelfth grades to enter Morehouse College at age fifteen.

In 1948 King graduated from Morehouse with a BA in sociology, and he later graduated from the Crozer Theological Seminary in Chester, Pennsylvania, with a Bachelor of Divinity degree in 1951. Four years later, on June 5, 1955, he earned his Doctor of Philosophy degree from Boston University. King would become pastor of the Dexter Avenue Baptist Church in Montgomery, Alabama, in 1954—at the time he was only twenty-five years of age.

Volumes have been written about the life and about the impact and continuing legacy of Dr. Martin Luther King Jr. His leadership as head of the Southern Christian Leadership Council (SCLC) as well as his political acumen in subtly pressuring Presidents Kennedy and Johnson to enact meaningful civil rights protections for blacks have been well chronicled. Therefore, our inquiry will limit its focus on King's pursuit of nonviolent civil disobedience to achieve racial parity—a pursuit that would cause his opponents to label him as a sellout to the white establishment, an Uncle Tom, or worse.

Early in his career as a pastor and a theologian, King became deeply influenced by the teachings and philosophy of Mahatma Gandhi—a philosophy that advocated civil disobedience to achieve social and political change. The first time King would put Gandhi's civil disobedience into public practice was the public-bus boycott in Montgomery, Alabama, from late 1955 through 1956—an event that would involve many of the most prominent figures of the civil rights era.

Under the prevailing system at the time in Montgomery, blacks entering public buses were required to fill the seats at the rear of the bus and gradually work their way forward toward the front of the bus, where white patrons were permitted to sit closest to the door of the vehicle. Should a white passenger enter and there not be a place for him or her to sit, the black passengers in the row nearest the door were required to move to the rear of the bus in order to make a new row of seats available for white passengers.

On December 1, 1955, Rosa Parks was sitting in the black row closest to the front of the bus when a white patron entered the bus. The bus operator, James Blake, ordered everyone in Parks's row to move toward the back of the bus to create a new row for subsequent white passengers. Parks refused to do so and was subsequently arrested for failing to obey the driver's command forever cementing Parks as a legendary pioneer of the civil rights movement.

The arrest of Rosa Parks for refusing to yield her seat to a white passenger provided King with the first opportunity to implement civil disobedience to protest the discriminatory seating practice on public transit. Almost immediately following Parks's arrest, King was appointed head of the Montgomery Improvement Association (MIA), charged with implementing a boycott to protest and thus change the current practice that relegated black bus passengers to the back and treated them as inferior and unequal to whites.

Over the course of the next year, King and his fellow boycotters refused to use the Montgomery public transportation system, crippling the economy with the loss of black patrons on the buses. Meanwhile, they engaged in civil disobedience to effect the meaningful change of allowing blacks to act as freely as whites, of allowing them to sit where they wished anywhere on a city bus without having to yield their seats to white patrons.

Often, at great risk to his personal safety, King refused armed protection from the scores of threats he endured in supporting the boycott and as head of the MIA. Many boycotters were routinely beaten, and King's house and several Baptist churches were firebombed during the dispute.

Finally, on June 4, 1956, a federal district court held that the system of racial segregation for bus passengers in Alabama was unconstitutional because of the manner in which black and white patrons were treated. Despite a brief injunction of the district court's decision, King and his fellow nonviolent demonstrators were rewarded for their efforts when the United States Supreme Court upheld the district court's decision on November 13, 1956—a move that led to the Montgomery city ordinance being revised to allow black bus passengers to sit virtually anywhere they chose without molestation.

As a result, the peaceful boycott instituted by Dr. King and enforced by blacks throughout the city of Montgomery had officially ended on December 20, 1956—a nearly yearlong struggle in which blacks refused to resort to violence to achieve desired social and political results. Dr. King's belief that nonviolent social disobedience could enact change was no longer a theoretical or intellectual exercise; the brave actions of thousands of unarmed blacks across the city of Montgomery, protesting peacefully in the face of violence and hatred spawned by racism, proved that oppression could be overcome by pacifist struggle.

Inspired by the success of the Montgomery bus boycott to achieve social change through civil disobedience, King elected to travel to India in 1959 to visit with Gandhi's family and inspect for himself how nonviolent struggle had led to equality in India and freedom from the oppressive hand of British colonialism. King was deeply moved by what he saw and heard during his pilgrimage to India, and he returned to the United States more resolved than ever to use nonviolence as a powerful means to the justifiable end of eliminating segregation and discrimination in the United States to ensure blacks could act just as equally as whites in society.

During his final evening in India, King would famously state in a radio interview:

Since being in India, I am more convinced than ever before that the method of nonviolent resistance is the most potent weapon available to oppressed people in their struggle for justice and human dignity. In a real sense, Mahatma Gandhi embodied in his life certain universal principles that are inherent in the moral structure of the universe, and these principles are as inescapable as the law of gravitation.[1]

Upon his return from India, King published an essay in *Ebony* magazine, where he reflected on what he had seen and learned during his monthlong pilgrimage as well as on the potential ramifications of having civil rights activists use civil disobedience in seeking equality for blacks in America.

To this end, King reflected on how the citizens of India and Great Britain were able to maintain a friendly rather than hostile disposition toward one another following India's independence from British colonial rule on August 15, 1947:

The aftermath of hatred and bitterness that usually follows a violent campaign was found nowhere in India. Today a mutual friendship based on complete equality exists between the Indian and British people within the commonwealth. The way of acquiescence leads to moral and spiritual suicide. The way of violence leads to bitterness in the survivors and brutality in the destroyers. But the way of nonviolence leads to redemption and the creation of the beloved community.[2]

King appreciated that the Indian and British people had allowed a friendship to exist with complete equality between them, even though the Indians had been subject to colonial rule for more than one hundred years, as well as that the transition from subjugation to independence had largely occurred because of civil disobedience. King was pleased he had been met with praise during his visit for his adoption of Gandhi's civil disobedience during the Montgomery bus boycott. Here King would note:

I was delighted that the Gandhians accepted us with open arms. They praised our experiment with the nonviolent resistance technique at Montgomery. They seem to look upon it as an outstanding example of the possibilities of its use in Western civilization. To them as to me it also suggests that nonviolent resistance *when planned and positive in action* can work effectively even under totalitarian regimes.[3]

Believing in the power of nonviolent protest as a compelling mechanism to achieve meaningful progress for an America segregated on racial lines, where blacks could not act as equals of whites in society, King would increasingly discuss civil disobedience following his return from India and for several years thereafter.

King would touch on the impact of civil obedience as a dignified method to bring social and political parity for blacks in America during a speech before 26,000 high school and college students—black and white—who had gathered in Washington, D.C., on April 18, 1959, to march in support of the *Brown* decision to eliminate racial segregation in the nation's schools.

Echoing a theme that would resonate throughout much of his public discourse on the future of America, King would observe that:

As I stand here and look out upon the thousands of Negro faces, and the thousands of white faces, intermingled like the waters of a river, I see only one face—the face of the future.

Yes; as I gaze upon this historic assembly, this unprecedented gathering of young people, I cannot help thinking—that a hundred years from now the historians will be calling this not the "beat" generation, but the generation of integration.[4]

While King had clearly articulated his vision for the future of America—a united states of America, where blacks and whites were intermingled like the waters of a river through social, cultural, and political integration, the question was how to change the collective mind-set of a country still confronted with segregation and increasingly violent confrontations between the police and those seeking to bring about true equality in the South. Here, King offered a path forward:

> For the southern Negro is learning to transform his degradation into resistance. Nonviolent resistance. And by doing so he is not only achieving his dignity as a human being, he is helping to advance democracy in the South.[5]

Rather than take up arms and use violence as the dramatic means to enact the end result of equality for blacks, King believed that the example set forth by Gandhi's civil disobedience would resonate in America, where blacks and whites could maintain a respectful relationship as equals rather than coexist as bitter enemies driven apart through violence and mistrust.

Although many blacks agreed with the approach advocated by King, which he promoted through numerous speeches and television and radio appearances, there was a growing minority that believed civil disobedience only strengthened, rather than weakened, the position of whites as the dominant members of society. Those who took exception with Dr. King largely believed that a stronger, bolder course of action was called for—a course of action where whites would accept the equality if not superiority of blacks through violent disobedience and armed conflict. Leading the charge for social and political change through violent struggle was an articulate and impassioned leader named Malcolm X.

Malcolm Little was born on May 19, 1925, to Louise and Earl Little in Omaha, Nebraska. Little's father, a former Baptist preacher in Marcus Garvey's United Negro Improvement Association (UNIA) would have a strong impact on Malcolm's philosophical and intellectual development. Although Little's father died early during his childhood, it is clear that he imparted to his son the lessons that were influenced by Garvey's teachings: distrust of white supremacy, political activism, and black separatism.[6]

Following a fractured childhood in which his mother was committed to a mental institution, Little and his siblings would be placed in the care of various welfare agencies; Little eventually moved to Boston, where he lived with his half sister. During his time in Boston, Little was arrested and convicted to serve ten years for burglary.

In prison he experienced a religious conversion after being exposed to the work of Elijah Muhammad and the Nation of Islam—a process that led him to read extensively and question the society around him. Upon his release from prison in 1952, Malcolm would jettison his last name Little in favor of X, which, in his words, was "a symbolic repudiation of a 'white man's name.'"[7]

An eloquent speaker, Malcolm X would begin to eclipse the name and image of his spiritual mentor, Elijah Muhammad. Becoming increasingly disillusioned with Muhammad's leadership, Malcolm X would resign from the Nation of Islam on March 8, 1964, to create the Muslim Mosque, Inc. Before his resignation from the Nation of Islam, Malcolm X gave an impassioned interview to Dr. Kenneth Clark* on the Public Broadcasting System (PBS) in the spring of 1963, in which he virulently criticized Dr. Martin Luther King Jr. as being both a tool and a pawn of whites. In the eyes of Malcolm X, the renowned civil rights leader was nothing more than an Uncle Tom acting white by trying to achieve societal change by working with whites.

For Malcolm X, the white man was the enemy rather than the friend of American blacks, a man to be hated rather than emulated. Consider the following exchange between Clark and Malcolm X about Dr. King:

CLARK: I see. Well, Reverend Martin Luther King preaches a doctrine of nonviolent insistence upon the rights of the American Negro. What is your attitude toward this philosophy?

---

* This is the same psychologist who persuasively testified regarding the inferiority complex blacks had developed as a result of the separate and unequal educational conditions before the Supreme Court's holding in *Brown v. Board of Education* in 1954.

MALCOLM X: The white man pays Reverend Martin Luther King, subsidizes Reverend Martin Luther King, so that Reverend Martin Luther King can continue to teach the Negroes to be defenseless. That's what you mean by nonviolent: be defenseless. Be defenseless in the face of one of the most cruel beasts that has ever taken a people into captivity. That's this American white man. And they have proved it throughout the country by the police dogs and the police clubs.

A hundred years ago they used to put on a white sheet and use a bloodhound against Negroes. Today they've taken off the white sheet and put on police uniforms; they've traded in the blood-hounds for police dogs, and they're still doing the same thing. And just as Uncle Tom, back during slavery, used to keep the Negroes from resisting the bloodhound or resisting the Ku Klux Klan by teaching them to love their enemy or pray for those who use them spitefully, today Martin Luther King is just a twentieth-century or modern Uncle Tom, or a religious Uncle Tom, who is doing the same thing today, to keep Negroes defenseless in the face of an attack, that Uncle Tom did on the plantation to keep *those* Negroes defenseless in the face of the attacks of the Klan in that day.[8]

The notion of the civil disobedience as either a virtuous path forward for Dr. King or, conversely, as a cowardly yet manipulative manner advocated by him so that blacks would remain subservient to whites in order to save those blacks—sellout Uncle Toms acting white in the mind of Malcolm X—deemed important for whites would mark the dichotomy in the two schools of ideological, social, cultural, and politi-cal thought as Dr. King and Malcolm X sought to transform American society.

Perhaps there is no better illustration of these diverging views than two speeches given in 1963 by Dr. Martin Luther King Jr. and Mal-colm X, respectively. The first is the iconic "I have a dream" speech that

Dr. King delivered on the steps of the Lincoln Memorial during the march on Washington on August 28. The second is the rebuttal speech by Malcolm X, delivered in Detroit, Michigan, during December of the same year.

The year 1963 marked the centennial of President Lincoln's Emancipation Proclamation. Also that year President Kennedy authorized federal marshals to integrate both the University of Alabama and the University of Mississippi over the fierce and violent objections of segregationists opposed to blacks and whites sharing educational facilities. Moreover, 1963 was the year when Birmingham Police Commissioner Bull Connor infamously turned dogs and fire hoses on peaceful demonstrators, in a scene that would both captivate and cause many Americans to feel shame and revulsion at the oppressive and violent actions taken in the South to preserve segregation. And on June 12, 1963, Medgar Evers, the thirty-seven-year-old field secretary of the NAACP, had been murdered on the front porch of his home, an action that would incite riots and protests across the country.

The "I have a dream" speech remains one of the most famous and often-quoted speeches in American history, given during one of the most tumultuous years in the struggle for civil rights. Reflecting on the increasing levels of violence and despair that had gripped many in the black community across the country, Dr. Martin Luther King Jr. famously ascended the steps of the Lincoln Memorial on August 28, 1963, where he would deliver a set of remarks before several hundred thousand people on the mall, words that would resonate with millions of his fellow Americans as he pled for justice, equality, and a world where blacks and whites could live together as peers rather than adversaries.

Perhaps reflecting on the teachings of Gandhi as well as his own success in the Montgomery bus boycott, which sought to enact meaningful social and political change through civil disobedience, King reminded his audience of the need to conduct their struggle for freedom with dignity and to avoid being marred with the stain of violence:

Let us not seek to satisfy our thirst for freedom by drinking from the cup of bitterness and hatred. We must forever conduct our struggle on the high plane of dignity and discipline. We must not allow our creative protest to degenerate into physical violence. Again and again, we must rise to the majestic heights of meeting physical force with soul force.[9]

And the struggle for freedom and justice, the struggle to bring about a world where blacks could act as equally as whites to decide on where they would live, go to school, and work, would not be waged by blacks alone—Dr. King envisioned a world where blacks and whites stood shoulder to shoulder to extinguish the flames of racial hatred together. Here he proffered:

The marvelous new militancy which has engulfed the Negro community must not lead us to a distrust of all white people, for many of our white brothers, as evidenced by their presence here today, have come to realize that their destiny is tied up with our destiny and they have come to realize that their freedom is inextricably bound to our freedom. This offense we share mounted to storm the battlements of injustice must be carried forth by a biracial army. We cannot walk alone.[10]

And as he concluded his remarks, King spoke of an America where the acting white slur would have no meaning, a society where individuals would be judged not by the color of their skin but by the content of their character. A society in which blacks and whites would view each other equally as fellow human beings rather than adversaries facing off along battle lines drawn by the colors black and white:

So I say to you, my friends, that even though we must face the difficulties of today and tomorrow, I still have a dream. It is a dream deeply rooted in the American dream that one day this nation will rise up and live out the true meaning of its creed—we hold these truths to be self-evident, that all men are created equal.[11]

In King's vision all men would be created equally to pursue the American dream, and they would neither act black nor white but as equal participants to fulfill their aspirations in society.

It is perhaps ironic that the very reason that Dr. Martin Luther King Jr.'s "I have a dream" speech was so successful and remains his most frequently quoted speech to date for its inspirational message is why Malcolm X chose to denigrate it: the language and imagery contained in the speech spoke of a world in which blacks would achieve equality and peaceful integration with whites through discussion and negotiation rather than violence.[12]

Perhaps Malcolm X witnessed the events that unfurled in 1963 and arrived at a different conclusion than King as to how best to confront the evils of segregation and hopelessness gripping many black communities across the country. Rather than seek progress and equality through negotiation and civil disobedience, the restlessness of Malcolm X and many of his followers led them to advocate a different way forward.

On November 10, 1963, Malcolm X delivered remarks entitled "Message to the Grass Roots," where he outlined the plight of blacks in America while also articulating a clear path forward to move beyond racism and segregation:

America has a very serious problem. Not only does America have a very serious problem, but our people have a very serious problem. America's problem is us. We're her problem. The only reason she has a problem is she doesn't want us here. And every time you look at yourself, be you black, brown, red or yellow, a so-called Negro, you represent a person who poses such a serious problem for America because you're not wanted. Once you face this as a fact, then you can start plotting a course that will make you appear intelligent, instead of unintelligent.[13]

The intelligence to which Malcolm X referred to was nothing short or shy of a revolution. Ridiculing the peaceful protest advocated by King and other civil rights organizations, Malcolm X offered his thoughts on how blacks could emerge victorious from the clutches of racial oppression:

> You don't have a turn the other cheek revolution. There's no such thing as a nonviolent revolution. . . . Revolution is bloody, revolution is hostile, revolution knows no compromise, revolution overturns and destroys everything that gets in its way. And you, sitting around here like a knot on the wall, saying, "I'm going to love these folks no matter how much they hate me." No, you need a revolution. Whoever heard of a revolution where they lock arms, as Reverend Cleage was pointing out beautifully singing "We Shall Overcome"? You don't do that in a revolution. You don't do any singing, you're too busy swinging.[14]

Malcolm X often showed contempt for King and other civil rights leaders who advocated civil disobedience, and he did so in very stark, racial terms that harkened back to Harriet Beecher Stowe's seminal work and that remain with us to the present day: a black man is an Uncle Tom if he seeks to assimilate with, work with, or otherwise interact with whites. Malcolm X and others who advocated violence as a means to achieve political and social change often denigrated Dr. King and his followers as being Uncle Toms and seeking to act white.

During the same speech Malcolm X is unequivocal in his lack of respect for Dr. King by equating him to an Uncle Tom who would be willing to sell out the black race in order to curry favor with whites. Consider the following declaration during "Message to the Grass Roots":

> Just as the slave master of that day used Tom, the house Negro, to keep the field Negroes in check, the same old slave master today has Negroes who are nothing but modern Uncle Toms, the twen-

tieth century Uncle Toms, to keep us passive and peaceful and nonviolent. That's Tom making you nonviolent.[15]

Lest there be any ambiguity as to whom Malcolm X had offered a direct affront, he continued:

> The slave master took Tom and dressed him well, fed him well and even gave him a little education—a *little* education; gave him a long coat and a top hat and made all the other slaves look up to him. Then he used Tom to control them. The same strategy that was used in those days is used today, by the same white man. He takes a Negro, a so-called Negro, and makes him prominent, builds him up, publicizes him, makes him a celebrity. And then he becomes a spokesman for Negroes—and a Negro leader.[16]

Malcolm X's imagery in this particular passage was designed to stir up anger and resentment toward Dr. King and other black leaders who failed to adhere to the ideological and political philosophy of Malcolm X and his followers. Rather than attack King on substance, Malcolm X chose to attack him based on populist perception: King was dressed a little too well compared to other blacks—he wasn't sufficiently black. King had a little more education than other blacks—he wasn't sufficiently black. The white establishment had taken an eloquent black leader and member of the clergy and made him a popular national figure who purported to speak as the leader of American blacks when, in fact, Dr. King was, in the eyes of Malcolm X and his disciples, a black man dressing, thinking, acting, and being white.

Malcolm X employed a metaphor similar to one employed in Ralph Ellison's *Invisible Man,* where the narrator in the story had been tasked with placing ten drops of black ink into a bucket of white paint. Once the paint had been mixed together, the blackness had disappeared entirely and the paint remained pure and white to the naked eye, despite the fact that blackness had been swirled within. Given that *Invisible*

Man had been published nearly a decade before, one wonders whether the imagery sought by Malcolm X was deliberate or a mere coincidence.

Regardless, I believe Malcolm X fully intended for his audience to perceive and believe that the method articulated by Dr. King to integrate society would only make blacks weaker, rather than stronger as a result. Consider the following from "Message to the Grass Roots," where Malcolm X discussed the historic march on Washington led by Dr. Martin Luther King Jr.:

> It's just like when you've got some coffee that's too black, which means it's too strong. What do you do? You integrate it with cream, you make it weak. But if you pour too much cream into it, you won't even know you ever had coffee. It used to be hot, it becomes cool. It used to be strong, it becomes weak. It used to wake you up, now it puts you to sleep. This is what they did with the march on Washington. They [civil rights leaders, especially Dr. King] joined it. They didn't integrate it, they infiltrated it. They joined it, became a part of it, took it over. And as they took it over, it lost its militancy. It ceased to be angry, it ceased to be hot, it ceased to be uncompromising.[17]

Malcolm X's references could not be more precise in his direct assault on those who sought to integrate the black and white races during the tumultuous 1960s. Malcolm X believed such integration would make blacks weaker rather than stronger members of society. Rather than encouraging blacks to act as equals of whites, Malcolm X encouraged blacks to act as their superiors in society. This superiority would result from blacks challenging and besting whites, rather than seeking to integrate and assimilate.

And while both leaders would remain uncompromising in their respective ideological beliefs about how best to move blacks forward, positions articulated in this pair of speeches from 1963, both men would later be assassinated at the height of their rhetorical and political power: Malcolm X was killed just shy of his fortieth birthday, on

February 21, 1965, and Dr. King was killed in Memphis, Tennessee, on April 4, 1968—also just shy of his fortieth birthday.

The sudden and violent deaths of two of the most eloquent and persuasive black leaders left many black Americans without a sense of purpose and filled many with hopelessness—a hopelessness that led to the rise of the Black Power movement and that was followed by an era of moral relativism as blacks struggled for the ability to exist and act as freely as whites in American society.

8

Black Power, Moral Relativism, and Radical Chic

The violent deaths of Malcolm X in 1965 and Dr. Martin Luther King Jr. in 1968 unleashed a counterculture revolution in many African-American communities across the United States. The sense that blacks would overcome racial oppression through integration or isolation evolved into a movement of Black Power that sought to bring about change through social agitation. The nonviolent path forward set by Dr. King had veered on a detour of violence that would mark a militant change in the attitudes of blacks toward whites for more than a decade from the mid-1960s to the late 1970s. Acting white during this pivotal point in American history was not only frowned upon by many blacks, especially in urban settings such as Los Angeles, Detroit, Philadelphia, and Newark, New Jersey, but the failure to assimilate into the Black Power movement could lead to a violent fate far worse than being ostracized at community gatherings.

While it is difficult to pinpoint an exact birth date of the Black Power movement in America, many social commentators point to two key and brave steps taken by James Meredith in Mississippi during the mid-1960s. First, Meredith became an early hero to the still-nascent civil rights movement by successfully enrolling as the first black student at the University of Mississippi on October 1, 1963. Over the strenuous objections of Mississippi's segregationist governor, Ross Barnett, Meredith was seated only with the assistance of federal marshals and the National Guard, which had been dispatched to maintain order and peace by President John F. Kennedy just days before his tragic assassination. Despite the presence of federal officials to safeguard Meredith's enrollment, several clashes erupted that resulted in two casualties and the injuries of dozens of soldiers and marshals. Perhaps Governor Barnett and those who sought to bar Meredith entry to the University of Mississippi feared something more than one black student joining the academic ranks of Ole Miss: perhaps their real concern was the fact that Meredith was acting white by doing so.

Despite the Emancipation Proclamation, the *Brown* decision, and the intervention of the Kennedy administration to seat Meredith, schools across the South had successfully barred entry to blacks seeking a higher education since they believed such education was the province of successful whites. The ripple effect caused by the entrance of one black student to Ole Miss could lead to a flood of blacks seeking to act as equals of whites, which could spread like a dark stain throughout Mississippi and across the South. The denial of a proper education was one of the last vestiges of slavery that segregationists clung to in order to prevent blacks from acting white; fortunately, President Kennedy and his attorney general stood firm to integrate the University of Mississippi, and James Meredith would become one of thousands of black graduates in the years to come.

Following his graduation from the University of Mississippi, Meredith would once again stand as a strong pioneer in the nascent civil rights movement when he decided to undertake a solitary "march against fear" from Memphis, Tennessee, to Jackson, Mississippi, a journey of more than 220 miles, to register black voters and show support for blacks to live in society free from fear of racial violence.[1] This time, Meredith would undertake his second walk for integration and against racial oppression alone; the federal troops that had protected his walk onto the Jackson, Mississippi, campus would not be there to offer similar protection for his journey from Memphis.

Tragedy struck Meredith on just the second day of his historic journey: he was ambushed and shot by the white supremacist Aubrey James Norvell on June 7, 1966. As Meredith lay writhing on the ground and implored those around him for help, an AP photographer captured Meredith's agony—both physical and mental—as he lay wounded while marching for freedom and equality, an image that would later capture the 1967 Pulitzer Prize for Photography.

The racially motivated shooting of James Meredith would prove an unsettling moment for leaders of the competing factions of the civil rights movement. Dr. Martin Luther King Jr., who had been in Chicago at the time of the shooting, urged calm and restraint against future violence. While Dr. King's message of conciliation was revered and respected by many, there was also a growing minority of blacks across the country who believed the true road toward an America with the rights of freedom and equality was paved with militant if not outright violent behavior.

As a group composed of members of the Southern Christian Leadership Council (SCLC), Congress of Racial Equality (CORE), and the Student Non-Violent Coordinating Committee (SNCC) resumed Meredith's freedom march, the tone of many of the participants became more strident. In particular, Stokely Carmichael, having recently assumed the reins as head of SNCC from the civil rights hero John Lewis, undertook a speech that is widely acknowledged as the first invocation of "Black Power" as a necessary ingredient to bring about change in the status of blacks as well as to condemn the lack of protection and justice for blacks in Mississippi.

Of particular significance here is the manner in which a former integrationist such as Carmichael changed his comments to a more militant and activist tone and tenor. Regarding Carmichael's more incendiary remarks, Robert L. Harris Jr. and Rosalyn Terborg-Penn write:

He [Carmichael] proclaimed what African-Americans needed was 'Black Power.' After the speech, Carmichael's lieutenant, Willie Ricks mounted the platform and whipped the crowd into a frenzy with the chant, 'What do we want?' and the response, 'Black Power.'[2]

The embers of long-pent-up frustration and resentment by the sluggish level of racial progress had been whipped into flames and brought new life to a civil rights movement that had largely devoted its activities to nonviolent means as a method to achieve demonstrable progress. As later described in a book by the political scientist Charles Hamilton, Black Power as defined by Carmichael was

> A call for black people in this country to unite, to recognize their heritage, to build a sense of community . . . to define their own goals, to lead their own organizations . . . to reject the racist institutions and values of this society.[3]

For his part, Dr. Martin Luther King Jr. had opposed the use of Black Power, remarking that the term endorsed violence and "black domination rather than black equality."[4] According to David Garrow's Pulitzer Prize–winning book, *Bearing the Cross*, which examines the civil rights movement, King and Carmichael allegedly had the following discussion in regard to Black Power:

> "Martin, I deliberately decided to raise this issue on the march in order to give it a national forum and force you to take a stand for Black Power." King responded, "I have been used before. One more time won't hurt."[5]

Unable to contain the combative sound-and-fury notion advocated by supporters of Black Power that resonated with a sizable minority of blacks across the country, conciliation would soon give way to another form of debate: confrontation.

With the rising militancy of proponents of Black Power came the desire to self-segregate, to exclude whites in order to gain black socio-economic and political power. One particular example of this was the manner in which the SNCC evolved from preaching racial harmony through the freedom rides of the early 1960s and the march on Washington in 1963 to, by the latter half of the decade, a more hard-line approach under Carmichael's leadership. For example, unlike the previously cited SNCC activities where whites were active partners and participants, the rise of Black Power led the group to exclude whites (particularly those from the North) from joining to preserve black purity. Working and partnering with whites would soon give rise to an increasingly temperamental view that one was not authentically black unless one shunned whites and focused on achieving racial power through Black Power—a doctrine embodied by the rise of the Black Panther Party.

Four months following the Meredith freedom march, where the notion of Black Power was first introduced, Bobby Seale and Huey Newton would form the Black Panther Party for Self Defense in Oakland, California, on October 15, 1966. In theory the Panthers were founded to empower and invigorate dispossessed African-Americans in urban areas, but in practice, the group advocated a more militaristic approach to achieve independence from whites.

More important, while originally echoing the black nationalist sentiments expressed by Marcus Garvey decades before, the Black Panthers came to represent a more violent, political, and militant counterculture to the progressive-integration movement of the 1960s. Indeed, as the membership of the Black Panthers spread from Oakland to Los Angeles, Chicago, Newark, Philadelphia, and points across the United States, their radical tone and tactics soon attracted the attention of J. Edgar Hoover, now the director of the Federal Bureau of Investigation. Despite Hoover's dire proclamation that the Panthers were "the greatest threat to the internal security of the country," the Panthers gained notoriety and grudging respect from many who admired their radical, often violent, means to advance racial parity.

But the demeanor of the Black Panthers struck a cultural chord in

America in the late 1960s that would resonate for nearly a decade. With their shunning of traditional conservative dress and grooming, the Panthers' influence would evolve dramatically from their original mission to protect blacks against police brutality to a barometer against which social, political, and cultural norms would be measured for many blacks. The motifs of black is beautiful and soulful and white is bland and bad would not only echo in many black households across America but also penetrate the American consciousness by instilling a new sense of pride and identity among blacks because of their ethnicity rather than their individuality. Blacks were encouraged not to act like whites, and they were further expressly encouraged to explore and cultivate their own distinct self-identification as powerful, militant, and proudly black.

This notion of self-identification of race as identity versus individual as identity is where a number of social commentators trace the modern cultural evolution of the acting white phenomena—a belief that those who were authentically black expressed themselves culturally as rooted in a collective race rather than as individuals who happened to belong to a particular ethnic group. The linguist John McWhorter examines this form of racial identification in his book of essays entitled *Authentically Black*. In the relevant section, McWhorter contends:

> [Writers] have chronicled the hijacking of education since the 1960s by a leftist distrust of traditional learning. Since then, a powerful current in education seeks to bolster students' "self esteem" against a demonized "Establishment" by encouraging them to "express themselves" rather than learn facts and be trained in careful reasoning and concrete skills.[6]

The emergence of Black Power and the subsequent battle against the white establishment by many would manifest in a variety of ways over the decades and in many areas that were detrimental to individual as well as collective advancement for many blacks. Why? Because many of the attributes and behavior traits necessary for success in America (applied learning in school, conservative dress and demeanor, hard-work ethic) were the very activities deemed to be "establishment" behavior that would lead a black person to charges of being less than authentically black and of acting white.

The popularity of blacks learning and speaking a different language from whites to preserve their "cultural" identity against that of the white establishment—a phenomena later known as Ebonics in the 1990s—traces its roots to the late 1960s and the rise of Black Power. Instead of acting and speaking as whites, a number of blacks would take pride in developing a dialect that was unique to many communities of color and that allowed one to speak and act black with authenticity.

While certain black educators have praised the virtues of Ebonics as an outlet and an alternative for blacks to communicate while remaining "authentic" to their race and culture, test scores and the widening achievement gap between black and white students offer a more sobering assessment on the impact on black children of their failure to learn basic English and math skills. Sadly, as McWhorter notes in *Authentically Black:*

> But the sense of standard English as a stiff, itchy costume rather than skin plays into a general sense of books and learning as something "else"—that is, "white." This is the prime culprit to black students' lagging grades and test scores, which persist regardless of class. . . . Overall the black educational establishment is focused more on decrying why black children *cannot* learn than how they *will* learn.[7]

Perhaps a more devastating analysis of the shunning of learning and the use of Standard English as uncomfortable white behavior is the evolution of Black English and the devalued influence scholastic advancement has had on black economic advancement since the late 1960s.

One of the preeminent scholars to examine the acting white phenomena against the black-white achievement gap is the Harvard

University professor Roland Fryer. Beyond his scholarship on the acting white issue itself, which we will examine in greater detail shortly, Fryer further sought to scrutinize whether or not the divergence in culture between blacks and whites led to a widening achievement gap between the races and whether the roots of this gap could be traced to the 1960s—and the emergence of Black Power as a cultural force in many black communities.

Along with the economist Steven Levitt, Fryer published a paper in August 2004 entitled "The Causes and Consequences of Distinctively Black Names."[8] Here, the economists sought to link the emergence of a distinctively black culture—tracing its roots to the emergence of Black Power in the late 1960s—to a decline in black academic and economic advancement. In their study, the authors drew their data from the Birth Statistical Master File maintained in the Office of Vital Records in the California Department of Health Services. They examined the names given to all 16 million children born in the state of California and entered on their birth certificates from 1961–2000 to answer two distinct questions: (1) Was there a divergence in the naming of black and white children during this time span? (2) If so, did the naming of children with distinctively black and/or white names lead to later cultural or economic discrimination?

On balance, the results were startling. In the early 1960s there was little divergence between the first names given to black and white children born in the state of California. Toward the end of the decade, coterminous with the rise of the Black Power movement, there was a wide disparity in the choice of first names given to children based on the ethnicity of the child. As the authors state from the outset:

> In the 1960s Blacks and Whites chose relatively similar first names for their children. Over a short period of time in the early 1970s, that pattern changed dramatically with most Blacks (particularly those living in racially isolated neighborhoods) adopting increasingly distinctive names. The pattern in the data appear most consistent with a model in which the rise

of the Black Power movement influenced how Blacks perceived their identities.[9]

The information culled from their statistical analysis is particularly striking: by the early 1970s the median black female in a segregated neighborhood went from choosing a name that was twice as likely to be given to a black child compared to a white child to a name that was more than twenty times as likely to be given to a black child—all within a narrow seven-year period![10]

Here the authors found that distinctively black names such as:

DeShawn, Tyrone, Reginald, Shanice, Precious, Kiara, and Deja are quite popular among Blacks, but virtually unheard of for Whites. The opposite is true for names like Connor, Cody, Jake, Molly, Emily, Abigail and Caitlin.[11]

Looking at the data another way, the authors found that between 1989 and 2000, of the 457 boys born in the state of California with the name Tyrone, 445 of those boys were black. Similarly, of the 277 girls born in the state with the name Shanice, 274 were black; conversely, of the 2,328 girls given the first name Molly, only six were black.[12] That blacks would marginalize themselves with uniquely black-sounding names while ceding the mainstream to whites in the name of Black Power or pride seems stunning to me. What is perhaps most tragic about this divergence from the mainstream, this attempt to avoid sounding white by choosing names that are authentically black, is the impact this has had on blacks seeking to enter the workforce.

While seeking to assess the consequences of choosing distinctively black names, Fryer and Levitt found that those individuals who did have distinctly black names were more likely to have been born into racial poverty and segregation. That is, the individual with a distinctly black name is more likely to have grown up in a household with a lower socioeconomic status, the result of which is that employers might discriminate against an applicant because of their name and perceived racial identity. Fryer and Levitt's fellow Harvard University economist, Robert Barro, assessed his colleagues' study to determine the prospects for individuals with distinctly black-sounding names in obtaining employment:

> Fryer and Levitt's study shows that the more black-sounding a person's name, the more likely the parents have a lower socio-economic status. Employers thus might infer that a job seeker with a black-sounding name is more likely to have grown up in a less educated and poorer family. If employers believe, rightly or wrongly, that such a background lowers the chance of job success, this may help explain why audit studies find that employers react negatively to black-sounding names on resumes, which contain education but little other socioeconomic information. Thus, a recent NBER [National Bureau of Economic Research] working paper by Marianne Bertrand and Sendhil Mullainathan found that call-back rates on identical (and made-up) resumes were substantially higher for white-sounding names such as Emily or Greg.[13]

While one study tracing the first names given to all children born in the state of California from 1961–2000 is by no means definitive on the impact of distinctly black names on the American society at large, I believe it is safe to assume that if similar studies were conducted nationwide, Fryer and Levitt's work would be largely replicated. Why would blacks willingly cede the mainstream to whites by naming their children with distinctly black-sounding names when the apparent consequence is condemning black children to prejudicial review by whites, who could perceive such individuals to be less well educated and as hailing from lower socioeconomic neighborhoods? Or, is the risk the parent is taking when giving a child a distinctively black name at birth, a name given so the child cannot be accused of having a white-sounding name and that can be viewed as celebrating black pride and culture, worth the potential cost the child will pay later in life?

While the Black Power movement is widely credited with the spike in distinctly black names, which are given as a manifestation of black pride and cultural identity, the movement also fueled the use of Black English, an idiom children learn in their homes and communities that supporters contend is another source of black pride. If one is speaking Black English, of course, one can hardly be accused of acting or sounding white. The rise of Black English in the late 1960s and early 1970s would explode in a national controversy on race during the 1990s, following a controversial resolution adopted by the Board of Education in Oakland, California, on December 18, 1996, regarding Black English.

Here, the Board of Education was worried about the widening gap between black and white scholastic achievement. Rather than confront underlying causes of poor academic performance by black students such as the proper development of math, writing, and study skills, the Board of Education instead concluded that meager test and academic results were the result of black students not being given instruction in Ebonics, their native language. In the most controversial section of the resolution, the Oakland Board of Education made the following declaration to arrive at their controversial conclusions. The excerpted relevant sections below deliver the startling findings arrived at by the Board of Education:

> WHEREAS, numerous validated scholarly studies demonstrate that African-American students as a part of their culture and history as African people possess and utilize a language described in various scholarly approaches as "Ebonics" (literally "Black sounds") or "Pan-African Communication Behavior" or "African Language Systems"; and

> ... WHEREAS, such recognition by scholars has given rise over the past fifteen years to legislation passed by the State of California recognizing the unique language stature of descendants

of slaves, with such legislation being prejudicially and unconsti-
tutionally vetoed repeatedly by various California state governors; and

WHEREAS, judicial cases in states other than California have
recognized the unique language stature of African-American
pupils, and such recognition by courts has resulted in court-
mandated educational programs which have substantially benefited African American children in the interest of vindicating
their equal protection of the law rights under the Fourteenth
Amendment to the United States Constitution; and

. . . WHEREAS, the interests of the Oakland Unified School
District in providing equal opportunities for all of its students
dictate limited English proficient educational programs recognizing the English language acquisition and improvement skills
of African-American students are as fundamental as is application of bilingual education principles for others whose primary
languages are other than English; and

WHEREAS, the standardized tests and grade scores of African-
American students in reading and language arts skills measuring
their application of English skills are substantially below state
and national norms and that such deficiencies will be remedied
by application of a program featuring African Language Systems
principles in instructing African-American children both in
their primary language and in English; and

WHEREAS, standardized tests and grade scores will be remedied by application of a program with teachers and aides who
are certified in the methodology of featuring African Language
Systems principles in instructing African-American children
both in their primary language and in English. The certified

teachers of these students will be provided incentives including, but not limited to salary differentials.

... BE IT FURTHER RESOLVED that the Superintendent in conjunction with her staff shall immediately devise and implement the best possible academic program for imparting instruction to African-American students in their primary language for the combined purposes of maintaining the legitimacy and richness of such language whether it is known as "Ebonics," "African Language Systems," "Pan-African Communication Behaviors" or other description, and to facilitate their acquisition and mastery of English language skills; and

... BE IT FURTHER RESOLVED that the Superintendent and her staff shall utilize the input of the entire Oakland educational community as well as state and federal scholarly and educational input in devising such a program.[14]

While the resolution was widely criticized upon its initial introduction, the notion that blacks were genetically predisposed to speak Ebonics as part of their unique language stature as descendents of slavery drew the most ire from opponents. While the section dealing with the genetic predisposition of blacks to speak Ebonics as their native tongue was later modified, the resolution sparked a fierce discussion that continues to the present day. It is difficult for me to read the resolution above without concluding that the Oakland Board of Education found that black children were somehow inferior to white children based on genetics rather than on the development of proper instruction and learning habits.

Moreover, the implicit suggestion that blacks are more comfortable speaking their "native" language is equally offensive. To reframe John McWhorter's question cited above, was the blame for poor black scholastic achievement to be placed at the hands of whites themselves, since blacks were uncomfortable speaking a language that they found itchy and white? As McWhorter aptly discerns:

> Much of the furious insistence that Black English bars black students from learning to read stems from how Victimology constrains black thinkers' creativity in formulating solutions to problems facing black America, out of a presumption that the only possible logical solutions will respond to white racism. . . . It is not an accident that the Ebonics approach was first developed in the mid 1960s as Victimology and its descendants took hold of black American culture, while the culture argument was not aired until the 1980s, and remains unacknowledged as the pivotal and decisive issue that it is.[15]

That Black English is part of black culture and Standard English is white English is perhaps the only logical outcome many blacks would arrive at when considering the perceived cultural divide that existed in the United States following the rise of Black Power in the late 1960s and well into the 1970s.

When the use of a distinctly black idiom is preferred in the home and the community at large while parents elect to choose black names for their children to demonstrate a level of black pride and awareness, the question persists in my mind: Is there an economic consequence of the overt manifestation of one's blackness to the exclusion of acting or sounding white?

It is here that we return once again to the work of Fryer and his examination of the acting white phenomena. In 2005, Fryer sought to quantify the economic and social costs associated with allegedly acting white while being black in America. A prolific author of scholarship on the topic, Fryer has written several works that stand in direct contrast to the work of those who either downplayed or dismissed outright the significance of the acting white stigma on academic achievement.

In a landmark paper entitled "An Economic Analysis of 'Acting White,'" published in 2005, Fryer and his coauthor, David Austen-Smith, formalized the economic consequences of peer stigmatization associated with acting white. Early in the work the authors trace the emergence of the acting white phenomena, a stigma that drew its roots from the rise of the Black Power movement from the late 1960s and into the 1970s. They assert:

> The notion that blacks view a set of distinctive behaviors (upward mobility, particular speech patterns, acquiescence to white authority) as "selling out," "acting white," or "Tomism" can be traced (at least) to the well-documented strife between house and field Negroes in everyday plantation life and seems to have taken hold by the advent of the Black Power movement in the late 1960s.[16]

More interesting, however, is the connection the two authors make between black racial solidarity and group membership from the time of slavery to the waning days of Jim Crow in the United States in the 1960s. During this era, higher-educated blacks such as doctors, lawyers, and teachers were likely to live in urban neighborhoods with fellow blacks with lower levels of education who were employed in blue-collar occupations. Following the civil rights movement, when systemic discrimination began to recede, a migration occurred in which higher-educated blacks began to live and work in integrated neighborhoods—a development that left many lesser-educated blacks concentrated in inner-city neighborhoods.

Or, the African-American community began to split in two, with higher-educated blacks gaining more power and prominence to the detriment of blue-collar and lesser-educated blacks, who remained in the inner city and became even more marginalized in society.[17] This division between blacks based on socioeconomics led Fryer and Austen-Smith to argue

[t]hat the very presence of high ability blacks and institutional barriers gave incentives to those on the margin to invest in group membership . . . [and] that the very presence of institutional discrimination and the lack of mobility eliminated the two-audience signaling problem and hence, the link between education and acting white."[18]

Accordingly, the link between education and acting white can manifest itself such that some blacks would elect to maintain their cultural identity and underperform in schools rather than apply themselves in the classroom for fear of the social and group exclusion caused by being accused of acting white.

As such, I believe there are two parts of the vicious cycle of the acting white phenomena that must be broken. First, black parents must think carefully about choosing distinctively black names for their children at birth since such names could subject the child to discrimination by future employers, who may believe that child hails from a lower socioeconomic background and therefore is not worthy of consideration for a potential job opening. Second, and equally as important, black parents should warn their children about the high value of receiving a proper education to succeed in America in the twenty-first century.

Rather than shun Standard English and the development of proper study skills as the purview of acting white, parents should reinforce the message that performing well in school isn't accomplished because of the color of one's skin. Instead, the lessons learned in school by acting right rather than acting white will prepare the student to pursue his or her dreams because that student has received the proper skills and training to be a success.

Finally, shunning school and the value of an education by refusing to act white while glorifying the culture of prison and violence enunciated in rap music has had a disturbingly negative impact on black communities across the country. Preserving one's blackness by electing to embrace cultural acceptance instead of by rejecting acting white has had a devastating impact on many blacks across the United States since the Black Power movement of the 1960s and the era of moral relativism and racial exclusion it ushered in, which remains largely in place as an imperfect legacy to the present day.

9

Affirmative Action

Despite the groundbreaking success of *Brown* in setting America on a course toward desegregation, America was still very much unequal in the manner in which blacks and whites interacted in society during the late 1950s and early 1960s. Even with the hard-fought victories before the Supreme Court beginning with *Brown* and continuing throughout the following decade, it would take more than a decade for the "colored" signs to be removed from water fountains, bathrooms, and lunch counters across America. Even as late as 1967, blacks were barred from interracial marriage in numerous states across the land.

And yet the *Brown* decision ushered in a new era when blacks could act as equally as whites to avail themselves in education, housing, and employment opportunities. Instead of an America where individuals were stigmatized for trying to act white, civil rights leaders pressed for one where individuals would be judged based on the content of their character, not the color of their skin. Rather than hope for Americans to stem their feelings of prejudice toward blacks overnight, civil rights leaders sought the force and protection of federal statutes to ensure liberty and equality, not segregation and oppression, would become the law of the land during the turbulent midpoint of the twentieth century.

To this end, Martin Luther King Jr. and other leaders of the civil rights movement acted swiftly in the light of the *Brown* decision to press the federal government to undertake significant steps to address past wrongs due to discriminatory policies. A new playing field was necessary in a slowly integrating America, one that would allow blacks to act and compete equally with whites for opportunities in such areas as employment, housing, and education. This new playing field? A nascent program called affirmative action—an innocuous concept that started in the 1960s by encouraging equal opportunity for employment in the federal government regardless of skin color. It would ultimately devolve into an advanced-quota and set-aside program that reserved slots based not on merit but on pigmentation for blacks and other ethnic minorities, allowing them to receive preferential treatment to attend schools and gain employment in the 1970s and beyond. Rather than promote a color-blind system where blacks and whites could act equally in society based on merit and qualification, the affirmative action debate has instead inhibited blacks and whites from acting as equals—and from viewing one another equally—in contemporary society.

Did the desire to address past discrimination through affirmative action instead codify a system that emblazoned a scarlet *I* for *Inferior* on the chests of successive generations of black children, who were then deemed incapable of acting as academic or industrial equals to whites? We begin our investigation here with the initial foray into affirmative action programs by a young president of the United States who, despite the fanfare given him for addressing civil rights early in his term, remained skeptical about alienating southern whites until his death in 1963.

Just months after being sworn in as the thirty-fifth president of the United States, John F. Kennedy signed Executive Order 10925 on March 6, 1961, which created the President's Committee on Equal

Employment Opportunity (which would eventually become the Equal Employment Opportunity Commission as part of the Civil Rights Act of 1964). Beyond creating the equal employment commission itself, President Kennedy urged the newly created entity to

> [s]crutinize and study employment practices of the Government of the United States, and to consider and recommend additional *affirmative* steps which should be taken by executive department and agencies to realize more fully the national policy of nondiscrimination within executive branch of government.[1] (emphasis added)

Perhaps most famously, Kennedy's executive order also called upon government contractors to

> . . . not discriminate against any employee or applicant for employment because of race, creed, color, or national origin. The contractor will *take affirmative action* to ensure that applicants are employed, and that employees are treated during employment, without regard to their race, creed, color, or national origin.[2] (emphasis added)

While Kennedy's executive order would give birth to the modern concept of affirmative action, his directive at the time was relatively innocuous; he had asked his administration to ensure that affirmative steps would be taken to stamp out discrimination while directing federal contractors to take affirmative action to ensure all employers were hired without regard to the color of their skin. Kennedy's original executive order would be twice modified by President Lyndon Johnson during his term in office to ensure that the federal government and its contractors would take affirmative action so that all job applicants were hired and treated fairly without regard to the color of their skin.

Building on the efforts undertaken by President Kennedy, Dr. Martin Luther King Jr. and other civil rights leaders urged federal leaders to undertake significant efforts to eliminate discrimination across America by federal statute. The *Brown* decision had put cracks in the ceiling of inequality that had stooped blacks for generations; a final push was necessary to smash the barriers of intolerance that had prevented blacks from acting as equals to whites once and for all. Ten years following the *Brown* decision, on July 2, 1964, the Congress and President Lyndon Johnson responded to the vigorous lobbying campaign of King and others by enacting the Civil Rights Act of 1964. This far-sweeping legislation put the force of law behind ending discriminatory behavior based on race, creed, or national origin. More important, would the power of the federal government now curb discrimination that had run rampant across the landscape of America to deny blacks the opportunity to achieve their dreams to act as equal participants in society alongside whites?

The drafters of the Civil Rights Act of 1964 wanted to be proactive in their mission. The statute not only barred discrimination based on the race, color, or creed of an individual but also took a further important and controversial step: Title VII of the act specifically called on the federal courts to undertake "*affirmative action* as may be appropriate" (emphasis added) to remedy past discrimination in the workplace.[3] What precisely were the courts to do to undertake "affirmative action as may be appropriate" to remedy past discrimination in the workplace? As the program expanded and was further interpreted by both the federal courts and presidents beyond President Kennedy, whose desire was to affirmatively hire individuals without regard to the color of their skin, it became a quota system for employment, education, and other forms of federal assistance, and the program would soon attach more significance to the color of one's skin rather than their specific qualifications for admission to a particular school or for being hired to work in a specific job—a precursor to the modern quota and set-aside system that has roiled America ever since.

President Lyndon Johnson would expand efforts to implement affirmative action by issuing two executive orders of his own, in 1965 and 1967 (Executive Orders 11246 and 11375), to ensure that the federal government and its contractors would take affirmative action to ensure that all job applicants were hired and treated fairly without regard to the color of their skin. In revising Executive Order 11375, President Johnson "obligated government contractors to set goals and timelines for employing previously 'underutilized' minority workers who were available and qualified for positions."[4] That a white president previously known for racist sentiments against blacks would embrace efforts in the public and private sector to set quotas and benchmarks for minority employment and educational opportunities is surprising. What is not surprising, however, is that the efforts to level the playing field and to allow blacks to act as freely as whites in society would ultimately lead to resentment and accusations of reverse racism when private and public entities would judge one's race rather than the sum of their accomplishments when seeking to fill a vacancy in employment or a seat at colleges and universities across the country.

The evolution of affirmative action from a mechanism for blacks to pursue opportunities on an equal footing with whites to a government preferential-quota program where blacks were favored at the expense of whites first occurred during President Johnson's administration. In 1967 Johnson directed his Department of Health, Education, and Welfare (HEW) to require colleges and universities across the United States that received federal funding to set affirmative action goals for minority faculty employment.[5]

During his tenure in office, President Richard Nixon expanded the HEW directive to push colleges and universities to do the following:

Recruit, employ and promote members of previously excluded groups, even if prior exclusion could not be traced to past discrimination actions. The HEW guidelines distinguished between goals that were indicators of compliance and quotas that might exclude others from equal opportunity.[6]

Ten years. In just ten years, it took the Supreme Court's decision in *Brown v. Board of Education* in 1954 followed by enactment of the

Civil Rights Act of 1964 to bring about a new American society where blacks could not be legally discriminated against and were instead free to act the same as whites in most segments of society.

And yet in the ten-year period between 1964 and 1974, Presidents Johnson and Nixon directed their executive-branch agencies to promote a system that failed to strengthen blacks' position to be equals of whites in the American landscape or to have their abilities assessed on merit and hard work; instead, the system rewarded the recruitment of those who may not have been qualified for employment or enrollment in school to satisfy the vacuous goals of "diversity." In doing so, it cemented the notion that blacks were inferior and unable to compete with whites on an equal playing field.

Despite their good intentions, the two chief executives promoted a set-aside and quota system to ostensibly "help" blacks achieve equality in America that would instead reduce, not elevate, the ability of blacks to act as the equals of whites. For many, the color-blind society sought by Dr. Martin Luther King Jr., where one was judged by the content of one's character rather than the color of one's skin, was very much in jeopardy; affirmative action programs had quickly evolved from equal access and opportunity for employment and education to one where blacks and whites were not treated equally, to its (unfortunate) result— they only fueled rather than reduced racial anxieties and resentment.

An early challenge to the legitimacy and efficacy of affirmative action programs in the field of education occurred in the 1978 Supreme Court case of *Regents of the University of California v. Bakke.* At its center was an aspiring white applicant to medical school, Allan Bakke, who sought and had twice been denied admission to the University of California at Davis School of Medicine. When he applied to attend UC Davis in 1972, Bakke was one of 2,664 applicants seeking admission for what he believed were one hundred seats in the entering class. Bakke subsequently discovered that there were two separate admissions programs at the school of medicine: one with eighty-four seats for applicants with competitive academic and board scores and one with sixteen seats that were to be filled using different academic and test-score criteria that were not nearly as stringent; with these seats the University of California had felt compelled to increase its admission of black, Asian, Latino, and other students who were barely represented on campus or were part of a special "disadvantaged" group.

When Bakke discovered that no white students had been admitted to the sixteen seats in the special-admissions program, for which the admissions criteria for acceptance was lower than the criteria of the applicant pool from which he had been rejected, he initiated litigation. In the ensuing lawsuit, he claimed that the University of California had violated the stipulation of Title VII of the Civil Rights Act of 1964, which forbid racial or ethnic preferences in programs supported by the federal government. Moreover, Bakke asserted that the university's decision to set aside slots reserved for minorities had denied him equal protection under the law as guaranteed by the Fourteenth Amendment.

Answering Bakke's charge, the University of California agreed that while racial classifications were in fact bad, the state had an equally compelling interest and concern for victims of past and continuing racial injustice. As such, the increase of diversity on campus would help create a future generation of role models for minority youths while increasing the numbers of minority medical practitioners who could provide services to minority communities.

Before examining the Court's decision in *Bakke* in greater detail, it is important to frame the issue from a broader context within the struggles of the civil rights movement, which had ended not ten years earlier. From 1896 to 1954—a span of some fifty-eight years—blacks were relegated to separate and inherently unequal conditions in schools, colleges, and universities across the country courtesy of the ruling held in *Plessy v. Ferguson.* Following the landmark decision in *Brown v. Board of Education,* the Supreme Court held that *Plessy v. Ferguson* had instituted systemic discrimination across the United States, where separate and equal accommodations not only were offensive to the protections afforded in the Constitution but also had led to a generation of young black students believing they were inferior to white students.

In just over twenty years following its decision in *Brown,* the Supreme

Court was once again asked to rule in a discrimination case pertaining to education. In the *Bakke* case, however, the Court wasn't asked to determine whether the struggles of the civil rights era had failed to promote a system where blacks could act as freely as whites to pursue the strengths and benefits of an education. Instead, the Court was asked to rule on the validity of a federally funded university admissions program where blacks and "specially disadvantaged" individuals were granted admission for precious seats at an institution of higher learning based not on their academic performance and fitness for study but on the institution's desire to promote diversity and to "help" minorities serve as future role models for youths and to work in minority communities.

In a narrow 5–4 decision, the Supreme Court held in *Regents of the University of California v. Bakke* that a university is free to consider racial criteria as part of the admissions decision so long as a fixed-quota system is not in place. Justice Lewis Powell cast the deciding vote and wrote the majority opinion. In essence, the Court held that racial quotas should be banned but that an applicant's race could be a factor schools considered when selecting incoming students for enrollment.

Rather than limit the use of race as a factor for admissions committees across the country, the *Bakke* decision only ruled out the use of a fixed-quota system for minority-student enrollment, and it allowed a candidate's racial ethnicity to be considered as part of a plan to increase diversity on campuses across the country. The initial efforts of President Kennedy to provide color-blind affirmative action to ensure blacks were treated equally under the law had devolved into racial quotas and then further into programs for racial diversity on campuses and places of employment; in this system the victories garnered in *Brown* to treat blacks equally under the color of law had deteriorated into a system where blacks were viewed as desirable for their diversity rather than their ability to act and compete equally as whites in society.

Moreover, the rationale displayed by the Regents of the University of California to admit more students of color, while well intentioned, was patently offensive to those who believed all students—black and white alike—should be admitted to attend the University of California school system based on their academic and extracurricular success rather than the color of their skin.

While I believe an increase of highly trained black doctors could, in fact, provide role models to students of color, to suggest that these same doctors would increase the number of minority doctors serving in minority communities is condescending on its face to me. The regents' rationale suggests that in an integrated America in the 1970s, minorities would choose to self-segregate and practice medicine only in communities of color. To follow this supposition further, Would minority doctors who had been admitted with lower scores than their white counterparts also provide a lower quality of care in black communities they ostensibly had been trained to serve?

While Allan Bakke ultimately prevailed in his litigation in 1978 and was seated at the University of California at Davis School of Medicine, successive generations of black students, such as myself, who lived not only in California but around the United States would be subjected to the insult and ridicule of being "affirmative action" admitees. In other words, the only reason many thought that a black or minority student had been admitted to a school was because of the color of their skin rather than the strength of their academic record. The result of such an admissions policy would be to brand black students with a badge of inferiority—the result derived from those who viewed blacks as unable to compete as academic equals with their white counterparts.

As a California native who grew up not far from the University of California at Davis, after the *Bakke* decision was handed down from the Supreme Court in 1978, I would be haunted by the legacy from its decision for decades to come—fostering my virulent opposition to affirmative action quota programs to the present day. During elementary and high school, the students in my suburban San Francisco town—black and white—were treated more or less as equals. I didn't think that I had friends who were black or friends who were white; most of us had known one another since kindergarten or before and viewed one another as friends, classmates, and teammates on the athletic fields together. Color had never entered into the equation as we lived our lives together.

When I attended high school, Stanford University had a voluntary program for minority students to enroll should they be considering a career in mathematics, science, or engineering. While never a strong student in the natural or applied sciences (I was ultimately an English major in college), the thought of being an astronaut had always appealed to me, and NASA had the Ames Research Center in the town next door; I applied to the Mathematics, Engineering and Science Achievement (MESA) program and was accepted. Stanford provided tutors, interesting lecture programs, and internship opportunities for program participants—a true affirmative action program designed to give students an equal opportunity to learn and excel in the sciences if they so chose. And to inoculate against charges of being racially exclusionary, MESA was geared to getting minority students interested in the sciences but was also open to those who were genuinely interested—a long about way of saying whites could enroll if they so chose.

It was only when I applied to college and it came time to check boxes on application forms that I was first confronted by my ostensibly racially neutral peers. I had been told on more than one occasion by my classmates that Stanford University and other elite private colleges and universities would admit black students if only they had a pulse. To say the least, I was stunned by such assertions: while not a National Merit Scholar or outstanding athlete, I had worked hard in high school and had a wide variety of extracurricular activities to supplement my academic credentials. And yet, less than a decade after the *Bakke* decision, a number of my classmates from Northern California had questioned my qualifications to attend college to my face, wondering if I was going to be an affirmative action or diversity pick. Apparently, they thought that the only way I would be able to attend a top-tier school would be through the color of my skin, and a heartbeat that registered in a pulse—my academic record and extracurricular activities were apparently immaterial to them. Sadly, this was an accusation and assertion that I would encounter repeatedly throughout my under-graduate and graduate school training.

Upon my subsequent enrollment to Haverford College in the fall of 1987, I was confronted by similar questions from classmates who, intentionally or not, denigrated my enrollment and asked whether affirmative action was behind my admission. This is the true legacy of *Bakke:* whether a black student is truly qualified or not is immaterial in the minds of many of their white students, employees, and colleagues—many just assume that your presence is strictly a result of affirmative action programs. Otherwise, an inferior candidate such as you, Ron Christie, would never have been admitted. This was a far cry from the legacy and sacrifice of Thurgood Marshall, the NAACP, and Dr. Martin Luther King Jr., who worked tirelessly so that students such as myself would be judged based on the content of their character rather than the color of their skin. The diversity wave ushered in by *Bakke* only led people to openly question my inferiority rather than accept me at face value. A young black man on the college campus of my alma mater couldn't have arrived on his own to act and participate as equally in class discussions as whites; affirmative action must be the true reason he's here.

By no means have I meant to infer this was the prevailing attitude at Haverford College—far from it, in fact. Haverford prides itself on bringing together bright, intellectually curious, and socially active students from across the country to learn and interact with one another, and it has succeeded in cultivating one of the best academic programs in America, of which I was honored to have been a part. At the same time, just a few isolated questions about my fitness and qualifications from a few unenlightened students led me to believe that, however well intentioned, quotas and affirmative action programs did more to denigrate the accomplishments of ethnic minorities and to plant the seeds of inferiority in their minds and those of their classmates than anything I could possibly imagine.

Here, I vividly recall a rally organized by the Reverend Jesse Jackson Sr. at Harvard Law School in 1990, as I wrapped up my junior year at Haverford, that forever turned me off to the notion of affirmative action quota and diversity programs. Jackson had arrived in Cambridge to bemoan the fact that there was no tenured women faculty members teaching at Harvard Law School. The crisis at Harvard had escalated after Derrick Bell, the first black tenured professor at the law school, had threatened to go on leave from Harvard unless and until the university hired a tenured black woman professor to its ranks. Of the sixty tenured faculty members of Harvard Law School at the time, three were black and five were women; Harvard had yet to have a tenured black woman on its faculty.

While internal deliberations proceeded at Harvard University to address the paucity of black faculty members teaching at Harvard Law School, the Reverend Jesse Jackson Sr. found an opening to interject himself into the debate. After the dean of the law school, Robert C. Clark, had met with Jackson but declined his offer to mediate the "crisis," Jackson took to the microphone to champion the cause for himself.

At a rally held at Harvard, Jackson assailed the "moral character" of Harvard Law School, declaring it was on trial for its failure to have a tenured black woman professor as a member of the faculty: "To say in 1990 that there is no African-American woman qualified for appointment to Harvard Law School is both an error and a gross insult to our intelligence. It is humiliating."[7] I remember thinking at the time that, while Harvard should have made more of an effort to recruit and attract more professors of color, calling the scarcity of such faculty members an "insult to our intelligence" and "humiliating" was a bit much. Shouldn't a private institution be allowed to hire its own faculty members without being bullied or accused of racism? Is this what affirmative action had devolved into: "hire more blacks or else you're a racist"? Something about that logic seemed terribly wrong.

But Jackson wasn't finished. Following a twenty-five-minute meeting with the dean of the law school, in which Jackson was assured Harvard was devoting significant efforts to hiring a tenured black woman to its faculty but that they would not be pressured into doing so, Jackson bemoaned such efforts as "cultural anemia." Even worse, Jackson offered the following vision of affirmative action in 1990:

> "We cannot just define who is qualified in the most narrow, vertical academic terms," he said. "Most people in the world are yellow, brown, black, poor, non-Christian and don't speak English, and they can't wait for some white males with archaic rules to appraise them."[8]

"Narrow, vertical academic" qualifications? "White males with archaic rules to appraise" blacks? One would suspect that Harvard University's faculty would be among the leaders of academic institutions around the world with professors with impeccable academic qualifications. To suggest that black faculty members should not be viewed equally as whites in assessing their qualifications is nothing more than admitting that a black faculty member is inferior and not able to withstand the rigorous qualification process.

And how had the entire firestorm over the hiring of black tenured women faculty members at Harvard begun in the first place? Jackson and others had objected to the affirmative action plan Harvard had filed with the federal government—a plan they believed demonstrated that the university had no further plans to hire a black faculty member for the following year.

How far afield the program had swayed from the original purpose envisioned by President Kennedy in 1961—for blacks to have the ability to compete equally with whites, with the federal government taking affirmative action to ensure that individuals would be treated equally under the law without regard to the color of their skin. In 1990 blacks would object to affirmative action plans that did not include a sufficient quota of black faculty members to be hired.

Incredibly, Professor Derrick Bell, himself the first tenured black faculty member hired at Harvard, offered the following commentary on the controversy while standing beside the Reverend Jackson: "Harvard needs and deserves a faculty based on more than what was deemed the ideal more than 50 years ago."[9] The ideal at the dawn of the twenty-first century should have been one where blacks and whites could act as academic equals based on their scholarship and intelligence rather than one that sought to systematize the inclusion of minorities based on their skin color. Ultimately, Bell would leave his position at Harvard and would transfer to New York University School of Law, where he remains to the present day. And shortly following Bell's departure in 1992, Harvard University hired Lani Guinier, a prominent civil rights lawyer and the future nominee for assistant United States attorney general, to become the first black female faculty member tenured at its law school.

Two decades following the *Regents of the University of California v. Bakke* decision in 1978, a regent of the University of California had had enough with the manner in which the state had administered affirmative action programs, and he sought to change the system. Ward Connolly, a black regent of the University of California, unveiled the California Civil Rights Initiative, or Proposition 209, in 1996; it aimed to change the status quo of affirmative action and quota programs in the state. Connolly had become convinced that affirmative action programs as administered by the University of California and other state and local entities were tantamount to racial discrimination.

Therefore, Connolly sought to eliminate all classification programs based on race, sex, and color administered by the state: California would act the same toward black, white, Asian, and female applicants— treat them equally and act without consideration for, giving preferable treatment to, or prejudice because of the color of an applicant's skin. Instead, blacks, whites, and others would have equal standing in the admissions process and would be admitted for their qualifications rather than the color of their skin.

In clear and concise language, the initiative simply proposed to amend the state of California's constitution by declaring that the state would not discriminate against or grant preferential treatment to anyone based on race, color, sex, or national origin. The true essence of President Kennedy's vision for affirmative action was being put forth once again: blacks, whites, Hispanics, women, and men should be viewed under the law equally, and the opportunities for all to act equally in society should be granted without prejudice and without regard for the color of one's skin.

After a bitter and closely contested campaign that spanned much of 1996, voters went to the polls on November 5, 1996, to support or reject Proposition 209 once and for all. Of nearly 10 million ballots cast, Proposition 209 was enacted into law with more than 54 percent of the electorate voting to eliminate preferential treatment based on race, color, and sex of the applicant in question.

Despite a myriad of legal challenges, the proposition became law, and the California constitution was amended accordingly:

CALIFORNIA CONSTITUTION
ARTICLE 1 DECLARATION OF RIGHTS

SEC. 31. (a) The State shall not discriminate against, or grant preferential treatment to, any individual or group on the basis of race, sex, color, ethnicity, or national origin in the operation of public employment, public education, or public contracting.[10]

Critics of Proposition 209 bitterly warned that the clock of progress would be turned back against blacks and other ethnic minorities with the elimination of racial-preference programs. But what is the legacy of such a controversial program that sought to treat people, regardless of their race or gender, as equal actors before the law in the state of California?

Eryn Hadley tackled this difficult question in an article for the *BYU Journal of Public Law*, "Did the Sky Really Fall? Ten Years After California's Proposition 209."[11] In particular, Hadley challenged the assertion that passage of the proposition would dilute the percentage of black and Latino students attending the University of California schools of higher education. Critics of the measure contended that blacks and other minorities needed quota and affirmative action programs to compete equally with whites; Connolly and proponents of the measure believed blacks and whites should stand as equal actors with equal opportunity to succeed or fail in regard to state admission and employment programs, regardless of the color of their skin.

To make her case, Hadley noted the prediction of the Proposition 209 critic Cynthia Lee that the percentage of black students attending the University of California at Los Angeles would drop from 6.9 percent to between 1.5 percent and 1.8 percent without strong affirmative action outreach programs in place. For the five-year period 1995–2000, data furnished by the University of California shows only a 1 percent reduction in the number of underrepresented minorities within the system following enactment of Proposition 209. Most surprisingly, however, is data that demonstrates dramatic *increases* in underrepresented minority students at several University of California schools, most notably UC Santa Cruz and UC Riverside. As Hadley argues:

> Although the more prestigious schools saw a significant decrease in admissions of underrepresented minorities similar to that predicted by Proposition 209's opponents, UC Santa Cruz and UC Riverside saw a drastic increase in admissions of underrepresented minorities. Students are being admitted on the strength of their credentials. UC Santa Cruz and UC Riverside continue to enroll a strong percentage of underrepresented minority students.[12]

In fact, once the University of California stopped looking at students based merely on the color of their skin to satisfy affirmative action programs, UC Santa Cruz and UC Riverside saw their black and Latino student enrollment flourish. During the five-year period 1995–2000, underrepresented minorities at the UC Riverside increased 87 percent, and the UC Santa Cruz saw underrepresented minorities increase by 27 percent. Why? Because when black and other candidates were being admitted to the schools in which their credentials matched those of their white and Asian counterparts, their enrollment numbers soared.

Moreover, the retention rates of black students in the University of California system also rose dramatically. As noted by Hadley:

> For example, at UC Berkeley, the six-year or less graduation rate of African-American and Hispanic freshmen entering in the fall of 1998, increased by 6.5% and 4.9%, respectively, compared to the graduation rates of their peers just two years earlier, before Proposition 209 was in effect.
>
> At UC San Diego, the average freshman GPAs for minorities all but converged with the GPAs of white and Asian students, just one year after Proposition 209 was implemented.[13]

Despite the dire predictions of detractors of Proposition 209, the data furnished by the University of California confirmed what proponents of the proposition had predicted all along: black and minority students are capable of academic performance in school that is equally as strong as that of their Asian and white peers when their admission is based on academic achievement and preparation rather than affirmative action programs that admit minority students to fulfill diversity goals.

THE WAY FORWARD

The battles fought by the early pioneers of the civil rights movement were waged to ensure that the practice of separate but equal accommodations in schools would be abolished so that black children would have an equal opportunity to compete with whites and act as equals in a new American society. Instead of codifying government rules and regulations to ensure blacks acted as the inferiors of whites in America, the *Brown* decision and subsequent actions by Presidents Kennedy and Johnson, along with the enactment of the Civil Rights Act of 1964, brought about a new start for blacks, long accustomed to oppression and inequality, to act on a newly created playing field.

Sadly, the efforts by some to alleviate white guilt brought about by decades of oppression toward blacks has instead manifested itself in the sacrifice of black self-agency and sufficiency. As Shelby Steele asserts in *The Content of Our Character:* "I think that affirmative action has shown itself to be more bad than good and that blacks . . . now stand to lose more from it than they gain."[14] We stand to lose more than we gain, Steele continued, because, in his belief:

> Under affirmative action, the quality [being black] that earns us preferential treatment is an implied inferiority. . . . Even when the black sees no implication of inferiority in racial preferences, he knows that whites do, so that—consciously or unconsciously—the result is virtually the same. The effect of preferential treatment—the lowering of normal standards to increase black representation—puts blacks at war with an expanded realm of debilitating doubt, so that the doubt itself becomes an unrecognized preoccupation that undermines their ability to perform especially in integrated situations.[15]

Thus, many whites perceive their black classmates and office peers not as being equal but as being inferior because they believe the standards must have been lowered somehow for that black person to be in a position of equal footing with them.

In a similar proposition put forth by the linguist John McWhorter in *Winning the Race:*

> . . . [a]t a top university as everywhere else, one's "blackness" is the first consideration and one's humanity the second, rather than the other way around. Meanwhile, whites are equally under the sway of an era that elevates exaggeration of victimhood, and pretending to concur with it, as permissible suspensions of common sense.[16]

Perhaps these sentiments offer a revealing portrait of why their peers accuse black students who work hard, study hard, and perform well in school of acting white. Perhaps the advent of affirmative action programs have perpetuated a stereotype that has become self-fulfilling: acting black is doing poorly and needing government assistance and quota programs to try—and fail—to pull even with whites. Acting white by doing well in school is the exception rather than the norm for blacks, since society has been accustomed for more than forty years to the idea that blacks need an extra boost just to try to stay even with whites.

Finally, the seeds sown by affirmative action over the decades have blossomed into a culture that prides itself on victimization, government quotas to move ahead, cultural self-exclusion, and disdain for self-identity—and, most tragically, acceptance of mediocrity and inferiority, where performing well academically is akin to a black child's acting white. That the struggles for equality brought about by *Brown v. Board of Education* have instead caused cultural acceptance of black inferiority is a phenomena that must be reversed. We owe our children and our society much, much more. And both deserve nothing less.

10

The Divide

Upwardly Mobile Black America
and the Urban Poor

. . .

Too white for Bed-Stuy, too black for Harvard, Chanequa
Campbell struggled between two worlds.

—*New York Post*, July 26, 2009[1]

The acting white phenomenon has now come full circle early in
the twenty-first century. Gone are the days when blacks
fought tirelessly and at great peril for their personal safety to
secure the right for their children to receive an education that would
allow them a true shot at achieving the American dream. The dark days
of the civil rights era are now behind us—the dogs have been leashed,
the water hoses cut off, and the guns and batons have been holstered.

And yet, more than fifty years following the historic *Brown v.
Board of Education* decision that outlawed separate but equal accommodations as offensive to the equal protection of law under the Constitution, a new form of segregation now sweeps across America. In a
disturbing trend, many blacks mock members of their own race who
seek academic excellence in the classroom and speak and dress well as
being nothing more than Uncle Toms and acting white.

A slur nearly expunged by two separate political and social movements led by Martin Luther King Jr. and Malcolm X has resurfaced
under the institutionalization of affirmative action programs brought

about by the Great Society. In a previous generation, when Booker T. Washington recommended blacks cede higher learning to whites, a wave of black leaders rose to defend the access to ballot box, civil rights, and the power of the humanities through education for all U.S. citizens. Today, a large segment of the black community is voluntarily ceding intellectual development without conscience.

Is this new paradigm nothing more than a return to the days of Jim Crow, when being black in America meant being uneducated, inferior, and subservient to whites? Why do many blacks castigate fellow members of their race who seek to improve their social and economic standing for doing nothing more than acting white?

The contemporary criticism of acting white has arrived and flourished in our schools and communities, and we must take steps to quell this poisonous stain, which rewards inferiority at the cost of upward academic, social, and political mobility. I should know: I've been tarred with the acting white slur my entire professional and academic life, placing me in a unique perspective to debunk those who assert that the acting white phenomena is nothing more than an urban legend.

Until fairly recently, the acting white myth was depicted to be just that—a myth unsubstantiated by sociological, economic, or scholastic review. In 1986, Professors Signithia Fordham and John Ogbu published their findings on what is considered the leading initial empirical study regarding the impact of allegations of acting white in academic settings. Fordham and Ogbu conducted a survey of several high school students in the District of Columbia, at a school they later dubbed "Capital High" to protect the identity of the program participants. In their review, they found that African-American students failed to live up to their academic potential for fear of the social and cultural stigma of being accused by their peers of acting white.[2] A few years later, Ogbu further solidified these conclusions in his 2003 book, *Black American Students in an Affluent Suburb: A Study of Academic Disengagement.*

It should be noted that early scholarship on the effect of acting white in the classroom was far from conclusive, however. In 2003, the

University of North Carolina professors Karolyn Tyson and William Darity Jr. conducted an eighteen-month study of eleven North Carolina schools to ascertain the perception of acting white among black students. Unlike the conclusions reached by Fordham and Ogbu, the North Carolina study found that black and white students had essentially the same motivation and attitude regarding academic achievement. In their view, acting white did not have a negative effect on African-American student achievement. Perhaps, the authors led their audience to believe, the acting white myth would remain just that. Despite the conflicting results of two major studies on the impact of acting white in academic settings, the notion that blacks act white by speaking, dressing, and behaving differently than other blacks was quite real at the dawn of the twenty-first century.

The year 2004 would prove instrumental in elevating the prominence of acting white as a stigma and deterrent for the many African-Americans who sought to break the binds of poverty and blue-collar occupations through self-reliance and the power of education. That year, just one year after the release of Tyson and Darity's study on the effects of acting white, two unlikely figures would push acting white to the forefront of American social and political consciousness. The first figure was eminently well known to the American people, and the second, while relatively unknown at that point in time, would become president of the United States a mere four years later.

Interestingly, the assessment of the success or failure of the opportunities presented to black children across America in the fifty years since the landmark *Brown* decision and whether a black child who was succeeding in the classroom was now merely acting white would come from a most unlikely source, one that would roil the country in controversy for months to come: William Henry "Bill" Cosby, Ed.D.

Cosby has long been regarded as America's dad from his prolific work as a pitchman for Jell-O pudding and Coca-Cola and as the star in early television programs such as *I Spy* and *The Electric Company*. Cosby is perhaps best known for two television programs he created:

the cartoon series *Fat Albert and the Cosby Kids* as well as *The Cosby Show,* which ran from 1984 to 1992 and remains in syndication today.

Unlike previous depictions of blacks on television, *The Cosby Show* portrayed an affluent upper-middle-class black nuclear family where the parents (a doctor and a lawyer) served as proper role models to their well-spoken and educated children. The premium placed on education by the fictitious Huxtable family was high: learning, dressing well, and holding oneself with dignity was not considered acting white, it was deemed acting properly to succeed in America. More than anything, *The Cosby Show* proved that the depiction of a successful African-American family could draw vast audiences at either end of the racial spectrum.

At the height of its popularity in the 1980s, *The Cosby Show* drew as many as 50 million viewers per episode. By contrast, Fox's *American Idol* program has been the most-watched show over the past several years. In 2007–08, for example, the show drew 28.8 million viewers per week.[3] The *Cosby Show* numbers proved that Americans, regardless of their race, were comfortable with welcoming an upwardly mobile middle-class black family into their homes each week, one for whom hard work, proper speech, and education and upward mobility was the norm rather than the exception.

While many Americans are aware of Cosby's comedic brilliance, fewer are aware of his work in the field of education. Cosby received an Ed.D degree in 1976 from the University of Massachusetts, where he wrote a dissertation entitled "An Integration of the Visual Media via 'Fat Albert and the Cosby Kids' into the Elementary School Curriculum as a Teaching Aid and Vehicle to Achieve Increased Learning." Long a proponent of African-Americans opening the locked doors and shattering the ceilings of advancement that existed before *Brown v. Board of Education,* Cosby was a strong believer in the power of education to lift blacks from the ghetto into the middle class of America.

Recognizing his work and vast achievements, the NAACP invited Dr. Cosby to deliver the keynote remarks at their gala to commemorate and celebrate the fiftieth anniversary of the *Brown v. Board of Education* decision, on May 14, 2004. Fifty years following this landmark decision, separate but equal school facilities had been outlawed in America, but had her black schoolchildren fully used their opportunities to perform as equals to whites? Separate but equal had been the barrier to black children's having the opportunity to succeed for more than fifty years from 1896 to 1954: how had the children of subsequent generations responded in the fifty years following *Brown?* Finally, were the scars of racial inferiority exposed by the doll test so far removed fifty years since the passage of *Brown* that blacks now viewed themselves in a positive manner and as coequals with whites, or did they still view being white as positive and being black as negative now that they had arrived in a newly integrated society?

Accepting the invitation to speak and reflect on the transformative nature of the *Brown* decision, Cosby surprised many in the audience and across the country for using his remarks to castigate the leadership of black parents, teachers, and politicians for their tolerance and failure to capitalize on the doors that had been opened by *Brown,* instead allowing successive generations of black children to shun the value of education as the key to unlock the doors to the American dream. Previous generations of black children had yearned merely for the opportunity to attend school without fear of castigation, violence, and strict adherence to racial segregation; many of today's black children viewed studying and performing well in school as acting white instead of as acting right among their peers.

Before a stunned audience, who perhaps believed it was set to be regaled rather than reprimanded by America's dad, Cosby condemned the lack of economic and social progress in many urban neighborhoods across America since previous generations had fought at great personal risk to their personal safety to ensure future black children had opportunities to act as equal rather than subservient to whites. Rather than take a bow or a lap in victory following fifty years of remarkable and demonstrable progress, Cosby instead famously told the audience composed of such luminaries as Dorothy Height and the Reverend Jesse

Jackson Sr. to stop blaming white people for injustice in their lives and accept personal responsibility for the missed opportunities for blacks to achieve financial, academic, and personal success.

Dubbed the "pound cake" speech, Cosby's remarks did not just electrify the audience at Constitution Hall in Washington, D.C. He sparked a powerful debate that served as a catalyst for his directly wading into the acting white controversy head-on just days later. The following excerpts offer a colorful yet powerful illustration of Cosby's passion for black self-empowerment and his disdain for pulling down others for acting white and for seeking an escape from adverse socioeconomic surroundings in favor of a better life. Of the brave pioneers who championed the *Brown* decision, Cosby thundered:

> Ladies and gentlemen, these people set—they opened the doors, they gave us the right and today, ladies and gentlemen, in our cities and public schools we have 50% drop out. . . . Ladies and gentlemen, the lower economic and lower middle economic people are not holding their end in this deal.[4]

Cosby took his fiery remarks one step further by seeking to extinguish the excuse that somehow whites were to blame for the predicament of blacks:

> We cannot blame white people. White people—white people don't live over there. . . . What part of Africa did this come from? We are not Africans. Those people are not Africans; they don't know a damned thing about Africa. With names like Shaniqua, Shaligua, Mohamed and all that crap and all of them are in jail. . . . Brown versus the Board of Education is no longer the white person's problem. We've got to take the neighborhood back. . . . Everybody knows it's important to speak English except these knuckleheads. You can't land a plane with "Why you ain't . . ." You can't be a doctor with that kind of crap coming out of your mouth.[5]

And perhaps most dramatically, Cosby chose the following words near the end of his address to lament the lack of progress and educational development of blacks since *Brown v. Board of Education*, since many African-Americans equated success in the classroom as acting white rather than as advancing up the rungs to higher socioeconomic success:

> Brown v. Board of Education, these people who marched and were hit in the face with rocks and punched in the face to get an education and we got these knuckleheads walking around who don't want to learn English. I know you all know it. I just want to get you as angry that you ought to be. . . . These people are not funny any more. And that's not my brother. And that's not my sister. They're faking and they're dragging me way down because the state, the city and all these people have to pick up the tab on them because they don't want to accept that they have to study to get an education. . . . Well, Brown v. Board of Education, where are we today? It's there. They paved the way. What did we do with it? The white man, he's laughing, got to be laughing. 50 percent drop out, rest of them in prison.[6]

Drawing scant praise and significant condemnation for his remarks before the NAACP event that evening, Dr. Cosby was merely at the beginning rather than the end of his journey to shine a bright light on many of the predicaments that ailed far too many African-Americans across the country—including the pejorative that a young black child with a book was acting white.

Both in speeches and in an appearance on TV, Cosby not only re-fused to back down in his critiques of those who sought to put the failure for black advancement at the feet of others but also refused to accept a scenario where blacks who sought to elevate their socioeco-nomic standing were doing nothing more than acting white.

Cosby took to the airwaves to defend himself against those who criticized his call for black empowerment and self-reliance by appear-ing on PBS's *Tavis Smiley Show* on May 26, 2004. Note the following exchange, where Smiley engaged Cosby on his less than politically correct comments holding blacks to account for their actions:

Smiley: But you kicked up a conversation here. You got America talking. That's what a presidential candidate ought to do.

Cosby: Ladies and gentlemen, do me a favor. Talk to each other. Talk to each other. I have too many positive stories also. When I said, 'take your neighborhoods back,' this can happen. You have to get out and talk to each other. And you have to realize what is good and what is not good and who's tweaking your children to buy things.

I mean, when girls are beating up other girls because the other girls were virgins, when boys are attacking other boys because the boys are studying and they say, *'You're acting white.'* Well, I got news for y[ou] . . . it's a disease all around.[7] (emphasis added)

Suddenly, the acting white discussion had left local schools, playgrounds, and barbershops and found its way to the national stage. A slur that had been murmured under one's breath in the school yard regarding another student was now being broadcast into millions of homes across America.

What had roused Bill Cosby to such ire and consternation? Hadn't *Brown,* affirmative action, and the rise of black power and pride unshackled the chains that had held blacks back from academic and cultural success? Perhaps the sad reality that led Cosby to his call to arms within the black community was the fact that many blacks intentionally spurned success as acting white rather than as honoring the sacrifice of previous generations who had given them the opportunity to prevail through hard work and discipline. As we shall soon discover, victimization and the desire to become socially acceptable to other blacks would inhibit the perseverance and dedication to succeed of blacks who feared being accused of acting white.

While the national dialogue and debate on acting white had been elevated with Cosby's "pound cake" speech and his subsequent discussion of the topic on the *Tavis Smiley Show,* just two months following Cosby's remarks a little-known state senator from Illinois would deliver the keynote address at the Democratic National Convention in Boston, Massachusetts, and denounce the demonization of black students for seeking educational advancement and for this "acting white"—providing further validation of a term many had dismissed as an urban myth.[8] Acting white had now entered the realm of national politics, where it has remained ever since.

Senator Barack Obama (D-IL), a charismatic candidate running for the United States Senate, had been asked by the party standard-bearer, Senator John Kerry (D-MA), to deliver the keynote remarks during his presidential nominating convention in Boston. In electrifying remarks heard around the world that would catapult Obama's political trajectory from Springfield, Illinois, to 1600 Pennsylvania Avenue in just four years, Obama touched on the racially sensitive pejorative of "acting white," used to refer to blacks in academic settings. While Cosby was widely criticized for his denunciation of the allegation that blacks were acting white by seeking to advance themselves through education and self-empowerment, the silence surrounding the senator's remarks was deafening in the days following his prime-time address:

> Go into any inner-city neighborhood, and folks will tell you that government alone can't teach kids to learn. They know that parents have to teach, that children can't achieve unless we raise their expectations and turn off the television sets and eradicate the slander that says a black youth with a book is acting white. They know those things.[9]

One speech. One searing indictment of black attitudes that equate academic success and proper speech with acting white in American society—Obama's remarks on the heels of Cosby's denunciations of the slur drew swift reaction from black intellectuals and social commentators. Ironically, Cosby would be repeatedly castigated and denounced for his criticism of the acting white pejorative, while Obama escaped such vitriolic commentary.

Henry Louis Gates Jr., director of the W. E. B. Du Bois Institute for African and African American Research at Harvard University, came to the defense of Cosby in a column published in *The New York Times* on August 1, 2004, just days following Obama's address to the Democratic National Convention.

In an op-ed entitled "Breaking the Silence," Gates offered the following commentary regarding the uproar Cosby had created by denouncing the acting white slur, which Obama had similarly done just days before:

> In a speech filled with rousing applause lines, it [Obama's denunciation of the acting white slander] was a line that many black Democratic delegates found especially galvanizing. Not just because they agreed, but because it was a home truth they'd seldom heard a politician say out loud.
>
> Why has it been so difficult for black leaders to say such things in public without being pilloried for "blaming the victim"? Why the huge flap over Bill Cosby's insistence that black teenagers do their homework, stay in school, master Standard English and stop having babies? Any black person knows that Mr. Cosby was only echoing sentiments widely shared in the black community.[10]

Beyond Professor Gates, Cosby also received a spirited defense of his remarks by the African-American essayist Clarence Page during an appearance on *PBS NewsHour* on September 27, 2004. In his televised remarks, Page attacked the notion of the acting white slur as well as Cosby's detractors when he commented:

> In African American folklore, the sea crab ranks among the dumbest of creatures who also offers a valuable lesson. When you catch a bucket or a basketful, you never have to put a lid

on because when one of the creatures tries to get out, the others will just pull it back in. Some of our fellow human beings aren't much smarter than that. When they see you working hard to achieve your dreams, they'll make fun of you just for trying. . . . Yes, today's hip-hop generation has basket crabs of its own, eager to put you down for somehow acting white when you try to get ahead as if blackness means you have to fail.[11]

In speaking of Senator Obama and Bill Cosby's remarks, Page would touch on a paradox that has followed many in the black community for generations: if one is somehow acting white to get ahead, being black and acting black means that one must be a failure in order to be deemed successful. Page further noted that prominent black professors such as Henry Louis Gates Jr. and Lani Guinier had observed that more black undergraduates at Harvard had hailed from immigrant families than from families descended from African-American slaves. According to Page: "Black immigrants from Africa, the West Indies, and elsewhere seem too busy pursuing American opportunities to waste time worrying about whether or not they are 'acting black.'"[12]

For their part, leaders such as Bill Cosby and the then senator Obama sought to change both the image and the perception of blacks and of being black to something more positive: academic and socioeconomic success is not something limited to whites or acting white, they asserted. Instead, these pioneers sought to instill in blacks, young and old, that success is color-blind. The choice is not to act white and be successful or act black and be a failure.

And yet while Professor Gates and a distinct minority spoke out in favor of Cosby's articulation of the corrosive social factors inhibiting progress in many black households across the country, they were drowned out by the caustic and vitriolic commentary of his detractors.

For one, many social commentators took exception with Cosby's belief that the acting white syndrome even existed. The *New York Times*

Magazine editor Paul Tough debunked Cosby's commentary with a stinging op-ed on December 12, 2004, entitled "The Acting White Myth." While noting that Cosby brought the concept of acting white to the national consciousness by invoking the phrase to describe black boys who attacked other black children who studied for acting white, Tough denied the existence of such a practice in reality. Citing the study conducted by the University of North Carolina professors Karolyn Tyson and William Darity Jr., referred to above, Tough noted that while Cosby invoked the notion of acting white to explain certain social behavior among black children that led to low academic achievement, "for the most part, it isn't true."[13] Tough continued by observing that use of the acting white rationale to explain poor academic results among black children provides

> an excuse by administrators to conceal or justify discrimination in the public-education system. The one school where the researchers did find anxiety about "acting white" was the one in which black students were drastically underrepresented in the gifted-and-talented classes. And significantly, at this particular school, the notion of the burden of "acting white" was most pervasive not among the black students interviewed by the researchers, but among their teachers and administrators, who told researchers that blacks are "averse to success" and "don't place a high value on education."[14]

Tough's analysis entirely missed the context drawn by Cosby, Professor Gates, and the then senator Obama and the point they sought to make: the stigma associated with acting white is not limited to academic performance in the classroom. Early scholars of the subject limited the parameters of the debate to whether the charge of acting white led to poor academic achievement by black children. Instead, what these and other critics were trying to eliminate was the perception, the stigma, that doing well in school, speaking proper English, and treating others with respect and common courtesy was, according to many black households, acting white. Academic performance was merely one component of a far larger social stigma in many segments of black society, where breaking the societal and generational chains of low socioeconomic ties to advance toward the middle class was denigrated as acting white.

Of *The New York Times* op-ed ostensibly debunking the existence of acting white, the prominent linguist John McWhorter argues in his book *Winning the Race: Beyond the Crisis in Black America* that the study conducted by Professors Tyson and Darity confirms rather than denies the existence of the acting white phenomena. He writes:

> Then there has been a study by Karolyn Tyson, William Darity Jr., and Domini Castellino that the *New York Times* glibly featured as disproving the "acting white" thesis. But, in fact, the study soundly confirms that the phenomenon exists—it simply nuances the issue of what schools it is most likely to play a part in. . . . In a different ideological climate, the paper could easily have been published as *proving* the 'acting white' thesis.[15] (emphasis added)

As the acting white slur gained prominence in discussions on national television and within the pages of *The New York Times,* I found it somewhat ironic that depending on the messenger, the mainstream-media reaction to it was dissimilar. Why was there widespread criticism surrounding Cosby's outrage of black children picking fights with others for acting white while Senator Obama received thunderous applause for similar utterances? Shouldn't the message rather than the messenger on a subject this important be the critical issue for the media and others to focus on?

In a vivid example of the discordant analysis given the "acting white" slur that had ignited a national conversation on what it meant to be black and successful in America, the Georgetown University professor Michael Eric Dyson wrote a *New York Times* bestseller entitled *Is Bill Cosby Right? (Or Has the Black Middle Class Lost Its Mind?)* in

2005, where he waded in directly to confront the issue of acting white. Rather than acknowledge the prevalence of the slur or its negative ramifications on many African-Americans seeking to change their academic and socioeconomic standing, Dyson instead takes Cosby to task (but not Senator Obama) for identifying the slur of acting white as a negative influence on intellectual development.

Here, Dyson dismisses out of hand the belief that African-Americans are any more or less inclined to be intellectual and seemingly rejects the notion of acting white without significant or reflective analysis:

> Cosby's insistence, in his infamous May 2004 speech and on National Public Radio's *Talk of the Nation* in July 2004, that black youth are anti-intellectual because they chide high achievement as "acting white," repeats what is the academic equivalent of an urban legend. . . . The notion that black youth who are smart and who study hard are accused by their black peers of "acting white" is rooted in a single 1986 study of a Washington, D.C., high school conducted by Signithia Fordham, a black anthropologist at Rutgers University, and John Ogbu, the late Nigerian professor of anthropology at the University of California at Berkeley.[16]

Signithia Fordham, coauthor of the original study on the notion of acting white, followed up on her original piece in the aftermath of the Bill Cosby controversy, some twenty years after her study and one year following the publication of Professor Dyson's book, by warning that by limiting our view of the acting white phenomenon and suggesting it exists only in academic circles rather than seeing it as a broader social stigma in the black community is mistaken in fact. In a far-ranging interview by *City* newspaper in Rochester, New York, conducted on February 8, 2006, Fordham took exception with those such as Dyson who sought to argue that the impact of the slur of acting white is minimal in black society:

It's misunderstood far more than it's understood. First, people limit it to the school context. Then they create a false dichotomy, kids who are seeking academic achievement and kids who are not. That is a component of "acting white," but "acting white" is much larger than that. It's part of the larger African American community. That's why I wrote about Rosa Parks. "Acting white" not only means conformity, it is also resisting prevailing norms and expectations. It's not just school.[17]

Instead, Fordham and McWhorter point to more broad and deeper issues that had penetrated the black consciousness to limit educational as well as socioeconomic advancement. First, in a searing essay entitled "Was Rosa Parks 'Acting White'?" printed as part of her interview with the *City* newspaper, Fordham examined whether the civil rights pioneer could well have been accused of acting white for refusing to give up her seat to a white passenger on December 1, 1955, on that fateful bus trip in Montgomery, Alabama. Fordham points to the real impact of acting white on blacks, both in 1955 and in the current day:

> When the other black passengers did not initially support [Parks] because she was upsetting the imposed and customary order of race relations and they feared white reprisals against the whole black community, were they responsible for the insult to her dignity?[18]

After posing the poignant question about what the imposed and customary order of race relations as perceived by blacks should be, Fordham further comments that

> Because black identity is the core of the response to the accusation of "acting white," I cannot embrace the idea supported by recent researchers . . . that all high-achieving students—regardless of race or class—are stigmatized and subject to ridicule and exclusion by their lower-achieving peers. I resoundingly

reject their conclusion that the problem of "acting white" is "not a black thing."[19]

Continuing to peel away the layers of the onion that Fordham had exposed to get to the real crux of the issue of acting white as being far more broad and entrenched in the cultural identity of blacks in society, McWhorter describes the notion of therapeutic alienation as being at the heart of the racial slight.

In the provocative book *Winning the Race: Beyond the Crisis in Black America,* McWhorter reveals a scenario where blacks assail those who act in or react to a particular instance in a manner that differs from expected cultural norms:

> But treating the act of doing well in school as disloyal became attractive under the new way of thinking that was settling into the black community. An open-ended wariness of whites became a bedrock of black identity, among a people deprived by history of a more positive, individual source of security and purpose. If this had not led black kids to start turning away from school as "white," it would have been surprising.[20]

This sense of betrayal to the greater good of the black community by those blacks who dared step out of the cultural norms and narratives that had been expected of them is a poison to which I have sought the cure for my entire academic, professional, and social life. In the following passage, McWhorter describes the cultural alienation and castigation I have experienced for electing to follow a path not taken by many, if not most, other blacks in my cultural, political, and academic views. Here he notes:

> For blacks, the idea that one's value as a black American was one's difference from whites, including a mission to teach them about racial injustice, fit right in with a new black identity based too often on being in opposition to The Man. To value oneself as "diverse" from whites is, actually, to avoid being an

individual actor, in favor of joining a herd of people united in cherishing *not* being something, rather than *being* something— attractive when one is not sure whether one is good enough to *be* something.[21]

McWhorter's analysis provides an excellent opportunity to depart from the ivory-tower interpretations of those who deny or minimize the existence of acting white in academic and cultural settings by using my own life experiences as a poignant illustration that the slight is very real and very much an issue in the United States today.

First, from my earliest days as an undergraduate at Haverford College, I was constantly challenged by my fellow black students about why I was not "sufficiently black" or whether I was embarrassed to be associated with other blacks. The transgression at issue? I had refused to participate in the social events sponsored and held at the Black Cultural Center (or BCC, as it was known when I was there). The idea that I was not sufficiently black or was acting white by choosing friends based on the content of their character rather than the color of their skin was a foreign concept to many of my fellow students of color during the late 1980s and early 1990s.

I sought to surround myself with friends with academic and social interests that I enjoyed—I never believed the diversity of the college experience meant that I should self-segregate to associate only with persons of color because somehow the color of our skin bound us together more than mutually shared interests and pursuits. As Fordham notes, the notion of black identity is tied into the use of the slur "acting white"—a truism I would discover repeatedly throughout my time at Haverford. Since I was not "sufficiently black" to associate with blacks at the exclusion of whites at a predominately white college and given the friends and social settings I sought to associate myself with, I was repeatedly told to my face in class and in the dining hall and around campus that I was doing nothing more than acting white.

And, though it was unbeknownst to me at the time, McWhorter's discussion of therapeutic alienation rang true in many encounters I had with fellow black classmates. There *was* a certain wariness of white classmates held by several of my black contemporaries that formed an unbreakable bond and identity for them at my expense and exclusion. In many instances while at Haverford I was made to feel that there was something wrong with me for breaking away from the African-American community. And yet nothing could be further from the truth. The ostracism I faced by some was due to a sense that somehow I was acting white while being not sufficiently black. Why?

I didn't want to live in a dormitory composed only of blacks, self-segregate in the dining center to sit primarily with blacks, and engage in social activities where only African-Americans were involved. I thought that the entire purpose of a liberal arts education was to interact with those from differing backgrounds—self-segregation seemed counter-productive. Allegedly open-minded black classmates of mine had no problem whatsoever of accusing me of being insufficiently black and acting white when my political, social, and cultural norms differed from theirs.

This trend and sense of cultural alienation continued as I graduated from Haverford College and obtained a job working as a legislative assistant to a junior member of the House of Representatives. From my earliest days in the Longworth House Office Building, I would discover that the richness of diversity on Capitol Hill did not exist within the ranks of the Republican Party: I was one of a handful of black legislative aides who served alongside a Republican member of Congress.

There certainly wasn't strength in numbers for me at the elected level in the Republican House membership. When I arrived in September 1991, there was only one black member of Congress who was serving in the House of Representatives. Representative Gary Franks (R-CT) was the first black Republican elected to the House since Oscar Stanton De Priest represented Chicago's South Side from 1929 to 1935.

Beyond the slights previously described at the hands of Representative Maxine Waters (D-CA), I would soon encounter open hostility from fellow black staff members working for Democratic members of Congress who were appalled that I would dare register as, let alone work for, a Republican.

As described by McWhorter, time and time again I would be attacked for being an individual actor, an individual exercising independent political thought rather than joining the herd of most blacks on Capitol Hill who cherished group identification and acceptance as members of the Democratic Party above all else. For my transgression and decision to join the ranks of a political party where I felt comfortable both on ideology and public-policy positions, I was castigated repeatedly for acting white, being inauthentically black and an Uncle Tom—all at the hands of blacks who would profess to their deep commitment to diversity and equal opportunity for all.

The sense of cultural alienation and exclusion for daring to express opinions that differed from what most other blacks subscribed to followed me from Capitol Hill to K Street and to the White House, where I served as an advisor to President George W. Bush and Vice President Dick Cheney. I had apparently turned my back on the black community by acting white for electing to serve our country in a Republican administration, I was repeatedly told. More recently, the intensity and level of vitriolic commentary toward me for ostensibly acting white has increased with the election and inauguration of President Barack Obama.

Since leaving the Bush administration in 2004, I have been sought out by many cable news networks for my political insights on their television programs. While I occasionally received a less than flattering letter or phone call for expressing my views on air, the tenor and frequency of such unsolicited feedback would intensify as Obama began his quest for the presidency.

Following Obama's historic election to the Oval Office, I remained vigilant in my review of the president's policies; in areas where I agreed with his approach, I said so on television and on National Public Radio, where I offer frequent political commentary. Rather than celebrate the opportunities that were afforded me by pioneers of the civil rights movement to think and act freely as an American, I was and remain a constant target of those who either accuse me of being an African-American acting white or of turning my back on the black race for my criticism of the new president's policies. Don't take my word for it: consider the following samples of vitriolic commentary found in a series of blogs and Web sites, found by doing a quick search of "Ron Christie" on the Internet:

> I am so ashamed that a black man would get on television in front of millions and show how ignorant he is about what he really is (a Black Man). All of your education and exposure should have allowed you to deliver comments that did not cut to the soul and disregard the efforts and sacrifice of those who came before us to make it possible to even be where you are today . . . This only proves that the republicans are fiscal conservatives but mutually exclusive to whites and Uncle Toms! (February 19, 2009)

> You will never be white, Ronnie. (February 27, 2009)

> Does everybody know that Ron Christie is . . . the whitest black man in America? (March 17, 2009)

> Ron, I am so sick of your . . . uncle tom statements! You make me sick!!! (March 23, 2009)

Or consider an e-mail I received after a recent appearance on television, where my black authenticity was put into question:

> Perhaps you can tell us why you and other like you, Clarence Thomas for one, do not like being black. I understand the making of money and the need to support yourself, but to sell out on

those that opposed civil rights since the beginning is quite sad as you are. . . . You will take positions opposed to your own interests—a paid uncle Tom.

Rather than provide satisfaction to those who posted the comments about me above by listing their names, I have elected to delete their identification. Nonetheless, these posts represent only some of hundreds of similar remarks that populate the Internet. Their message and intent is clear: if one strays from the conventional political, social, and cultural norms exercised by a majority of African-Americans, one will be immediately labeled an Uncle Tom or one who acts white. Such views are hardly a laudable sign of progress as America turns the corner from the twentieth century, which was marked by more than fifty years of Jim Crow, segregation, and inadequate educational opportunities for blacks, to the dawn of the twenty-first century, when this form of racial hatred should be well behind us.

Accordingly, Shelby Steele offers the following analysis in his examination of those blacks who refused to follow the group-think, herd mentality of racial apologists and those who thought of blacks as perpetual victims rather than as equal participants in society. Acting white according to these two views is equated with a strong educational footing, hard work, and ultimate success in one's endeavors, while acting black fulfills a stereotype of inferiority, of lack of intellectual curiosity, and of dependence on others to achieve success rather than self-reliance. Steele reveals:

> From the abolitionist era to the present, the terms of racial reform in America have always been set by a coalition of white liberals and black leaders. And since the sixties, interventionism that would engineer blacks to equality has been the virtuous idea of this coalition. But, in supporting interventionism, I think the black leadership has forsaken the black mandate to achieve true and full equality with all others for the perquisites of interventionism—the preferential patronage of jobs, careers, grant money, set asides, di-

versity consulting businesses, black political districts and so on. . . . This bargain has transformed the civil rights establishment into something of a grievance elite, largely concerned with turning the exceptionalism practiced by institutions in regard to blacks into the patronage of racial preferences.[22]

As we shall see in the chapter to follow, many in black communities across the country desire to marginalize those who would dare support the patronage of jobs, academic admissions, and government set-asides in the name of affirmative action and diversity and are not only labeled as acting white but also castigated for "selling-out" for doing so. It is here that we turn our attention to the slur of not only acting white but selling out that dilutes rather than enhances the ability of many blacks to act as true equals with whites in society.

11

Justice Clarence Thomas

An Uncle Tom Acting White by Selling Out?

In our discussion of the acting white phenomenon, one consistent thread has remained true throughout: in the aftermath of the civil rights movement and the rise of black power in the late 1960s and early 1970s to the present day, one who disavows affirmative action programs and who refuses to engage in lockstep with the black cultural identity (such as it is) in regard to music, politics, or any other matter is not only often afflicted with the moniker of acting white but also with an equally offensive label, that of sellout, which suggests one is busy "selling out" the race by acting white.

In his *New York Times* "Notable Book," the conservative black author and social commentator Shelby Steele offers poignant and incisive insight into the plight faced by black conservatives today—those who elect to deviate from "conventional" black thought. His commentary is interesting because it asserts that many African-Americans view their fellow black conservatives as sellouts or Uncle Toms—a phenomenon with which I am rather familiar. Steele observes:

The idea of a black openly outside the framework of liberalism is still odd in the United States. Such a person seems to be disqualifying himself from the fruits of America's struggle for racial redemption, standing against his own racial self-interest.[1]

Taking this analysis one step further, Steele elaborates:

> An Uncle Tom is someone whose failure to love his own people makes him an accessory to their oppression. . . . Because of historic vulnerability and the resulting insistence on conformity around a single strategic explanation of group fate, black America has not yet achieved a two-party politics. Thus, black conservatives do not yet comprise a loyal opposition; they are, instead, classic dissenters.[2]

The theme evident here is that black conservatives are Uncle Toms who turn their backs on the plights of fellow blacks by refusing to adhere to conventional black thought (should such a definition be available) and are somehow inauthentically black because they act white.

Steele points to a common representation of successful black conservatives in the mainstream media as once again being either insufficiently black or at odds with the alleged struggles of inferiority faced by a majority of blacks in the country today. To illustrate this point he draws attention to a column written by the husband-and-wife team of journalists Steve and Cokie Roberts regarding then congressman J. C. Watts delivering the Republican response to President Clinton's State of the Union Address in 1997. In full disclosure, I consider Watts a friend and a mentor of mine, while the Roberts have been quite hospitable to me over the years as well.*

---

* I have appeared on television periodically with Cokie Roberts, and her brother, Thomas Hale Boggs Jr., was my mentor while I practiced law at Patton Boggs LLC. Steve Roberts and I serve as adjunct professors together at the George Washington University Graduate School of Political Management.

Nonetheless, consider the condescending manner, inadvertent or not, in which they discuss black conservatives such as Watts and former Secretary of State and General Colin Powell:

> After praising Watts's [remarks] . . . for its focus on "black individualism and self-reliance," they quickly reversed fold. They said Watts, like Colin Powell, was "lucky" to have had "hardworking parents," but that unlike Powell, he had forgotten "that many African-Americans have not been so fortunate."[3]

This level of paternalism is as depressing as it is unsurprising. For one, shouldn't all children in America be fortunate to grow up in a household where one's parents are hardworking? The insinuation that a black child growing up in a household with a hardworking parent or parents is somehow the exception rather than the norm in modern society is patently insulting. The resulting commentary that Watts had "forgotten that many African-Americans have not been so fortunate" demonstrates the extent to which many whites and blacks alike view those blacks who eschew the conventional route as hapless victims whose lack of socioeconomic progress is tied to systemic racism at the hands of others.

I know Watts to be a man of great empathy, compassion, and accomplishment, and he would hardly have turned his back on those less fortunate than himself. But Watts, like many other black conservatives, refused to blame society for his success or failure; he instead took pride in working hard to provide for himself and his family rather than seeking government intervention or benevolence. His reward? Disdain from his fellow members of the Congressional Black Caucus, many of whom treated him with open contempt for being a conservative while receiving condescending praise from the likes of the Roberts, who questioned whether he could understand the plight of other blacks that he had somehow "left behind."

While many black conservatives are accused of acting white, turning their backs on the race, or being sellouts, perhaps no one draws the ire of those who purport to be the guardians and enforcers of main-stream black thought more than the associate justice of the United States Supreme Court Clarence Thomas. The story of how Thomas would succeed the civil rights icon Justice Thurgood Marshall to become the second black jurist confirmed to the United States Supreme Court is well documented.

The story of why Justice Thomas is so reviled when his life embodies the path to equality and success dreamed of by key architects of the civil rights movement such as Dr. Martin Luther King Jr., Thurgood Marshall, and countless others is less clear—except when you consider that his detractors denigrate him for his success because it was allegedly gained by acting white, by pulling the ladder of opportunity up behind him so other blacks could not succeed—all while selling out his race.

I suspect few of the countless black entertainers, politicians, academics, and others who frequently assail Thomas's assent to and tenure on the United States Supreme Court have a clue that Thomas's life embodies the spirit of the dream of real equality for blacks in America following years of oppression and segregation. Born in 1948 in abject poverty in a shack with no electricity or running water on a spit of land known as Pin Point, Georgia, Thomas's beginnings were quite austere rather than privileged.

Thomas was abandoned by his father when he was two years old, and he was left in the care of his grandparents when his mother was unable to care for her sons on the paltry salary of $10 per week. Raised under the strict tutelage of his grandfather, Thomas and his brother were taught to rely on no one or nothing for their success other than themselves and the fruits borne of their hard work, as the future justice would relate in his 2008 autobiography, *My Grandfather's Son*.

Although he was raised in poverty, Thomas would excel in school, and he was offered a scholarship to attend the College of the Holy Cross and, later, the Yale University Law School. Instead of having been raised as a staunch conservative, Thomas entered Holy Cross at the rise of the Black Power movement, and he was often found sporting combat fatigues. A member of the black student union while at Holy Cross,

Thomas, who had initially aspired to become a Catholic priest, had his faith in Catholicism dashed when a fellow student reveled in the assassination of Dr. Martin Luther King Jr. on April 4, 1968. From that day forward, Thomas began an introspective soul searching that stressed more individuality and less immediate acceptance of a particular group's ideological perspective—a characteristic that remains unchanged to the present day.

From the pages of his autobiography as well as from frequent speeches he has given over the years, Justice Thomas reveals that his early opposition to affirmative action programs and his shift from black radical to intellectual conservative took place following his graduation from Yale Law School. Cognizant that the law school had a separate affirmative action admissions program to bring black and other disadvantaged minority students to Yale, Thomas would poignantly discover that Yale's diploma would have two distinctive values in regard to future employment: one standard was ascribed to the diploma for white graduates and another for black graduates. Unable to find a job immediately upon his graduation, Thomas would assess the value of his diploma as nearly nothing; he would later affix a fifteen-cent label to the frame of his law diploma, which remains to the present day.

Raised during times of segregation, Thomas was often castigated by his white peers for doing well in class—a form of discrimination that would follow him throughout his entire academic and professional career. One story that sticks with me concerns a horrific event that happened to the justice years ago, when he had attended a Catholic high school named Saint John Vianney, which he relayed to me in a poignant manner as we sat in his chambers at the Supreme Court more than a decade ago.

While working for the then congressman John Kasich (R-OH) on Capitol Hill, I had the opportunity to work with and befriend Virginia Thomas, a senior staff member working for the then house majority leader Dick Armey (R-TX); Thomas also happened to be the justice's wife. I had mentioned to Ginny one day that I had admired her husband's career, and she encouraged me to write him a letter telling him just that—a letter she promised to deliver, if written.

A few weeks after delivering the letter, I appeared one Saturday morning on C-SPAN's *Washington Journal*—a program that featured two Hill staffers under the age of thirty-five, I believe, to react to the current events in the news. Moderated by an anchor, the show featured one Republican and one Democrat staff member, who offered their ideological views and perspectives.

Unbeknownst to me, Justice Thomas was a fan of C-SPAN, and he happened to watch my appearance that particular morning. When I arrived to work the following Monday, I had hardly taken my seat when I received a phone call from a most unexpected source: the justice's office called and wondered if I had any time *right now* to cross the street from Capitol Hill to the Supreme Court to meet with the justice for "a few minutes." With my heart racing, I bounded down the steps of the Longworth House Office Building and across the street to the court.

With little fanfare, I was ushered into the justice's Chambers and found the justice waiting for me, standing before his desk. After introducing ourselves, he mentioned that he had seen my "debate" on C-SPAN and had appreciated the letter I had written him. After sharing my experiences growing up in California, attending Haverford College, and working on Capitol Hill, the justice reciprocated in kind by sharing his life's story and experiences with me.

One hour slipped into the next, and our conversation spanned topics ranging from the workings of the Supreme Court to the writings of the conservative Hoover Institute economist Thomas Sowell. Then, in a very emotional manner that brought tears to his eyes, Justice Thomas shared how segregation and discrimination had shaped his resolve and spirit during his early years living in the segregated South.

Attending Saint John Vianney, a Catholic high school in Savannah, Georgia, when he was a young man, the justice struggled to adapt to the demanding workload, and his grades began to improve—particularly in his Latin studies. Only a few black students attended Saint John's during that time in the segregated South, and Thomas relayed to me how his classmates not only resented his presence but also referred to the legendary Cleveland Browns' running back Jim Brown as "nigger" and how one classmate had handed him a note that read "I like Martin Luther King" on the outside and that, when Thomas unfolded it, read on the inside: "Dead."

Determined not to let the racism of his classmates get to him, Thomas set his sights on winning the prize for excelling in Latin—a statue of Saint Jude, the patron saint of hopeless cases. After winning both a Latin bee and the statue, Thomas told me how proud he was to take the prize back to his dorm, where he could show his fellow students he wasn't hopeless in his Latin studies, after all.

With tears brimming in his eyes, Justice Thomas next shared with me what happened when he returned just a few moments later to his dorm: someone had taken his Saint Jude statue and broken the head off. After gluing the head back on, someone decided to break it off again a few days later. As he spoke quietly, the justice motioned his arm and shared that he had taken the statue with him to every job he had had since—including its current location within his chambers at the Supreme Court.

I share that story with you for two reasons. First, I believe the Saint Jude–statue story reflects the early challenges faced by a young black student who was resented for acting white by performing well in school. Rather than acknowledge and congratulate him on his accomplishment, his prize was defaced entirely because Thomas had "acted white" by outperforming his white classmates. Second, I believe the Saint Jude statue is a metaphor for the arc of the justice's life and career: no matter how hopeless or daunting the challenges placed before him, he always prevailed. Or, no matter how much his detractors have tried to minimize his accomplishments and castigate him for acting white and being an Uncle Tom and sellout to his race, the justice has always maintained his dignity in the most difficult and trying of times.

Consider Justice Thomas's path to the Supreme Court in itself and how his trajectory to the bench embodies much of the challenges faced by independent-thinking blacks who have been afflicted with the acting white moniker. Thomas did well in school and was denigrated for his success—blacks weren't supposed to do well in school during segregation, and he was acting white by doing well.

Further still, when he had been accepted to Yale Law School, Thomas was dismayed to hear that the school had used an affirmative action program to admit black and other minority students who had traditionally never been admitted in large numbers—with lower admissions standards than their white classmates. Instead of being judged on his academic performance at the College of the Holy Cross, the future justice believed people had minimized his presence by believing—correctly or not—that he had been admitted because of the color of his skin rather than the content of his character and intellect. This assessment proved true once Thomas had graduated from Yale, when his white classmates were successful in their quest for employment and he was not. Thomas believed that employers placed a premium on white graduates and that they assumed that black graduates had only been admitted because of affirmative action programs and were not sufficiently prepared to compete as equals of whites.

And once Thomas decried the efficacy of the affirmative action programs to assist blacks as a badge of their inferiority, he was attacked and accused of trying to pull the very ladder he had allegedly climbed successfully away from subsequent generations of black youths. A strong-minded black man who performed well in school and opposed affirmative action and the mainstream of black political and social norms was nothing more than a black man acting white. Justice Thomas fit the bill perfectly, and his opponents found their opportunity to try to destroy him during his confirmation hearings before the United States Senate as it was being deliberated whether to elevate him to serve as a justice on the highest court in the land.

We need not discuss much of the events and the controversy surrounding the justice's confirmation in 1991 except to briefly mention how the then–circuit court judge had defended himself in the wake of his detractors, who sought to derail his appointment to the Supreme Court. Despite the fact that he had been confirmed before the Senate several times over the past several years to work in the Reagan administration as well as to sit on the United States Court of Appeals, D.C. Circuit, the sexual-harassment allegations of a former colleague, Anita Hill, sought to doom Thomas both before the court of public opinion and before the majority of the United States Senate, who would be required to vote in favor or reject his nomination to become the next associate justice of the Supreme Court.

Following Hill's testimony, which riveted millions of Americans to their television sets, Judge Thomas defended his honor and integrity while also poignantly describing the fate of a black man who elected to follow an independent path rather than the path blacks were expected to follow—the fate of a black man acting white, who, many believed, had sold out his race in the process.

Thomas conveys a similar impression in his memoirs as he reflects upon the manner in which the Senate Judiciary Committee was to sit in judgment over his life. He recalls the famous scene from one of my favorite books, *To Kill a Mockingbird*, where the white lawyer Atticus Finch seeks to defend a black man named Tom (ironically enough) who stood accused of raping a white woman in the segregated South. Thomas quotes the closing argument Atticus Finch delivered before the jury, in which Finch passionately proclaims:

> The witnesses for the state . . . have presented themselves to you gentlemen, to this court, in the cynical confidence that their testimony would not be doubted, confident that you gentlemen would go along with them on the assumption—the evil assumption— that *all* Negroes lie, that *all* Negroes are basically immoral beings, that *all* Negro men are not to be trusted around our women, an assumption one associates with minds of their caliber.[4]

In citing this passage, Thomas recounts the manner in which whites perceived blacks from the days of slavery through segregation, which we have discussed thus far: blacks were assumed to be ignorant, immoral, and not equal with whites. A black man seeking judgment based on his accomplishments rather than on the color of his skin and a black man seeking to chart an independent course rather than the one he was expected to follow were considered nothing more than a black man acting white—a man who had to be stopped.

Thomas's outrage about the manner in which the Senate Judiciary Committee had humiliated him for essentially acting white while being black is manifest in the emotional speech he gave to conclude his testimony, which would eventually cement his confirmation to the Court. Of the hearings and the process, Thomas thundered to those present in the committee and to the millions watching on television across the United States:

> This is a circus. It is a national disgrace. And from my standpoint, as a black American, as far as I am concerned, it is a high-tech lynching for uppity blacks who in any way deign to think for themselves, to do for themselves, to have different ideas, and it is a message that, unless you kowtow to an old order, this is what will happen to you, you will be lynched, destroyed, caricatured by a committee of the U.S. Senate rather than hang from a tree.[5]

Those blacks perceived to be acting properly within the mainstream of the acceptable political, cultural, or social norms are to be celebrated. Those expressing an independent streak and differing ideas about how blacks should define and achieve success without playing the victimization card are accused of selling out, of acting white and betraying their race. Journalist Juan Williams summarizes the destructive confirmation process that Justice Thomas was forced to endure in a searing op-ed:

> Here is indiscriminate, mean-spirited mudslinging supported by the so-called champions of fairness: liberal politicians, unions, civil rights groups and women's organizations. They have been

mindlessly led into mob action against one man by the Leadership Conference on Civil Rights. . . . He has been conveniently transformed into a monster about whom it is fair to say anything, to whom it is fair to do anything. . . . In pursuit of abuses by a conservative president the liberals have become the abusive monsters.[6]

We know the allegations put forth by Hill, but what was the "mudslinging supported by the so-called champions of fairness" that Thomas had to endure for being an independent-thinking black man often accused of being an Uncle Tom or acting white for his failure to adhere to mainstream black cultural ideology?

In his provocative book *Sellout: The Politics of Racial Betrayal,* Randall Kennedy devotes an entire chapter to Justice Clarence Thomas, entitled "The Case of Clarence Thomas," in which he examines the controversy and the vitriolic comments that have followed the justice ever since. In just the opening pages of the chapter, Kennedy captures much of the mean-spiritedness and hatred that Williams notes had been hurled by the alleged champions of the civil rights movement, unions, women's groups, and others who were less than evenhanded when dealing with a black conservative who didn't follow their narrative for social, cultural, and political change.

For one, the liberal activist and Bennett College president Dr. Julianne Malveaux famously opined: "I hope [Clarence Thomas's] wife feeds him lots of eggs and butter and he dies early like many black men do of heart disease."[7] Or consider Pearl Cleage's assertion from 1993:

He is an enemy of our race. . . . [T]he fact that Thomas is a brother should make us hold him to an even higher standard, not provide him with a way to weasel out of taking responsibility for being a traitor.[8]

Perhaps the most ironic comment of all came from New York congressman Major Owens in 2005, after the Supreme Court narrowly ruled in a 5-4 decision that the redistricting plan to create majority black districts, adopted by the state of Georgia, was unconstitutional—a case in which Justice Thomas voted with the majority of the Court. After several members of the Congressional Black Caucus and the NAACP decried the decision of the Court as a resegregation of America and a setback for minority electoral gains advanced since the civil rights movement, Owens offered his assessment of the Court's decision and Thomas's role to *Jet* magazine:

> New York City congressman Major R. Owens took to the floor of the House to criticize leadership and the selection of Justice Clarence Thomas to the high court.
>
> "Our leadership and people we select as leaders is critical," railed the Congressman. "Many in the leadership knew very clearly what were the positions of Justice Thomas, yet they supported him [for the high court] because he was an African American.
>
> "Anybody who is educated, any African American who achieves becomes a person we look up to, becomes a person we will not criticize."⁹

The contradictions and hypocrisy of Congressman Owens's comments above are galling yet quite revealing about the manner in which certain black leaders think about those they perceive as selling out their race by acting white. For one, Thomas was criticized for casting his vote in a landmark case based not on the facts presented to the Court or the deliberations of the justices on the constitutionality of the redistricting plan in question but based on the fact that he was the lone black justice on the Court and thus hadn't "done the right thing." In this case, one may infer that doing the right thing would have been casting his vote in favor of crafting congressional districts through gerrymandering and creative line drawing to preserve majority black seats in Congress. Black jurist casting vote to further issues to benefit blacks rather than the Constitution? Good. Black jurist casting vote to eliminate discrimination of congressional district based merely on skin color? Acting white.

Nonetheless, the most stunning commentary offered by Congressman Owens is the apparent standard to which black leaders (whomever they might be) will adhere to in respecting and refusing to criticize other blacks. Once again, in Owens's view: "Anybody who is educated, any African American who achieves becomes a person we look up to, becomes a person we will not criticize." By that logic, Justice Clarence Thomas should be the very person the Congressional Black Caucus and presumably the NAACP and other civil rights groups should support rather than scorn. Anyone who is educated? Justice Thomas received his undergraduate degree from Holy Cross with honors and went on to graduate from Yale Law School. Any African-American who achieves? A young lawyer who came to Washington, D.C., served in several high-ranking government positions before being confirmed by the United States Senate to serve as a judge on the United States Court of Appeals, D.C. Circuit, and ultimately as the associate justice of the United States Supreme Court would seemingly qualify as a black man who had achieved success.

And finally, anyone who fulfills the criteria set forth by Congressman Owens qualifies that individual to become a person worthy of being looked up to and of not being criticized? Owens fails to live up to even his own standards when one considers the commentary he offered from the floor of the House of Representatives in regard to Justice Thomas's nomination to the high court and his pleading to his counterparts in the United States Senate to reject Thomas's elevation to the Supreme Court. As noted by Kennedy in *Sellout,* Congressman Owens had less than flattering comments to make about the educated black man who had achieved much and who was ostensibly worthy of praise rather than criticism:

Imploring the Senate to block Thomas's elevation to the Supreme Court, Congressman Major Owens asked his colleagues to "try to imagine how the French would have felt if the collaborator Marshal Petain had been awarded a medal after the liberation of France in World War II, or if in Norway Quisling had been made a high official in the government," or if, after the War for Independence, Benedict Arnold had been promoted to the level of a general.[10]

So much for the sincerity of the congressman's self-identified test, by which successful blacks were to be judged and praised rather than criticized by "black leadership" organizations such as the Congressional Black Caucus. Owens instead took the opportunity to castigate rather than celebrate then judge Thomas's potential elevation to the Supreme Court as a move akin to putting a traitor into a position of high honor and distinction. Presumably Thomas's transgression back in 1991 had little to do with his academic or professional success. Instead, as we have predictably seen thus far, a black man who excels academically yet shuns affirmative action and a man who marches to an independent beat rather than falls lockstep in rhythm with mainstream black cultural, political, and social thought is labeled an Uncle Tom, a sellout, and one who is acting white.

But the critics of Justice Thomas who used the criteria set forth above by Congressman Owens were not limited to only one member of the Congressional Black Caucus before his confirmation. In fact, Congressman John Lewis (D-GA), a hero of the civil rights movement, was severely critical of Justice Thomas's appointment, notwithstanding Congressman Owens's assertion that a successful, accomplished, and well-educated black would draw praise rather than criticism from the Congressional Black Caucus. Consider the following remarks offered by Congressman Lewis just before Justice Thomas's confirmation to the Supreme Court in 1993: "What you have here is a nominee who wants to destroy the bridge that brought him over troubled waters."[11] The condemnation from the man who had been famously beaten on a bridge in Selma, Alabama, an event that seared the oppressiveness and brutality of Jim Crow into the consciousness of America a generation before, was particularly incisive.

Consider further the charges leveled by fellow Congressional Black Caucus member Louis Stokes (D-OH) in regard to Clarence Thomas's qualifications to sit on the Supreme Court. Nearly echoing the comments of journalists Steve and Cokie Roberts, Congressman Stokes asserted that the future associate justice of the Supreme Court had somehow turned his back on his race and forgotten where he came from. Here, Stokes proclaimed:

> The difference between Judge Thomas and most black Americans who have achieved, in spite of poverty, adversity and racism, is that most of them have not forgotten from whence they have come. Whenever possible, they have used their educations and positions of achievement to help eliminate from our society these barriers to equal opportunity, liberty, and justice. It is almost unheard of to see them utilize their educations and positions to impede the progress of those less fortunate than they.[12]

So much for Congressman Owens's criteria for drawing praise rather than scorn from the Congressional Black Caucus. Despite the justice's education, achievement, and intellect, he was criticized for his failure to adhere to the rigid ideological litmus test that has hindered black achievement since the end of the civil rights movement: if one dares to break free of the lockstep ideological and cultural norms that blacks are expected to follow, one will be accused of acting white, betraying the race, and being a sellout to those they have "left behind."

Finally, before we turn our attention to another transformative black leader who, unlike Justice Thomas, has received nearly universal praise from the so-called black establishment, it is important to conclude our review of selling out while acting white by bringing to light an editorial written in 2005 by the *Milwaukee Journal Sentinel,* ostensibly about the nomination of Judge Samuel Alito but actually about the "blackness" of Justice Clarence Thomas.

On October 31, 2005, the editors of the *Milwaukee Journal Sentinel* wrote an op-ed critical of President Bush's nomination of Samuel Alito to replace retiring Justice Sandra Day O'Connor to become the next associate justice of the Supreme Court, entitled "A Nomination That Will Divide." In discussing the diversity and composition of the new Court should Alito be confirmed, the paper launched a thinly veiled attack on Justice Thomas, questioning whether he was truly black, when the paper noted:

> In losing a woman, the court with Alito would feature seven white men, one white woman and a black man, who deserves an asterisk because he arguably does not represent the views of mainstream black America.[13]

The notion that Justice Thomas deserves an asterisk next to his name because he was insufficiently or inauthentically black since his views do not represent those of mainstream black America is an incredible statement to be made in general, least of all by an editorial page of one of the country's leading newspapers. Justice Scalia is not criticized for taking views that are out of the mainstream for Italian-Americans any more than Justice Ruth Bader Ginsburg is assailed for harming women or those from the Jewish faith.

In fact, I suspect it would be difficult for the *Milwaukee Journal Sentinel* to express exactly how to define what the views of mainstream black America are. What is easier to define, however, is that a conservative black jurist who opposes affirmative action programs, places a premium on results rather than excuses, and refuses to believe in a monolithic black leadership or ideology is one to be accused of being a sellout or acting white while turning his back on fellow blacks. Why? Consider the case of retired general and former secretary of state Colin Powell.

Powell, the first black to become national security advisor under President Ronald Reagan, would become the first black to serve as secretary of state in the cabinet of President George W. Bush. Interestingly, given that Powell's rise in the power corridors of Washington, D.C., occurred during Republican rather the Democrat administrations, criticism of Powell from the so-called black-leadership establishment has been virtually nonexistent, and, unlike Justice Thomas, General Powell has hardly ever been accused of acting white or selling out his race. Once again, the question is why Justice Thomas and General Powell, two highly educated and successful black men, have been treated entirely differently by those who purport to represent mainstream black views and the media at large. One is labeled as an Uncle Tom who acts white, the other is not.

I believe Randall Kennedy is correct in his assertion that affirmative action is the third rail of black American politics; whereas Justice Thomas repudiated affirmative action as a crutch that denigrated blacks as inferior, General Powell never (publicly) criticized affirmative action or set-aside programs.

As a result, while nearly 90 percent of blacks in America are registered Democrats, they appear willing to overlook Powell's political affiliation and to avoid labeling him an Uncle Tom and describing him as acting white while selling out the race because he refused to touch the third rail of black political and cultural norms—a rail, once touched, that leads to the denigration that one is selling out the race, all while being an Uncle Tom and acting white.

How can this destructive cycle ever be broken? Perhaps the election of America's first black president, who decried the insult of stating that a black child with a book is acting white, will prove illustrative in turning around a monolithic cycle of victimization that has rendered many blacks in America less equal, less competitive, and in a greater position of inferiority now than at the beginning of the twenty-first century or any point since the landmark accomplishments of the civil rights movement more than fifty years ago. Insults and pejoratives must yield to hard work and constructive engagement in order for the acting white slur to recede into the past.

12

The President Who
Happens to Be Black
versus a Black President

The Coming Rise of
Colorless Values—or Not?

On November 4, 2008, Senator Barack Obama achieved what many Americans of all races thought might never be achieved: the junior senator from Illinois was decisively elected to be the forty-fourth president of the United States. As the euphoria from this historic achievement settles down, however, a pressing question regarding the Obama presidency must be confronted in earnest: will Barack Obama become America's black president, or will he serve as the president of the United States who happens to be black?

The road to the Oval Office for Mr. Obama was paved by some blacks and whites who accused the junior senator from Illinois of acting white as he campaigned to become the most powerful man in the world. The dynamic and charismatic senator, unlike the Reverends Jesse Jackson and Al Sharpton before him, had failed to make race the central issue in his bid for the presidency. Obama adroitly avoided casting his candidacy in terms of his racial identity and the struggles of the civil rights movement, opting instead to serve as a catalyst of hope and change after eight years of the presidency of George W. Bush.

Perhaps for Reverend Jackson and other apologists for racial victimization, Obama's tactics, approach, and outlook rubbed them the wrong way—not unlike those in the African-American community who chose to castigate black Republicans for not following the group mentality and accepted ideology preferred by many in the African-American community. Perhaps Reverend Jackson, long accustomed to having white politicians kiss his ring while seeking his endorsement and the alleged endorsement of the African-American community as they sought the presidency, chafed at the manner in which Obama effectively ignored and neutralized his fellow denizen from Chicago.

Whatever the case, it all proved too much for Jackson as Obama's star rose and Jackson's approach, to marginalize and proselytize based on alleged racial grievances, was exposed for the fraud it was. On September 18, 2007, an opportunity presented itself for Jackson to place himself back on the national stage and stand in the limelight he so craved, and he further took the opportunity to castigate Obama for acting white in the process.

At the time, the nation was riveted by the case of the so-called Jena Six, a group of African-American teenagers who had assaulted a white classmate after a number of nooses and other racially inflammatory symbols were found at a Louisiana high school. Never mind that a subsequent investigation revealed that the black teens assaulted their white classmate without cause—only later did the black teenagers seek protection behind the noose incident as the source for their provocation. For Jackson, the made-for-television narrative of the Jena Six was a perfect opportunity for him to garner attention: racial oppression, victimization, and calls for justice to right alleged wrongs.

Senator Obama resolved to remain largely removed as the controversy and intensity behind coverage of the Jena Sex grew with each successive day. While Jackson and his determined band of supporters marched and called attention to the issue, Obama remained focused on his quest to best fellow senator Hillary Rodham Clinton in the critical South Carolina primary. Perhaps interpreting events in the present through glasses colored by racial transgressions in the past, Jackson responded accordingly when asked about the Jena Six case and how he would respond were he running for president of the United States: "If I were a candidate I'd be all over Jena . . . Jena is a defining moment, just like Selma was a defining moment."[1]

Before discussing Obama's response to Jackson's assertion, it is important to pause and reflect on the allegorical significance between Selma, Alabama, and Jena, Louisiana, that Jackson used to drive a racial wedge between himself and candidate Obama. On March 7, 1965, some 525 civil rights activists led by John Lewis gathered to march in favor of African-Americans' having equal access to the ballot box in the United States.

As the marchers gathered at the Edmund Pettus Bridge early that morning, state troopers cautioned them that they were demonstrators and had less than two minutes to disperse. Mere seconds had elapsed before the troopers assaulted the peaceful group that had assembled, hitting them with tear gas, whips, batons, and insults in an event that transfixed the nation through the lens of television cameras, which brought the ugly fury of racial discrimination into millions of homes across the country in a disgraceful event that would be known as Bloody Sunday. Disgusted by the scenes of hatred inflicted on the largely black marchers at the hands of the white troopers, millions of Americans galvanized behind the cause for equal access for all to vote, and Congress responded by passing the Voting Rights Act of 1965 just months later, which President Lyndon Johnson signed into law on August 6, 1965.

Fast-forward, then, to the incident in Jena, Louisiana, in 2006 that the Reverend Jesse Jackson had compared with the atrocities that had taken place in Selma some forty years before. Jena, a small town of some three thousand residents, became renowned around the world for several incidents at the local high school that sparked a series of racially tinged events. After several nooses were found hanging in a tree that was a popular gathering spot for African-American students to seek refuge from the heat, the school became engulfed in racial controversy. The white students found responsible for hanging the nooses were subject to severe disciplinary action and were subsequently suspended from school.

On December 4, 2006, Justin Barker, a seventeen-year-old white student, was attacked by a group of six black teenagers in what the school superintendant described as a premeditated attack against Barker. A subsequent investigation by the United States attorney revealed that there was no connection between the noose hangings and the beatings. Although thousands, including Reverend Jackson, marched in Jena, alleging that the black youths had been harshly punished while the noose hangers received far lighter treatment, Jackson's hypocrisy and attempt to put fuel on the fire of a sensitive racial cauldron are equally disgusting. Despite the fact that the United States attorney investigating the matter found no connection between the seventeen-year-old white student who was viciously attacked by six black class-mates and the noose incident, Jackson could not help himself by doing what he does best: injecting himself into an issue and then seeking to shame others for racism and discrimination. It is particularly revolting that Jackson would morally equate the peaceful demonstration in Selma that turned into a vicious riot where hundreds of innocent people were beaten and hurt to an incident in Jena, Louisiana, some forty years later where an innocent white student was viciously attacked by six black assailants.

As for Obama, he remained largely silent on the "marches for jus-tice" and other incidents in Jena that Jackson had either organized or participated in. When pressed to make a statement on the issue, Sena-tor Obama chose his words carefully and offered the following, as re-ported by CNN:

In a statement released Wednesday afternoon, Obama said his previous statements about the Jena Six case "were carefully thought out," with input from his national campaign chairman and Jackson's son, Rep. Jesse Jackson, Jr., D-Illinois.

"Outrage over an injustice like the Jena 6 isn't a matter of black and white. It's a matter of right and wrong," he said in the statement.[2]

Whether by design or specific intent, Jackson saw his opening to garner attention for himself, moving immediately to capitalize on his
good fortune. Consider the following account from September 19,
2007:

> The Rev. Jesse Jackson criticized Democratic presidential candi-
> date Barack Obama on Tuesday over his reaction to the arrest of
> six black juveniles, in Jena, Louisiana . . . accusing the Illinois
> Senator of "acting like he's white" according to a South Caro-
> lina newspaper.[3]

While Reverend Jackson claimed that he didn't recall making the
comments about Obama "acting like he's white," he never disputed
the account, either. Was Obama's transgression that he sought to examine the case before the law in a color-blind manner so that justice could
be properly adjudicated, or was the comment a deeper reflection of the
reverend's displeasure with the manner in which Obama had conducted
his campaign, in which he refused to make his racial identity the central
thrust of his candidacy? We shall examine these questions in closer detail momentarily.

The Reverend Jackson's racist comments toward Obama "acting like
he's white" sparked similar comments from less-than-enlightened individuals. Less than a year later, Obama was once again hit with the
charge that he was conducting his presidential campaign while seeking
to act white—this time at the hands of the activist Ralph Nader. In a
wide-ranging interview on the topic given to the *Rocky Mountain News*
on June 25, 2008, Nader accused Obama of trying to "talk white" while
appealing to white guilt. In criticizing Obama for failing to address poverty and other issues that ostensibly adversely affected African-Americans
across the country, Nader offered the following assessment:

> I haven't heard him have a strong crackdown on economic exploi-
> tation in the ghettos. Payday loans, predatory lending, asbestos,

lead. What's keeping him from doing that? Is it because he wants to talk white? He doesn't want to appear like Jesse Jackson?[4]

Nader added more insult to injury when asked what it meant for the presumptive Democratic candidate to be "talking white." Plunging deeper into the racist hole he had dug for himself, Nader explained his remarks by noting:

> He [Obama] wants to show that he is not threatening . . . another threatening African-American politician. He wants to appeal to white guilt, not by coming on as black is beautiful, black is powerful. Basically he's coming on as someone who is not going to threaten the white power structure, whether it's corporate or whether it's simply oligarchic. And they love it. Whites just eat it up.[5]

Not another Jesse Jackson? Not talking black, taking pride in black identity? A nonthreatening African-American politician who fed white guilt—to the apparent approval of whites?

In analyzing Nader's remarks, it is hard to discern which is more disturbing to interpret: Nader's overt racism and condescension toward the standard-bearer of the Democratic Party or the manner in which the media largely chose to look the other way by ignoring his remarks. One can only imagine what the outcry might have been if a white Republican had accused the junior senator from Illinois of acting as if he were white. The critical question, of course, is why the media would permit such an overt double standard in coverage when an African-American castigates another for acting white and when a white man does the same to a black.

Sadly, I believe the charge from Jackson as well as Nader that Senator Obama had been acting as if he were white stuck in the minds of many in the African-American community. For one, I had been privy to several conversations where the allegation was raised that Obama was not "sufficiently black." As the 2008 Democratic primary battle heated up, I was a part of many intense discussions in my corner barbershop near Washington, D.C., in which the authenticity of Obama's black credentials were debated. Over the buzz of clippers and the clicking of scissors I heard the charge repeated again and again that Obama was not a "real black man," "not authentic," and a "half-breed," like the fictional Spock character from the *Star Trek* television show.

My protestations to the contrary that Obama had been born of a black father were tossed aside: "He's still half-white," I was often told. But the true reason and rationale was often revealed after a few penetrating questions: Obama's authenticity was called into question because he had gone to Columbia University as a college student before heading off to Harvard Law School to receive his juris doctor degree. Obama wasn't really black and chose to act white in their minds because he had chosen to excel academically, speak with proper English, and to avoid subscribing to the victim complex that laid much of the blame and guilt behind poor African-American achievement at the feet of whites.

In a penetrating essay written years before Obama's candidacy to become president of the United States, the linguist John McWhorter cut to the heart of the issue of why many blacks such as President Obama, Shelby Steele, and Thomas Sowell will always be accused of being less than authentically black and of acting white by the likes of Jesse Jackson Sr. and the patrons in my barbershop. McWhorter took the unique perspective of analyzing the authenticity question through the prism of W. E. B. Du Bois's notion of double consciousness—this time in the context of blacks in modern American society. In this contemporary analysis of Du Bois's double consciousness, McWhorter accurately notes the following:

> To wit, a tacit sense reigns among a great many black Americans today that the "authentic" black person stresses personal initiative and strength in private but dutifully takes on the mantle of victimhood as a public face.[6]

Failure to play the victim card while evading alleged white oppression would lead to blacks being charged *by fellow blacks* as acting white and being less than authentically black.

Thus I would challenge the Reverend Jesse Jackson, or any one of his supporters for that matter, to name one significant accomplishment he has achieved on behalf of the race he portends to represent—not the number of marches in front of television cameras before receiving a "settlement" that seemed to line the pockets of Jackson and his associates rather than the public at large, but a demonstrable and tangible goal that was accomplished that had nothing to do with blacks being oppressed or held back at the hands of whites. Linking Du Bois's struggle for whites to perceive blacks as worthy of responsibility to Jesse Jackson's frequent attempts to portray blacks as the victims of white racism to achieve desired results, McWhorter writes:

> Du Bois's strategy was to show whites that blacks had proven that they were worth bringing into the fold. Jesse Jackson's strategy is to show whites that to not bring blacks into the fold makes them immoral, and that this means that whether or not blacks present ability, diligence, or moral solidity beforehand is beside the point. This has been the leitmotif of Civil Rights discourse for over three decades now. Politics meets the New Double Consciousness: blacks under forty-five have known little else.[7]

Having just turned forty-one years old myself, I understand entirely where McWhorter is coming from. Worse still are the parallels between the behavior exhibited by Jackson in contemporary society and Booker T. Washington's seeking to burnish his own pockets and reputation while purportedly speaking on behalf of the black race. Try as I might, I can't help wondering whether history might be repeating itself: a black leader is seeking appeasement over accomplishment, oratory over demonstrable progress and results. Only this time, there does not appear to be another leader with the magnitude and strength of a

Du Bois to overcome the destructive line of thinking advanced with the help of the mainstream media and those in the teachers unions, civil rights organizations, and others, that blacks are somehow unable to break free of the chains of oppression without the assistance of government programs and white benevolence. Those few blacks who break free of the mainstream and cultural norms that many whites and blacks have held should form the parameters for success for African-Americans in contemporary society, but they are deemed to be acting white, an Uncle Tom, or not authentically black.

How else to explain the derision and demeaning treatment toward the associate justice of the Supreme Court Clarence Thomas or the retired four-star general Colin Powell? Both men grew up in challenging circumstances and both men overcame early adversity to reach the pinnacles of their respected professions. Rather than take pride in the significant barriers each man had broken by becoming only the second black justice on the United States Supreme Court or the first African-American national security advisor and secretary of state, many blacks castigate them as acting white while being less than authentically black. It is true that a certain number of Justice Thomas's detractors are those who were troubled by the unproved allegations of sexual harassment proffered by Professor Anita Hill during his Supreme Court confirmation hearings. At the same time, a significantly higher percentage of those who denigrate the justice did and do so for his allegedly acting white and ostensibly turning his back on fellow blacks.

As previously noted above, the acting white charge is not just leveled by the likes of Jesse Jackson Sr. toward Barack Obama. Consider also the malevolence directed at the retired four-star general Colin Powell, the first African-American to become national security advisor and secretary of state. Powell doing so in a Democrat administration? Fine. Powell doing the same in the White House of President George H. W. Bush and his son, President George W. Bush? Sellout acting white, who is less than authentically black.

And yet while Obama sought the presidency he was vexed with a difficult contradiction with which he was forced to grapple. On the one hand to reach the most powerful job in the world he had to convince people of color that he was sufficiently authentic as a black man and that he wasn't acting white. On the other hand Obama had to convince many white Americans that he would be the first president of the United States who happened to be black rather than America's first black president.

To address the first issue, Obama had a difficult uphill challenge. Many in the Congressional Black Caucus supported his main rival for the nomination, Senator Hillary Rodham Clinton. Love for the Clintons had always been strong in the African-American community, and Toni Morrison had famously proclaimed Bill Clinton to be America's first black president years ago. Whether they felt Obama was acting white or inauthentically black, many prominent black politicians had thrown their support behind Hillary Clinton early in her presidential campaign, believing that the contest would be over by February 2008, with Clinton handily the victor.

For his part, Obama subtly sought to quell any questions within the black community of his authenticity and to refute any accusations that he was acting white while seeking the presidency. Thus Obama did what many black politicians had done before him: appeared in churches, barbershops, and at other cultural landmarks associated with "authentic" African-Americans. Obama also shrewdly cultivated the support of previous Clinton loyalists, asking them to abandon her campaign to join his "historic" campaign. One by one, Obama picked off revered civil rights icons such as Representative John Lewis, the organizer of the march on Selma many years ago, and the House majority whip James Clyburn (D-SC), who had stood alongside Reverend Martin Luther King Jr. as they fought for equality and integration in South Carolina. The reputations of Lewis, Clyburn, and other black luminaries were unassailable—these distinguished individuals would never be accused of acting white, and they provided Obama with subtle yet critical cover against the likes of Jesse Jackson Sr., who had accused Obama of "acting like he's white."

At the same time, Obama wisely kept race hustlers such as the Reverends Jesse Jackson and Al Sharpton far removed from his campaign in either an official or advisory capacity—lest anyone accuse him of playing the race card to fuel his campaign. The mainstream American media, early and ardent cheerleaders of the Obama candidacy, began to publish and broadcast reports that Obama's race would not be a factor in his bid for the presidency. Instead, we were told, Obama represented a break with the past, the promise of America's first black president, since he transcended race by becoming "postracial." The story line proved too intriguing for many in the media, resulting in countless stories that appeared in print and on the airwaves discussing the postracial candidacy of Obama. One couldn't act white or become America's black president if one transcended race, now could they?

An early yet typical example of the media's breathless postracial coverage of Senator Obama appeared in *The New York Times Magazine* on August 10, 2008. The front cover of the magazine queried, "Is Obama the End of Black Politics?" as if there is such a thing as black politics. The story on the inside, written by Matt Bai, posed in its headline a similar question: "What Would a Black President Mean for Black Politics: Post Race." Ironically, the article written to illustrate how Obama's candidacy was postracial only revealed further evidence of why many blacks had viewed the candidate as either acting white, being inauthentically black, or both.

In an instructive passage, Bai uncovers the dilemma facing many black voters as they considered supporting Obama's candidacy for the presidency:

> But maybe it wasn't only what you didn't know about Obama. What did he know about you? Obama was barely 2 years old when King gave his famous speech, 3 when Lewis was beaten about the head in Selma. He didn't grow up in the segregated South as Bill Clinton had. Sharing those experiences didn't mean Obama, with his nice talk of transcending race and baby-boomer

partisanship, could fully appreciate the sacrifices they made, either.[8]

I found Bai's analysis striking both because of the insights it provided into the thinking of many blacks in America in 2008 as well as the inability of some to move beyond a time when blacks were struggling to become equal participants in society. For all the talk that the civil rights struggles were about equality for all, access to the ballot box, and freedom to live as one chose, the stunning contradictions between what leaders from that era had fought for and their difficulty in embracing those who had benefitted from their struggles decades later is quite illustrative. If one hadn't marched with King, eaten at segregated lunch counters, or been the victim of racial discrimination, did that mean younger blacks who had grown up without those struggles were open to the charge, made by older blacks who could not accept or understand, that they were being less than authentically black or, even worse, acting white?

Later in the article, which describes how the junior senator from Illinois ostensibly transcended his race, the author makes yet more stunning revelations both about Obama's viability as a candidate and about some blacks who were reluctant to view the content of his character and who instead made certain assumptions about Obama based solely on the color of his skin. Once again, the Reverend Jesse Jackson Sr. figured prominently and was at the center of the controversy.

Only months removed from the dustup in which Jackson had famously accused Obama of acting white, the reverend once again took to the airwaves to criticize the presumptive nominee for president from the Democrat Party. This time, Jackson's comments were far more crude than his acting white commentary, but they revealed the level of hostility held by Jackson and others who harbored animus toward the candidate who refused to make race the central theme of his campaign for the presidency.

During a Father's Day speech on the South Side of Chicago in 2008, Obama had famously chastised and challenged a group of black fathers for failing to live up to their responsibilities as parents. Upon hearing the news of Obama's remarks, Jackson, who was awaiting a television appearance on the Fox News channel and did not realize his microphone had been turned on, told a fellow guest that he wouldn't mind personally castrating Obama. As noted in the piece by *The New York Times Magazine*:

> To Jackson, this must have sounded a lot like a presidential candidate polishing his bona fides with white America at the expense of black ones—something he had steadfastly refused to do even during his second presidential run in 1988.[9]

For me, the aside only further illuminates the thinking behind Jackson and others believing that Obama had been guilty of acting white during his campaign—once again, Obama, in their view, was less than authentically black and guilty of acting white for his refusal to curry favor with one race at the expense of another. In other words, Jackson's two failed presidential bids were grounded in his belief that he was running to represent "black" America rather than seeking elective office to become the leader of the United States of America without regard for citizens' skin color.

And for all the talk of the postracial aspect of Obama's candidacy, the comments by Jackson reveal fear, jealously, or the inability of certain *blacks* to move beyond viewing the world in terms of black and white rather than in terms of a person as an individual with particular strengths and weaknesses unique to that individual. Obama's early victories in primary and caucus states indicated that the country was willing to cast the lever for a black candidate, even in a state with a strong-majority white population. Perhaps the reluctance of Jackson and other lukewarm Obama supporters who were black only confirmed that they viewed those without "authentic" black credentials as doing nothing more than acting white. As noted by Bai in this regard:

> Black leaders who rose to political power in the years after the civil rights marches came almost entirely from the pulpit and

the movement, and they have always defined leadership, in broad terms, as confronting an inherently racist white establishment, which in terms of sheer career advancement was their only real option anyway. . . . [The] newly emerging class of black politicians closer in age to Obama and Jesse [Jackson] Jr. seek a broader political brief. Comfortable inside the establishment, bred at universities rather than seminaries, they are just as likely to see themselves as ambassadors to the black community as they are to see themselves as spokesmen for it, which often means extolling middle-class values in urban neighborhoods, as Obama did on Father's Day. Their ambitions range well beyond safely black seats.[10]

This analysis, of course is exactly why Jesse Jackson Sr. failed at his repeated bids for president while Obama prevailed in his first contest: Obama ran on a theme of hope and change rather than racial divisions and barriers. He stressed the importance of his political views and ideology rather than his racial identity as a rallying cry for supporters. And perhaps most important, Obama recognized that in order for America to succeed in the twenty-first century and beyond, her youngsters needed to be well educated so they could unleash the power of American innovation and productivity. As Obama famously noted in the prime-time convention speech that launched his political ambitions for higher office in 2004, he understood that America also needed to eradicate the slander that held that a black child with a book in hand was nothing more than a black child acting white.

In the end, I think it is fair to say that Obama prevailed in his bid for the presidency because he surmounted the two difficult challenges we discussed at the outset of this chapter. First, he was able to convince an overwhelming majority of African-American voters that he was authentic, that he wasn't acting white by seeking the presidency but instead understood the challenges facing them in their communities, and that a vote for Obama would bring about change for the country in a historic manner, by electing the first black president who understood blacks' needs. Second, I believe a strong number of whites cast their ballots for Obama because they believed he was an individual who would not polarize the nation along racial lines but who instead would become the president of the United States who happened to be black but who would best represent them and the country at large.

Nearly two years following his election, at the midterm of the president's first term, the question persists whether Obama has successfully governed as America's first postracial president or whether he has injected race into his style of governance, which has taken black and white America by surprise. Many believe that the candidate who ran on the theme of hope and change, free from partisan strife and the racial strife that has gripped this country from its infancy, has polarized rather than unified the country along racial lines.

I believe there are three specific incidents that give rise to the accusation, merited or not, that the president has divided rather than united the country along racial lines—the territory of racial division and victimization that many Americans thought had been left behind with his election. The first two incidents involve Eric Holder, the first African-American attorney general at the Department of Justice, and the third incident directly involves the forty-fourth president of the United States himself.

Not even one month had passed before the Obama administration had been sworn into office before the American people had their first glimpse on how the new administration would handle sensitive matters of race. During his remarks on February 18, 2009, to commemorate the celebration of Black History Month at the Department of Justice, the attorney general took to the podium and immediately delivered a set of remarks that were surprisingly polarizing rather than uplifting given the venue and the fact that those who had gathered were present to celebrate rather than debate issues of race. To this end, given the opportunity to honor the significant accomplishments of persons of color— the least of which included the election of the nation's first black president and confirmation of the first black attorney general, Holder instead took America to task on matters of race. Lecturing to the assembled audience before him as well as the American people as a whole, Holder intoned:

> Though this nation has proudly thought of itself as an ethnic melting pot, in things racial we have always been and continue to be, in too many ways, essentially a nation of cowards. Though race related issues continue to occupy a significant portion of our political discussion, and though there remain many unresolved racial issues in this nation, we, average Americans, simply do not talk enough with each other about race.[11]

A nation of cowards? Holder's words and stunning rebuke on matters of race were in direct contrast to the euphoric celebrations that still reverberated around the country of America's election of the first president of the United States who happened to be black yet postracial. Had Holder forgotten the divisiveness from the previous summer, when two prominent politicians had accused the now president that he had been campaigning while acting and talking as if he were white? Or, hadn't the election and elevation of Obama signified a departure from traditional judgments based on race/ethnicity toward a rise of colorless values?

Apparently not. As for President Obama himself, he was vexed and unnecessarily placed in a difficult position in regard to race very early in his term at the hands of his attorney general. During his campaign, Obama had successfully avoided discussions on matters of race—including charges of acting white, to which he largely demurred and declined comment. Now the president was forced to address the topic although he waited more than two weeks to do so.

In an interview published by *The New York Times* on March 7, 2009, Obama noted that he would have advised his attorney general to "have used different language" when Holder called America a country of "cowards" in regard to race relations. In a prophetic passage from the interview with *The New York Times,* Obama offered his own view of the value and efficacy of conversations on race relations:

"I'm not somebody who believes that constantly talking about race somehow solves racial tensions," Mr. Obama said. "I think what solves racial tensions is fixing the economy, putting people to work, making sure that people have health care, ensuring that every kid is learning out there. I think if we do that, then we'll probably have more fruitful conversations."[12]

For a newly inaugurated president who did not want constantly to talk about race, America was very much consumed with discussions of race following the controversial remarks given by his top law enforcement officer, Attorney General Eric Holder. Perhaps the conservative economist Walter Williams summed up the comments of the attorney general best. In a piece written days after Holder's remarks, Williams offered the following commentary to debunk the notion that America needed yet another conversation on matters of race:

> The bottom line is that the civil rights struggle is over and it is won. At one time black Americans didn't share the constitutional guarantees shared by whites; today we do. That does not mean that there are not major problems that confront a large segment of the black community, but they are not civil rights problems nor can they be solved through a "conversation on race."
>
> . . . If black people continue to accept the corrupt blame game agenda of liberal whites, black politicians and assorted hustlers, as opposed to accepting personal responsibility, the future for many black Americans will remain bleak.[13]

In just a matter of a few months, the Obama administration found itself frequently evoking discussions of race in such a manner that people began to look at the president not as the first president who happened to be black but instead as America's black president. This perception was fed, in part, by comments given by the president in an interview with *The New York Times* in March 2009. In the relevant section the president stated: "We could probably be more constructive in facing up to sort of the painful legacy of slavery and Jim Crow and discrimination."[14]

For a country that had just elected its first black president, evoking images of Jim Crow and the painful legacy of slavery would seem to diminish rather than elevate the progress made over the past one hundred and fifty years. Few could argue that the country had evolved from the painful days of slavery, Jim Crow, and discrimination by constructively addressing individuals on their own merit and accomplishments rather than the color of their skin. Were more conversations on race particularly necessary? If they were, couldn't President Obama have reflected upon the fact that the United States had just elected its first president who happened also to be an African-American? Perhaps take pride that the United States Senate confirmed his nomination of Eric Holder to become the first attorney general of the United States who also happened to be black? Or that his predecessor in office, President George W. Bush, had nominated the first man and woman to become secretaries of state who also happened to be black?

Indeed, America had much to be thankful for just within the past ten years alone in regard to constructively putting past racial division aside. Representative James Clyburn had been elected by his peers in the House of Representatives to become the first majority whip, second in line to the Speaker of the House in 2005—a gentleman who also happened to be black. Massachusetts's votes had sent Deval Patrick to the State House in Boston to become the first governor of the Commonwealth of Massachusetts who happened also to be black. The Republican National Committee had just elevated former Maryland governor Michael Steele to become the first head of the Republican Party who also happened to be black.

The stunning reversal of fortune for African-Americans in the United States at the beginning of the twenty-first century was to be admired—a fact that Williams picked up on when he reflected on the attorney general's reference to America as a nation of "cowards" in regard to race and wished that President Obama would have issued a more serious rebuke to focus the nation's attention forward rather the backward.

Holder was certainly correct to observe that there was a time in the not-too-distant past when African-Americans did not enjoy the same constitutional liberties as whites—but fortunately those days are largely behind us. Most poignantly, Williams intoned that if blacks continue to listen to the race "hustlers" and apologists who blame the inability of certain blacks to succeed in society based largely on matters of race, their future prospects would be bleak. Obama's decision to back the words of his attorney general rather than admit that the struggles of the civil rights era had largely been left in history would open the eyes and ears of the president's constituents, many of whom had believed President Obama was the leader of the free world, one who had not only transcended race but also moved the country beyond many of its painful wounds, inflicted from hundreds of years of racism and discrimination. I truly believe that if the president had the opportunity to rewind the clock and respond, he would have more politely but assertively assured the American people that we had come together to solve issues of race and that reflection on past events would not necessarily bring us closer together in the future.

Largely forgotten in the historic nature of the 2008 presidential election was the ugly manner in which the New Black Panther Party had supported President Obama while at the same time issuing racial taunts and threats and engaging in intimidating behavior aimed at white voters. As reported by the conservative columnist Michelle Malkin, senior leaders from the New Black Panther Party were busy on the eve of the election issuing threats and other racial invectives against those who would dare vote against Mr. Obama. Of particular interest was a statement read by Minister Jajee Muhammad, national field marshal of the New Black Panther Party, that had been issued by Dr. Malik Shabazz:

"We will not allow some racists and other angry whites, who are upset over an impending Barack Obama presidential victory, to intimidate blacks at the polls," Muhammad said. "Most certainly, we cannot allow these racist forces to slaughter our babies or commit other acts of violence against the black population, nor our black president."[15]

And yet on the very day when millions of Americans went to the polls to cast their ballots for Barack Obama after his campaign carefully cultivated his racial transcendence, the New Black Panther Party was caught on videotape intimidating white voters in Philadelphia. One Panther was brandishing a nightstick while standing in front of a polling station, while another Panther was clearly overheard saying, "That's right, you're going to be ruled by a black man."

During the first week of January 2009, the Justice Department filed a civil suit against the New Black Panther Party and three of its members. Specifically, the Department of Justice alleged that the party and the individuals named in the suit had violated the Voting Rights Act of 1965 by scaring voters away from a polling station through the use of racial slurs and by brandishing a nightstick and appearing in uniform. As the litigation wound its way through the legal system, neither the named defendants nor the New Black Panther Party itself responded to the complaint or appeared in federal court on their own behalf. Many expected a default judgment to be filed on behalf of the Justice Department since the Panthers had failed to appear in federal district court in Philadelphia.

This is where things began to get interesting. Rather than press ahead for a default adjudication, the Justice Department did the unthinkable in May 2009: they allowed two of the defendants to walk away without further penalty and allowed the third defendant, Minister King Samir Shabazz, to be served only with an injunction that prohibited him from displaying a weapon within one hundred feet of a Philadelphia polling station for the next three years—never mind that current law already prohibits brandishing weapons at polling stations.

Bartle Bull, the publisher of the left-leaning *Village Voice* and himself a civil rights attorney who observed the actions of the Black Panthers in Philadelphia, called their behavior "the most blatant form of voter intimidation I've ever seen."[16] And yet the Holder Justice Department allowed both the three named defendants and the New Black Panther Party to walk away. Why? I went back to candidate Obama's statement issued following the Jena six controversy to look for guidance as to why his Department of Justice would fail to prosecute three individuals who appeared to violate the Voting Rights Act of 1965—particularly since the then senator Obama had told the American people his administration would look at situations not in terms of black and white but in terms of right and wrong. Moreover, the then senator Obama had introduced legislation designed to eliminate the very form of voter intimidation witnessed in the case from Philadelphia. Testifying before John Conyers, chairman of the House Judiciary Committee, Senator Obama offered the following:

> There is no place for politics in this debate. . . . Both parties at different periods in our history have been guilty in different regions of preventing people from voting for a tactical advantage. We should be beyond that.[17]

Indeed. All the more reason why many Americans would question how the Justice Department could allow individuals to intimidate voters based on the color of their skin when just forty years before many blacks had similar problems gaining access to the ballot box.

As the debate on this issue unfolded, it turned out that the decision not to prosecute further came with the acquiescence of the attorney general and over the strenuous objections of six career prosecutors at the Department of Justice who had been overruled by Associate Attorney General Thomas Perrelli—an Obama political appointee. Writing about the internal deliberations to drop the charges in *The Wall Street Journal,* John Fund disclosed that one of the six career lawyers, Appellate Chief Diana Flynn, had recommended in an internal memo that the department should proceed with litigation to "prevent the paramilitary style intimidation of voters."[18] Rather than quell efforts to intimidate voters based on the color of their skin, some Americans questioned how the Obama administration could apparently turn a blind eye to efforts to suppress voter enfranchisement that was reminiscent of the clubs and taunts that were turned on John Lewis and the peaceful marchers on the Edmund Pettus Bridge in Selma, Alabama, years before.

As of this writing, the Department of Justice has failed to comment more directly other than to say that the dismissal was "based on a careful assessment of the facts and the law," a position several members of Congress and the United States Commission on Civil Rights have refused to accept.[19] A banner headline I saw on the Internet captures, I believe, the sentiment of many Americans about the manner in which the Justice Department and the Obama administration dismissed the case and the charges without further commentary: "Is This Post-Racial? . . . Obama Protecting Black Panther Criminals?"[20] I hope this headline is not true, and I am hopeful the Department of Justice will reexamine the case before any statute of limitations expires to ensure that all Americans can and will be treated equally under the law, regardless of the color of their skin.

While the New Black Panther Party incident left many in the country questioning whether the Obama presidency was truly postracial, the president would directly insert himself into the middle of a tense racial situation that left many questioning why President Obama would inject himself in a racial dispute when he had been careful throughout his career to avoid doing so. Ironically, the man both criticized for acting white and being less than authentically black would create a racial firestorm by making comments at a nationally televised press conference that would reverberate across the United States for months to follow.

A TEACHABLE MOMENT ON RACE

July 16, 2009, would prove to be a pivotal early day in the administration of the forty-fourth president of the United States. Hundreds of miles away from the Oval Office, an event was rapidly unfolding that would not only soon engulf the president and his staff but also spark a vigorous debate on race relations in the United States during a time when many Americans had been led to believe the Obama administration would take America on a path toward a postracial society.

As the president tended to business at the White House, Professor Henry Louis Gates Jr., the diminutive yet powerful Harvard professor and director of the W. E. B. Du Bois Institute for African and African American Research, had just arrived home to Cambridge, Massachusetts, following a long trip overseas to China to conduct research for his upcoming PBS documentary. Encountering difficulty opening the front door of his home, Gates and his driver pushed against the jammed entranceway so that Gates could drop off his luggage and pack fresh clothes for a long-awaited vacation on Martha's Vineyard with family and friends. A passerby noted two men pushing against the front door and called the Cambridge police to alert them of the potentially suspicious activity under way. Gates's driver had departed by the time the police arrived, but what happened next is disputed both by Professor Gates and the Cambridge police sergeant James Crowley. Their confrontation, which quickly escalated and led to the professor's arrest, gripped the nation for months to follow, since the country was confronted once again with a serious matter of race during the administration of the first president who happened to be black and was thought to be postracial. Here is how Professor Gates described his ordeal to the *Washington Post:*

> After returning from a week in China researching the genealogy of cellist Yo-Yo Ma, Gates found himself locked out of his house, and he and his driver began pushing against the front door. The sight of two black men forcing open a door prompted an emergency call to police.
>
> The white officer who arrived found Gates in the house (the driver was gone) and asked him to step outside. Gates refused, and the officer followed him in. Gates showed him his ID, which included his address, then demanded that the officer identify

himself. The officer did not comply, Gates said. He then followed the officer outside, saying repeatedly, "Is this how you treat a black man in America?"

The police report said that Gates was "exhibiting loud and tumultuous behavior" and that the officer, Sgt. James Crowley, identified himself. "We stand by whatever the officer said in his report," said Sgt. James DeFrancesco, a spokesman for the Cambridge Police Department. He would not comment on Gates's version of his arrest.

The department said that Crowley tried to calm Gates, but that the professor would not cooperate and said, "You don't know who you're messing with."[21]

A minor dispute between a black Harvard scholar and a white police officer was about to escalate into a worldwide conversation on race that would never have taken place had President Obama not directly immersed himself into a political cauldron he would have been better advised never to have touched.

As the debate slowly unfurled in the opinion and editorial pages across the country and on the airwaves of radio and television, President Obama remained silent and far removed from the relatively minor controversy. On the evening of July 22, 2009, the president conducted a press conference designed to rally public support for his efforts to reform the nation's health-care delivery system, which had stalled in the Congress.

Near the end of the conference, Obama decided to field one last question by the reporter Lynn Sweet, from his hometown paper, the *Chicago Sun-Times,* on his opinion of the arrest and subsequent dismissal of charges against Professor Gates. Here is the official transcription from the White House of the comment that was the spark that ignited the powder keg that had long been just beneath the collective American consciousness on matters of race in America early in the twenty-first century:

Q: Thank you, Mr. President. Recently Professor Henry Louis Gates Jr. was arrested at his home in Cambridge. What does that incident say to you and what does it say about race relations in America?

THE PRESIDENT: Well, I should say at the outset that "Skip" Gates is a friend, so I may be a little biased here. I don't know all the facts. What's been reported, though, is that the guy forgot his keys, jimmied his way to get into the house, there was a report called into the police station that there might be a burglary taking place—so far, so good, right? I mean, if I was trying to jigger into—well, I guess this is my house now so—(laughter)—it probably wouldn't happen. But let's say my old house in Chicago—(laughter)—here I'd get shot. (Laughter.)

But so far, so good. They're reporting—the police are doing what they should. There's a call, they go investigate what happens. My understanding is at that point Professor Gates is already in his house. The police officer comes in, I'm sure there's some exchange of words, but my understanding is, is that Professor Gates then shows his ID to show that this is his house. And at that point, he gets arrested for disorderly conduct—charges which are later dropped.

Now, I don't know, not having been there and not seeing all the facts, what role race played in that, but I think it's fair to say, number one, any of us would be pretty angry; number two, that the Cambridge Police acted stupidly in arresting somebody when there was already proof that they were in their own home; and number three, what I think we know separate and apart from this incident is that there is a long history in this country of African Americans and Latinos being stopped by law enforcement disproportionately. That's just a fact.

As you know, Lynn, when I was in the state legislature in Illinois, we worked on a racial profiling bill because there was indisputable evidence that blacks and Hispanics were being stopped disproportionately. And that is a sign, an example of how, you know, race remains a factor in this society. That doesn't lessen the incredible progress that has been made. I am standing here as testimony to the progress that's been made.

And yet the fact of the matter is, is that this still haunts us. And even when there are honest misunderstandings, the fact that blacks and Hispanics are picked up more frequently and oftentimes for no cause casts suspicion even when there is good cause. And that's why I think the more that we're working with local law enforcement to improve policing techniques so that we're eliminating potential bias, the safer everybody is going to be.[22]

I believe these remarks uttered from a lectern in the East Room of the White House on a warm evening in July 2009 severely damaged the president's ability to project himself to the American people as being postracial. Many Americans were puzzled by President Obama's apparent willingness to assess the Cambridge police officer's actions as "acting stupidly," a remark the president would eventually recant and apologize for. Many believed that as the nation's chief law enforcement officer, he owed a responsibility to view his fellow Americans as equal citizens under the law, blind to the color of their skin.

The reaction to the president's remarks around the nation and around the world was swift: editorial and opinion pieces took the dispute between Professor Gates and Sergeant Crowley from the confines of print and television and to intense personal discussions that aroused family dinner tables, office hallways, and checkout lines in the supermarkets. *Obama was right; Obama was wrong,* the debates raged for more than a week as the topic of race in America, now with its very first black president, overwhelmed all other political and policy discussions facing the country.

Overnight the discussion on how the president proposed to overhaul the nation's health-care delivery system was replaced with, How does the president propose to move forward in America on matters of race when the dispute between Gates and Crowley was hardly a clear-cut case of black and white, right versus wrong?

Wisely, albeit more than a week after his initial comments, the president took the proper course of action by stepping forward to apologize for his remarks while also inviting the two antagonists in the initial dispute to the White House for a "beer summit" on race. While I suspect that President Obama wished he had never waded into the conflict in the first place, the president deserves credit for embracing an issue that he had largely sidestepped during his young political career: matters and issues involving race. For a senator accused on more than one occasion of acting white as he sought the presidency, President Obama deserves credit for seeking to quell a racial firestorm largely of his own creation, especially since he had previously avoided public comments that brought his own ethnicity into focus and open discussion. Even though he had been criticized previously for being insensitive to the issues facing the black community (whatever those specific issues might be remains a mystery to me) and had been denigrated as acting white for being not sufficiently or authentically black, the president acted responsibly by trying to bridge a racial fissure that threatened to evolve into a deeper one early in his presidency.

As we shall see in the following chapter, however, many of the president's supporters could be said to have crossed the delicate line established by President Obama on matters of race as he sought to put the Gates-Crowley controversy behind him. Perhaps emboldened by the nearly nonstop television and print coverage of the dispute, some of the president's supporters both inside and outside government sought to portray subsequent honest policy disagreements by the president's political opponents as being racist and indicative of long-seated racism.

Given President Obama's courageous decision in 2004 to castigate those who would assail young black students with a book in their hands for acting white, the decision by some of his supporters within the administration and on Capitol Hill to accuse the president's opponents as being racist could be damaging as Americans reflect upon

Obama's first years in office and question whether the election of the country's first black president has done more harm than good to ameliorate relations between various ethnic groups and to constructively move the country forward rather than backward in its efforts to put the dark stain of racial discrimination behind it rather than revisit old issues.

13

The Death of a Racial Slur

The New Underground Railroad—Transporting
Black People to Real Equality

So where are we now? Our sweeping review of American history over the past one hundred and fifty years has shown a steady rise in the use of derogatory language directed toward blacks who act, think, dress, or associate in a manner that is not consistent with what the perceived ideological or societal norms would dictate. *Uncle Tom. Sellout. Not sufficiently black. White man's nigger—* all slights used and expanded on over the generations to denigrate those blacks who dared stray from the conventional norms established and enforced by those who purport to speak for the black race.

The successes of the civil rights struggle for equality have also brought about a new entitlement mentality for many within the black community that has hindered rather than inspired academic, social, and political process. Rather than compete as equals of whites and others in the classroom, many blacks across the country favor the reduction of admission standards for members of their race in the interest of diversity and multiculturalism—all the while denigrating those black students who perform well in school or shun affirmative action as acting white.

This breakdown in the collective black consciousness has been met with disastrous results since *Brown v. Board of Education* opened the schoolhouse doors for many blacks previously denied an education. Rather than celebrate the opportunities brought about by the struggle, many blacks have since sought to self-segregate in neighborhoods, schools, and places of worship. The rise of the Black Power movement in the late 1960s and early 1970s celebrated the creation of a new language for blacks to better express themselves while it castigated those who sought to learn proper English as acting white.

The second black member to become elevated to the United States Supreme Court would not only be labeled an Uncle Tom sellout who was acting white, but a certain number of his detractors mused that his views did not represent most of the black community—as if such a barometer exists in white or Latino communities as to what best represents societal norms.

The criticism of General Colin Powell and Condoleezza Rice as being sellouts and acting white by serving in a Republican administration overlooks the significance of America's having its first black national security advisor and secretary of state and its first female black secretary of state. In the minds of these enforcers of political correctness, real accomplishment pales in comparison with being authentically black and not acting white to move ahead.

This polarization of thought, if left unchecked, will do more to divide the United States of America on matters of race than any other division at any point in the history of this country since the dark days of segregation. This is a real rather than perceived threat—the era of the Obama presidency was supposed to usher us forward to being truly postracial in our cultural, societal, and political evolution. Instead, many Americans are seeking shelter behind similar retrenchments— the rise of nooses, swastikas, and other racially offensive objects have appeared with alarming frequency across the country in school dormitories, police departments, office buildings, and even places of worship.

Have decades of racial set-asides, multicultural demands for separate housing accommodations and graduation ceremonies, and diversity hires for black professors fueled the fires of racial intolerance? And, finally, have those citizens, both black and white, who denigrate black academic success as acting white sought to perpetuate a stereotype that a black acting properly is one who is unable to read or speak proper English and who leaves secondary and postsecondary school unarmed with the intellectual tools to compete and survive in the twenty-first century?

I believe there is a path forward to place our racial disagreements behind us to achieve real equality across racial lines and fulfill the dream of Dr. Martin Luther King Jr., where Americans will evaluate one another based not on the color of their skin but on the content of their character. As such, I believe there are several key steps that we must collectively embark upon as a society in order to proceed down the road less traveled and that will make the difference between Dr. King's dream and fulfilling his dream of putting the racial divisiveness behind us once and for all.

We Must Stop Making Excuses
for Inexcusable Behavior

The charge of acting white must be eradicated once and for all. The entire notion that it is acceptable in many white and black communities to question whether one is "black enough" or "acting white" is entirely inexcusable and has perpetuated numerous negative stereotypes that have persisted since the days of slavery in America.

First, we as a society can no longer tolerate the acting white slur because of the underlying assumptions the term implies. As we have seen, from the days of Harriet Beecher Stowe's *Uncle Tom's Cabin* to the present, there is a certain assumption about what it is to be black versus white in America.

With a broad brush, many have associated being black with being uneducated, lazy, unmotivated, and poor. Being white, on the other hand, could be associated with being successful, driven, motivated, and wealthy. When in 2004 the comedian Bill Cosby and the then senator Barack Obama assailed the notion that a black child with a book is acting white, they were challenging a set of assumptions that had been prevalent for generations: black children weren't expected to excel in school because they weren't smart enough, motivated enough, or capable of being equal to whites.

To use a phrase made famous by the former president George W. Bush, we will progress as a country and take the road less traveled by eliminating the "soft bigotry of low expectations" for black children and for their ability to succeed in the classroom and the workplace without government set-asides, affirmative action programs, or government intervention that substitutes artificial equality for equality brought about by hard work and by raising the bar of expectations black students will be forced to meet. This will be a difficult and painful process, but it is one that must be undertaken to establish a benchmark and a baseline for success in eradicating the academic curse that black students who test and perform well in the classroom are acting white.

The former president and I had the opportunity to discuss the acting white slur late in 2009 and how best to eradicate it from our lexicon once and for all. President Bush reflected upon his time as governor of Texas, when certain people were willing to shuffle black students from grade to grade without testing their progress to ensure that the students were learning and building upon their academic foundations. I was struck when President Bush told me that the reason he fought so hard to enact the No Child Left Behind law early in his presidency is that he had found that children of color in Texas could excel academically in the classroom when shown love and encouragement from both parents and teachers alike. In other words, the president had discovered that students of color, instead of being mocked as acting white by working hard in the classroom, were motivated by stronger tools to encourage success: love and encouragement.

These were the basic tenets President Bush signed into law that have remained controversial ever since: instead of allowing students to be shuffled from grade to grade without accountability, No Child Left Behind required assessments of students in grades 3–8 annually and in high school once to measure success or failure both of schools across

America and the students therein. Rather than seek to close the achievement gap between black and white students through lofty rhetorical language and promised admonitions of academic rigor, the new statute specifically sought to eliminate the black and white achievement gap through hard work and measured success.

While the law has been criticized for imposing unfunded federal mandates on local school district and for merely being an exercise to teach students to take the test, the results have been unmistakable over the years: according to the *Nation's Report Card* in 2005, reading and math scores for black nine-year-olds and math scores for black thirteen-year-olds were at an all-time high. Moreover, the achievement gaps in reading and math between black and white nine-year-olds were at all-time lows.[1]

In essence, the allegation of acting white is nothing more than the perpetuation of the soft bigotry of low expectations for black students that has been accepted as part of our society by blacks and whites for too long. We must strive for the day when a black student with a book in hand is praised for their diligence and study rather than castigated for trying to move ahead by acting white. This transformation will not be easy, but it will gradually occur over time as parents and teachers show their students love for academic and intellectual curiosity and reprimand those who criticize.

I strongly believe that these students, once measured not by the color of their skin but by their academic, intellectual, and social skills, will rise to the top in their chosen vocations and eradicate the notion that their success was brought about by their acting white; instead, these students, who are acting right by pursuing their dreams, hold the key to the future, which is unlocked by the power and strength provided by a quality education.

Blacks Must Be Responsible for Their Own Actions and Stop Blaming Others for Their Lack of Progress.

Concurrent with the responsibility we must take as a culture and a society to eradicate the notion that academic achievement and success are indicative of acting white, we must also eliminate the tolerance for those who wish to blame others in society—instead of looking in the mirror—for lack of academic, social, or financial success. As we have seen in our historical review, it has been easy for many over the generations to blame others for a perceived lack of success rather than to closely examine the actions and consequences of those actions an individual has chosen.

The early pioneers of the civil rights movement fought courageously to set aside the accepted separate and inherently unequal conditions for blacks and whites in America that had been codified into law with the *Plessy v. Ferguson* decision from 1896. For nearly sixty years, until the decision was overruled by *Brown v. Board of Education* in 1954, blacks were relegated to being second-class citizens and were denied equal opportunity to learn, live, interact, and work as the equals of whites in society.

Following the landmark decision in 1954, doors that had been firmly locked in place to deny blacks entry as equal participants in society were gradually pried open, often with the threat of force from federal troops sent in by presidents in the late 1950s and early 1960s to ensure black students could take their seats in secondary and postsecondary schools. And yet, as Bill Cosby famously lamented during the fifty-year anniversary of the *Brown* decision in 2004, many of the painful gains and achievements brought about by these early pioneers were being squandered by many blacks who blamed whites or others for their lack of success. Remember the words of Cosby from his famous "pound cake" speech given during the aforementioned gala in 2004:

> Ladies and gentlemen, the lower economic and lower middle economic people are not holding their end in this deal. In the neighborhood that most of us grew up in, parenting is not going on. In the old days, you couldn't hooky school because every drawn shade was an eye. And before your mother got off the bus and to the house, she knew exactly where you had gone, who had gone into the house, and where you got on whatever

you had one and where you got it from. Parents don't know that today. . . .

We cannot blame white people. White people . . . white people don't live over there.[2]

Perhaps the strength of the Black Power movement was that it instilled a new sense of pride and purpose in blacks following the violent assassinations of Dr. Martin Luther King Jr. and Malcolm X during the transformative years of the civil rights movement in the 1960s. At the same time, this movement also saw the acceptance of a new black cultural identity that shunned interaction and coexistence with whites while fostering the rise of Ebonics and the desired cultural connection with Africa yearned for by leaders such as Marcus Garvey years earlier.

Coupled with the rise of affirmative action, government set-aside programs, and multiculturalism, the sense of blacks as victims has done considerable harm in my view to the goal of strengthening our position in society by having blacks enter the doors that were opened by the *Brown* decision. This form of cultural and racial self-destruction must stop in order for blacks to gain true equality in society with whites. Once again, this will be a difficult road and a road less traveled, but it is one that will make all the difference as America evolves in the twenty-first century.

It is easy for many to blame high black unemployment, lack of academic or financial success, and inadequate housing on residual racism in America. And such blame is the road most often taken; rather, the road less traveled must be taken for us to break the cycle of dependency on government and others and to begin the cycle of self-sufficiency and hard work advocated earlier by Dr. Cosby and others. Without the power of an education, blacks are relegated to lower-wage jobs, forced to live in lower socioeconomic neighborhoods, and have less of an opportunity to break free from the strains of poverty and hopelessness. The doors that had been opened by *Brown v. Board of Education* are being shut in the minds of many who have proudly asserted that they are authentically black and that performing well in school is acting white. And, since these individuals will inevitably slip behind those who apply themselves in their academic training and their subsequent vocations, these individuals will blame whites and society at large for their lack of advancement.

It is time for American society to stop tolerating this form of "black as victim" if it is to advance and be cohesive. We must break free as a society from this cycle of victimization as surely as blacks broke free from the chains of slavery that bound them to involuntary servitude. This time, in the early-twenty-first century, there are those within black communities who now voluntarily don the chains that bind them to poverty and hopelessness because they choose to shun education and blame others for their lack of progress. This must stop, and as a society we must no longer tolerate those who blame "the man" or whites for the lack of black achievement in America. Instead, we must confront our friends, relatives, neighbors, and colleagues who seek to play the victim card and instead ask them if their individual actions and the consequences of those decisions has led them to their current level of success or lack thereof.

Beware of the Perils Brought by the Era of Obama; There Is No Such Thing as Being Authentically Black

Few would have predicted that the electrifying performance given by Senator Barack Obama (D-IL) at the 2004 Democratic National Convention on behalf of the presidential nominee, John Kerry (D-MA), would catapult him to the Oval Office less than five years later. In his speech Obama famously declared: "Go into any inner-city neighborhood, and folks will tell you that government alone can't teach kids to learn. They know that parents have to parent, that children can't achieve unless we raise their expectations and . . . eradicate the slander that says a black youth with a book is acting white." And yet during his dizzying ascendancy to become the forty-fourth president of the United States, Obama would be subjected to countless speculation and criticism as to whether or not he was sufficiently or authentically black.

This slight, along with that of being a sellout or acting white, must be eradicated from our lexicon once and for all. Obama, a Harvard-trained lawyer who would emerge from the South Side of Chicago as a community organizer only to become elected to the Illinois State Senate and ultimately the United States Senate, is a testament to the notion that working hard, applying oneself, and ultimately achieving success is not acting white but acting properly.

And yet once Senator Obama's presidential campaign gained traction, the whispers that had persisted in barbershops, beauty salons, and elsewhere made their way to the national dialogue of discussion—was the junior senator from Illinois authentically black? Obama first tackled this delicate issue early in his campaign for office when he made an appearance before the National Association of Black Journalists Conference, held on July 10, 2008, in Las Vegas, Nevada. For a campaign famously known for being on time and on schedule, Obama had arrived to his presentation an uncharacteristic ten minutes late, and then the candidate strolled on the stage and offered the following: "I want to apologize for being a little bit late. . . . But you guys keep asking whether I'm black enough."[3]

Speaking before an ostensibly friendly audience, the junior senator from Illinois evoked laughter from many black members in attendance by evoking the notion of "CPT," or "colored people's time." In other words, blacks are expected to be less than punctual in meeting their appointments, and Obama thought he could get a laugh from the crowd by pointing to his tardiness as indicative of his true blackness. While I understand the sentiment, the criticism still runs deep: why is it acceptable for blacks to be late because they are black and whites are not held to the same, and I daresay lower, standard?

Gwen Ifill, the noted journalist and managing editor and moderator of PBS's *Washington Week* television program, published a book on Inauguration Day entitled *The Breakthrough: Politics and Race in the Age of Obama,* in which she tackles his "blackness" problem. Interestingly, Ifill points to an August 2007 column written by the *Miami Herald* commentator Leonard Pitts Jr., who had decided to chronicle the "black enough" references to Obama dating back to 2003. In his informal survey, Pitts found 464 occasions where Obama's name had been linked to the phrase.[4]

We can think back to our earlier discussion regarding Obama's blackness and recollect that both Jesse Jackson Sr. and Ralph Nader questioned whether Obama either acted white or thought he was white as it related to the manner in which he (Obama) was conducting his campaign. The "sufficiently black" moniker is almost the exact counterreflection of acting white: one who is not sufficiently black can be assumed to be acting in such a way that one could equate the behavior with acting white. This is wrong, and this must stop.

We must take the road less traveled to recognize that only when we view one another as fellow human beings rather than as individuals who are sufficiently black or who act white can we end much of the racial divisiveness that permeates our society. To emphasize this point, I remember traveling to Martha's Vineyard during the summer of 2009 to attend a conference sponsored by Harvard University's W. E. B. Du Bois Institute for African and African American Research entitled "Equality in the Age of Obama."

The morning of the conference, August 20, I made my way to Back Door Donuts for breakfast and a hot cup of coffee. Entering the shop, a table of well-dressed African-Americans stared at me as I made my way toward the line that stretched throughout the store.

"Are you that political commentator Ron Christie from television?" a young lady sitting at the table asked me. After acknowledging that I was, an older gentleman sitting with her said: "That isn't what we fought for." Not wishing to cause a scene in the restaurant, I merely responded that we were all free to choose our party affiliation based on our own personal beliefs. When the gentleman replied that he was sorry that I was a Republican, I countered by saying that I was sorry he chose to overlook the fact that the civil rights movement paved the way for people like me to be free—free to make my own decision not to be bound by the ideological dictates of how one should vote or act based on the color of my skin.

Excusing myself and moving further along in the line, I felt the gentleman's eyes upon me while I paid for my coffee and moved to leave the shop. Before I could reach the door, he surprised me by inviting me back to his table and apologizing. "You're right," he said. "That was what the movement was about. Freedom to choose." Disarming each other with engaging smiles, we shook hands, and the gentleman took the time to introduce me to his family before we continued our conversation.

I use this story as an illustration that proves the road paved by John Lewis, Kenneth Clark, Thurgood Marshall, and Dr. Martin Luther King Jr. was meant to allow individuals to be judged by the content of their character rather than the color of their skin, to have the freedom to agree or disagree based not on skin color but on political or ideological reflection. This is why the "authentically black" charge must no longer be considered socially acceptable but inexcusable and must be dropped from our lexicon.

Case in point, the entertainer Harry Belafonte, a man who had taken the brave steps to raise sufficient funds to bail Dr. Martin Luther King Jr. out of jail during the 1960s, would resort to highly inflammatory language when referring to prominent black Republicans early in the administration of President George W. Bush. In an article posted by Marc Morano in the Cybercast News Service, the journalist revealed the following:

> Celebrity activist Harry Belafonte referred to prominent African-American officials in the Bush Administration as "black tyrants" at a weekend march, and he also compared the administration to Adolf Hitler's Nazi Germany.[5]

Sadly, Belafonte was only at the start, rather than the end, of his castigation of black Republicans serving in the Bush administration, a charge I was particularly attuned to. Belafonte continued:

> [If] a black is a tyrant, he is first and foremost a tyrant, then he incidentally is black. Bush is a tyrant and if he gathers around

him black tyrants, they all have to be treated as they are being treated.[6]

Black tyrants. Blacks being insufficiently or inauthentically black. It appears only within the black community that one is either sufficiently or authentically a member of one's race. I can't recall hearing such an allegation being used to describe whites, Asians, or Hispanics. This racial anomaly appears to exist only within black communities and is used as a threat and a weapon to bludgeon those who fail to follow the social, cultural, political, and ideological path blacks are expected to follow. This monolithic perspective will only perpetuate the acceptance of denigrating those who study hard as acting white and of refusing to explore diverse perspectives that differ from one's own. As former civil rights leader and NAACP head Julian Bond told Gwen Ifill:

> Segregation made us all alike. It made us think alike. . . . We lived together. We read the same newspapers, our own newspapers, so we had a group consciousness that has dissipated to some degree by the demise of segregation. So we are a different people now than we would have been, say, thirty, forty, fifty years ago.[7]

Just as segregation forced many blacks to think alike during the early and mid–twentieth century, we must change our ideological mind-set in the early twenty-first century to allow differing views, perspectives, and schools of thought within the black community instead of questioning one's blackness or authenticity. The celebration of diversity rather than the scorn associated with whether one is truly black will help bury this slur once and for all.

Disagreement with the President in the Era of Obama Is Not Tantamount to Racism

No one can deny the historical significance of the 2008 presidential election. The election of America's first black president will do more to inspire countless children that they can truly achieve the American dream regardless of the color of their skin and will inspire them to change the direction of this country in ways that we can't yet contemplate.

At the same time, President Obama's election must be understood in context—supporters must not project that racism has ended in America, and detractors must not postulate that a black man in the Oval Office will avoid causing more tension among racial groups. Unfortunately, as the euphoria of the election and the inauguration of the forty-fourth president of the United States gave way to the daily international and domestic demands of the job, a disturbing development took place that currently threatens to upset decades of racial progress between blacks and whites in America.

I believe the American political tone and tenor of discussion took a wrong turn during the summer of 2009, when a certain number of the president's supporters on Capitol Hill and elsewhere sought to castigate those who disagreed with Obama's health-care and global-climate-change policies as being racist instead of as having honest policy disagreements. For an incoming administration that reveled in the postinaugural assessment that President Obama, once criticized as acting white by detractors both black and white, would serve as America's first "postracial" president, the charges of racism by his supporters toward those who opposed his signature domestic policy initiatives proved a most unwelcome development.

Perhaps the flash point occurred on September 9, 2009, when the president arrived to address a rare joint session of Congress to garner its support as well as the support of the American people for his vision to overhaul the nation's health-care delivery system. At one point during the president's speech, when President Obama noted that illegal aliens would not be eligible to benefit from the new health-care reform measure, the gathered elected officials, including the president himself, were startled to hear Representative Joe Wilson shout out to the president: "You lie." For a Congress that had deteriorated in its relations with members of opposite political parties, Wilson's outburst marked a new low;

incivility and indecorum had descended upon Capitol Hill like a dense fog.

Almost immediately following his outburst, Congressman Wilson offered his apology to White House Chief of Staff Rahm Emmanuel, who passed along Wilson's contrition to the president, who accepted Wilson's apology. End of story? Sadly, this marked the beginning of the racial discord that would emanate from Capitol Hill and beyond to dominate discussions in newspaper columns and cable news outlets for months to follow.

For example, Maureen Dowd, the caustic columnist from *The New York Times,* led the charge to assert that the congressman from South Carolina had meant something far more sinister when he shouted out "You Lie" to the president. In her own words, Dowd declared:

> But fair or not, what I heard was an unspoken word in the air: You lie, boy! . . . For two centuries the South has feared a take-over by blacks or the feds. In Obama, they have both.[8]

Dowd continued by quoting the former Democratic National Committee Chairman Don Fowler's column:

> It may be President Obama's very air of elegance and erudition that raises hackles in some. "My father used to say to me, 'Boy, don't get above your raising,'" Fowler said. "Some people are prejudiced anyway, and then they look at his education and mannerisms and get more angry at him."[9]

The most inflammatory aspect of Dowd's column is the fact that she inserted words into the mouth of Congressman Wilson that he had never uttered during his outburst to President Obama on the floor of the House of Representatives during Obama's health-care address: "You lie, *boy*" (emphasis added). Her defenders will assert that Dowd was making an assumption that Congressman Wilson had meant to add "boy" to the end of his "you lie" remarks to express an unspoken sentiment—a sentiment assumed and perhaps only heard and articulated by Dowd herself.

For whatever reason, Dowd elected to insert a racially tinged comment where the congressman had neither insinuated nor implied anything beyond the fact that he believed that the president had been less than truthful in regard to whether illegal immigrants would have access to the proposed health-care initiative. Whether or not it was her intended consequence, Dowd's column ignited yet another powder keg in regard to race in America—more incendiary comments and conversations were set to follow as a result of the outburst she fabricated for Wilson.

Just days after Congressman Wilson's remark and Maureen Dowd's column, certain members of the Congressional Black Caucus escalated matters. Representative Hank Johnson (D-GA) threw more kerosene on the fire, fueling the racial debate clearly unwanted by the White House, when he offered:

> That Wilson's scream could signal the return of "folks putting on white hoods and white uniforms again, riding through the countryside."[10]

Unfortunately yet another resident of the state of Georgia, the thirty-ninth president of the United States, would weigh in with his own assessment of the Joe Wilson incident in language that went further than the comments expressed by many in the heated discussions on race in the era of Obama articulated thus far. President Jimmy Carter offered the following commentary regarding Representative Joe Wilson's outburst:

> "I think an overwhelming portion of the intensely demonstrated animosity toward President Obama is based on the fact that he is a black man," Carter told NBC. There exists the belief "among many white people not just in the South, but around the country," he continued, "that African-Americans are not qualified to

lead this great country. It's an abominable circumstance, and grieves me and concerns me very deeply."[11]

What is perhaps most "abominable," to use the words of President Carter, is that Dowd, Congressman Johnson, and Carter himself felt comfortable insinuating that honest political opposition to President Obama revealed a thinly disguised return to the days of the Ku Klux Klan roaming the countryside, a return indicating that whites could not accept that President Obama was a legitimate leader capable of leading the United States of America. In her column "Playing the Racial Deck," the syndicated columnist Kathleen Parker offered the following in regard to the sudden surge of calls of racism by supporters of the president:

> It's worth noting that Obama's approval rating was nearly 70 percent in January, dropping to 45 percent [in September 2009]. Did all of those people suddenly become racist? Or are they, as [Congressman] Wilson claims to be, passionately concerned about the rapid growth of government and debt? . . .
>
> Whatever prompted Wilson's rude display, it ultimately revealed our hair-trigger response to any remark or action involving an African-American. It is the height (or depth) of racism to suggest that any opposition to Obama's policies is race-based.[12]

This shortsighted effort to stifle political free speech with charges of racism must stop. Political discord has been at the root and the birth of the American existence since the Declaration of Independence. That Barack Obama sought to subject himself to the ultimate spotlight and microscope by running to become the president of the United States meant that he was willing to incur the scrutiny, criticism, and praise that the forty-three former occupants of the office had endured.

President Obama and his spokesman, Robert Gibbs, refused to inject race into the debate as to whether criticism over his policies amounted to racism on the part of his detractors. Still, the president could have gone much further to diffuse the debate when he had accepted the apology of Representative Wilson but allowed members of the Congressional Black Caucus to assert that criticism of him amounted to racism.

And yet the president and his supporters failed to address the overtly racial comments in regard to his candidacy and eventual election to office when Senate Majority Leader Harry Reid (D-NV) was revealed to have uttered racially insensitive comments about Obama in a book published earlier this year. In *Game Change,* a behind-the-scenes account of the 2008 presidential election, the Senate majority leader offered his assessment of Obama's prospects to win:

> [Reid] was wowed by Obama's oratorical gifts and believed the country was ready to embrace a black presidential candidate, especially one such as Obama—a "light-skinned" African American "with no Negro dialect, unless he wanted to have one," as he later put it privately.[13]

Just before the publication of the book, on January 9, 2010, Reid offered a public apology in which he noted: "I deeply regret using such a poor choice of words . . . I sincerely apologize for offending any and all Americans, especially African Americans for my improper comments." Rather than condemn Senator Reid for his remarks, President Obama, the Congressional Black Caucus, and the NAACP took the senator's apology at face value and considered the matter settled, despite widespread criticism that Democrats had used a double standard by ignoring inflammatory racial comments made by fellow party members but by being particularly vocal should such comments come from a Republican.

In the case of Reid's assessment that Obama has the ability to shift in and out of a "Negro" dialect poses an interesting question: What exactly does it mean to have a Negro dialect? Was the majority leader saying that then senator Obama was acceptable to the nation because he was light skinned and acted white?

President Obama's silence on Majority Leader Reid's comments immediately after they were published is particularly revealing. Perhaps the president was reluctant to wade into another racial controversy so soon following his infamous "beer summit" the previous summer with Professor Gates and Cambridge police officer Crowley. More likely, the president was merely continuing his pattern of avoiding racial issues—particularly those involving him personally. That Obama and his allies would allow the Senate majority leader to essentially accuse him of acting and talking white without challenge was a missed opportunity to bury the racist sentiment held by many over the generations.

Without question, President Obama is a unique and transformational figure in the political and cultural history of America. Just as the then senator Obama called for the elimination of the slur and the belief that a young black child with a book was acting white, I believe he must stand firm once again to tamp down a trend that threatens to polarize America along racial lines in ways the country has not seen since the 1960s. The president of the United States of America is the most powerful job in the world. Surely the occupant of such office can step forward to remind the Americans he leads that, while racism still remains in our country, criticism of him is not automatically racist.

The election of the first president of the United States who happens to be black offers the country a unique opportunity to make significant steps forward to achieve Dr. King's dream of a color-blind society. I believe that President Obama could use the power and station of his office to engage in constructive dialogue with his fellow Americans on matters of race, including calls to eliminate slurs that divide us along racial and color lines.

While these problems will not be solved overnight, I believe America stands ready to bury questions of whether one is sufficiently black or acting white and instead to ask whether our children are fulfilling the dream and vision set forth by brave leaders from the civil rights era who fought generations before to ensure that blacks are ready, willing, and able to compete as equals to whites in American society. As we honor their legacy, we must demand nothing less than that the charges of acting white will recede into history and that black and white children will achieve true parity and equality once and for all.

Appendix of
Primary Documents

BOOKER T. WASHINGTON'S
ATLANTA EXPOSITION ADDRESS (1895)

Mr. President and Gentlemen of the Board of Directors and Citizens: One-third of the population of the South is of the Negro race. No enterprise seeking the material, civil, or moral welfare of this section can disregard this element of our population and reach the highest success. I but convey to you, Mr. President and Directors, the sentiment of the masses of my race when I say that in no way have the value and manhood of the American Negro been more fittingly and generously recognized than by the managers of this magnificent Exposition at every stage of its progress. It is a recognition that will do more to cement the friendship of the two races than any occurrence since the dawn of our freedom.

Not only this, but the opportunity here afforded will awaken among us a new era of industrial progress. Ignorant and inexperienced, it is not strange that in the first years of our new life we began at the top instead of at the bottom; that a seat in Congress or the state legislature was more sought than real estate or industrial skill; that the political convention or stump speaking had more attractions than starting a dairy farm or truck garden.

A ship lost at sea for many days suddenly sighted a friendly vessel. From the mast of the unfortunate vessel was seen a signal, "Water, water; we die of thirst!" The answer from the friendly vessel at once came back, "Cast down your bucket where you are." A second time the signal, "Water, water; send us water!" ran up from the distressed vessel, and was answered, "Cast down your bucket where you are." And a third and fourth signal for water was answered, "Cast down your bucket where you are." The captain of the distressed vessel, at last heeding the injunction, cast down his bucket, and it came up full of fresh, sparkling water from the mouth of the Amazon River. To those of my race who depend on bettering their condition in a foreign land or who underestimate the importance of cultivating friendly relations with the Southern white man, who is their next-door neighbor, I would say: "Cast down your bucket where you are"—cast it down in making friends in every manly way of the people of all races by whom we are surrounded.

Cast it down in agriculture, mechanics, in commerce, in domestic service, and in the professions. And in this connection it is well to bear in mind that whatever other sins the South may be called to bear, when it comes to business, pure and simple, it is in the South that the Negro is given a man's chance in the commercial world, and in nothing is this Exposition more eloquent than in emphasizing this chance. Our greatest danger is that in the great leap from slavery to freedom we may overlook the fact that the masses of us are to live by the productions of our hands, and fail to keep in mind that we shall prosper in proportion as we learn to dignify and glorify common labour, and put brains and skill into the common occupations of life; shall prosper in proportion as we learn to draw the line between the superficial and the substantial, the ornamental gewgaws of life and the useful. No race can prosper till it learns that there is as much dignity in tilling a field as in writing a poem. It is at the bottom of life we must begin, and not at the top. Nor should we permit our grievances to overshadow our opportunities.

To those of the white race who look to the incoming of those of foreign birth and strange tongue and habits for the prosperity of the South, were I permitted I would repeat what I say to my own race, "Cast down your bucket where you are." Cast it down among the eight millions of Negroes whose habits you know, whose fidelity and love you have tested in days when to have proved treacherous meant the ruin of your firesides. Cast down your bucket among these people who have, without strikes and labour wars, tilled your fields, cleared your forests, builded your railroads and cities, and brought forth treasures from the bowels of the earth, and helped make possible this magnificent representation of the progress of the South. Casting down your bucket among my people, helping and encouraging them as you are doing on these grounds, and to education of head, hand, and heart, you will find that they will buy your surplus land, make blossom the waste places in your fields, and run your factories. While doing this, you can be sure in the future, as in the past, that you and your families will be surrounded by the most patient, faithful, law-abiding, and unresentful people that the world has seen. As we have proved our loyalty to you in the past, in nursing your children, watching by the sick-bed of your mothers and fathers, and often following them with tear-dimmed eyes to their graves, so in the future, in our humble way, we shall stand by you with a devotion that no foreigner can approach, ready to lay down our lives, if need be, in defense of yours, interlacing our industrial, commercial, civil, and religious life with yours in a way that shall make the interests of both races one. In all things that are purely social we can be as separate as the fingers, yet one as the hand in all things essential to mutual progress.

There is no defense or security for any of us except in the highest intelligence and development of all. If anywhere there are efforts tending to curtail the fullest growth of the Negro, let these efforts be turned into stimulating, encouraging, and making him the most useful and intelligent citizen. Effort or means so invested will pay a thousand per cent interest. These efforts will be twice blessed—blessing him that gives and him that takes. There is no escape through law of man or God from the inevitable:

The laws of changeless justice bind Oppressor with oppressed;

And close as sin and suffering joined We march to fate abreast . . .

Nearly sixteen millions of hands will aid you in pulling the load upward, or they will pull against you the load downward. We shall constitute one-third and more of the ignorance and crime of the South, or one-third [of] its intelligence and progress; we shall contribute one-third to the business and industrial prosperity of the South, or we shall prove a veritable body of death, stagnating, depressing, retarding every effort to advance the body politic.

Gentlemen of the Exposition, as we present to you our humble effort at an exhibition of our progress, you must not expect overmuch. Starting thirty years ago with ownership here and there in a few quilts and pumpkins and chickens (gathered from miscellaneous sources), remember the path that has led from these to the inventions and production of agricultural implements, buggies, steam-engines, newspapers, books, statuary, carving, paintings, the management of drug stores and banks, has not been trodden without contact with thorns and thistles. While we take pride in what we exhibit as a result of our independent efforts, we do not for a moment forget that our part in this exhibition would fall far short of your expectations but for the constant help that has come to our educational life, not only from the Southern states, but especially from Northern philanthropists, who have made their gifts a constant stream of blessing and encouragement.

The wisest among my race understand that the agitation of questions of social equality is the extremest folly, and that progress in the enjoyment of all the privileges that will come to us must be the result of severe and constant struggle rather than of artificial forcing. No race that has anything to contribute to the markets of the world is long in any degree ostracized. It is important and right that all privileges of the law be ours, but it is vastly more important that we be prepared for the exercise of these privileges. The opportunity to earn a dollar in a factory just now is worth infinitely more than the opportunity to spend a dollar in an opera-house.

In conclusion, may I repeat that nothing in thirty years has given us more hope and encouragement, and drawn us so near to you of the white race, as this opportunity offered by the Exposition; and here bending, as it were, over the altar that represents the results of the struggles of your race and mine, both starting practically empty-handed three decades ago, I pledge that in your effort to work out the great and intricate problem which God has laid at the doors of the South, you shall have at all times the patient, sympathetic help of my race; only let this he constantly in mind, that, while from representations in these buildings of the product of field, of forest, of mine, of factory, letters, and art, much good will come, yet far above and beyond material benefits will be that higher good, that, let us pray God, will come, in a blotting out of sectional differences and racial animosities and suspicions, in a determination to administer absolute justice, in a willing obedience among all classes to the mandates of law. This, coupled with our material prosperity, will bring into our beloved South a new heaven and a new earth.

■ ■ ■

PLESSY V. FERGUSON

SUPREME COURT OF THE UNITED STATES
163 U.S. 537
May 18, 1896

Prior History

THIS was a petition for writs of prohibition and certiorari, originally filed in the Supreme Court of the State by Plessy, the plaintiff in error, against the Hon. John H. Ferguson, judge of the criminal District Court for the parish of Orleans, and setting forth in substance the following facts:

That petitioner was a citizen of the United States and a resident of the State of Louisiana, of mixed descent, in the proportion of seven eighths Caucasian and one eighth African blood; that the mixture of colored blood was not discernible in him, and that he was entitled to every recognition, right, privilege and immunity secured to the citizens of the United States of the white race by its Constitution and laws; that on June 7, 1892, he engaged and paid for a first class passage on the East Louisiana Railway from New Orleans to Covington, in the same State, and thereupon entered a passenger train, and took possession of a vacant seat in a coach where passengers of the white race were accommodated; that such railroad company was incorporated by the laws of Louisiana as a common carrier, and was not authorized to distinguish between citizens according to their race. But, notwithstanding this, petitioner was required by the conductor, under penalty of ejection from said train and imprisonment, to vacate said coach and occupy another seat in a coach assigned by said company for persons not of the white race, and for no other reason than that petitioner was of the colored race; that upon petitioner's refusal to comply with such order, he was, with the aid of a police officer, forcibly ejected from said coach and hurried off to and imprisoned in the parish jail of New Orleans, and there held to answer a charge made by such officer to the effect that he was guilty of having criminally violated an act of the General Assembly of the State, approved July 10, 1890, in such case made and provided.

That petitioner was subsequently brought before the recorder of the city for preliminary examination and committed for trial to the criminal District Court for the parish of Orleans, where an information was filed against him in the matter above set forth, for a violation of the above act, which act the petitioner affirmed to be null and void, because in conflict with the Constitution of the United States.

MR. JUSTICE BROWN, *after stating the case, delivered the opinion of the court.*

This case turns upon the constitutionality of an act of the General Assembly of the State of Louisiana, passed in 1890, providing for separate railway carriages for the white and colored races. The first section of the statute enacts "that all railway companies carrying passengers in their coaches in this State, shall provide equal but separate accommodations for the white, and colored races, by providing two or more passenger coaches for each passenger train, or by dividing the passenger coaches by a partition so as to secure separate accommodations: Provided, That this section shall not be construed to apply to street railroads. No person or persons, shall be admitted to occupy seats in coaches, other than, the ones, assigned, to them on account of the race they belong to."

By the second section it was enacted "that the officers of such passenger trains shall have power and are hereby required to assign each passenger to the coach or compartment used for the race to which such passenger belongs; any passenger insisting on going into a coach or compartment to which by race he does not belong, shall be liable to a fine of twenty-five dollars, or in lieu thereof to imprisonment for a period of not more than twenty days in the parish prison, and any officer of any railroad insisting on assigning a passenger to a coach or compartment other than the one set aside for the race to which said passenger belongs, shall be liable to a fine of twenty-five dollars, or in lieu thereof to imprisonment for a period of not more than twenty days in the parish prison; and should any passenger refuse to occupy the coach or compartment to which he or she is assigned by the officer of such railway, said officer shall have power to refuse to carry such passenger on his train, and for such refusal neither he nor the railway company which he represents shall be liable for damages in any of the courts of this State."

The third section provides penalties for the refusal or neglect of the officers, directors, conductors and employes of railway companies to comply with the act, with a proviso that "nothing in this act shall be construed as applying to nurses attending children of the other race." The fourth section is immaterial.

The information filed in the criminal District Court charged in substance that Plessy, being a passenger between two stations within the State of

Louisiana, was assigned by officers of the company to the coach used for the race to which he belonged, but he insisted upon going into a coach used by the race to which he did not belong. Neither in the information nor plea was his particular race or color averred.

The petition for the writ of prohibition averred that petitioner was seven eighths Caucasian and one eighth African blood; that the mixture of colored blood was not discernible in him, and that he was entitled to every right, privilege and immunity secured to citizens of the United States of the white race; and that, upon such theory, he took possession of a vacant seat in a coach where passengers of the white race were accommodated, and was ordered by the conductor to vacate said coach and take a seat in another assigned to persons of the colored race, and having refused to comply with such demand he was forcibly ejected with the aid of a police officer, and imprisoned in the parish jail to answer a charge of having violated the above act.

The constitutionality of this act is attacked upon the ground that it conflicts both with the Thirteenth Amendment of the Constitution, abolishing slavery, and the Fourteenth Amendment, which prohibits certain restrictive legislation on the part of the States.

1. That it does not conflict with the Thirteenth Amendment, which abolished slavery and involuntary servitude, except as a punishment for crime, is too clear for argument. Slavery implies involuntary servitude—a state of bondage; the ownership of mankind as a chattel, or at least the control of the labor and services of one man for the benefit of another, and the absence of a legal right to the disposal of his own person, property and services. . . .

2. By the Fourteenth Amendment, all persons born or naturalized in the United States, and subject to the jurisdiction thereof, are made citizens of the United States and of the State wherein they reside; and the States are forbidden from making or enforcing any law which shall abridge the privileges or immunities of citizens of the United States, or shall deprive any person of life, liberty or property without due process of law, or deny to any person within their jurisdiction the equal protection of the laws.

The object of the amendment was undoubtedly to enforce the absolute equality of the two races before the law, but in the nature of things it could

not have been intended to abolish distinctions based upon color, or to enforce social, as distinguished from political equality, or a commingling of the
two races upon terms unsatisfactory to either. Laws permitting, and even requiring, their separation in places where they are liable to be brought into
contact do not necessarily imply the inferiority of either race to the other, and
have been generally, if not universally, recognized as within the competency
of the state legislatures in the exercise of their police power. The most common instance of this is connected with the establishment of separate schools
for white and colored children, which has been held to be a valid exercise of
the legislative power even by courts of States where the political rights of the
colored race have been longest and most earnestly enforced.

One of the earliest of these cases is that of Roberts v. City of Boston, 5
Cush. 198, in which the Supreme Judicial Court of Massachusetts held that
the general school committee of Boston had power to make provision for the
instruction of colored children in separate schools established exclusively for
them, and to prohibit their attendance upon the other schools. "The great
principle," said Chief Justice Shaw, "advanced by the learned and eloquent
advocate for the plaintiff," (Mr. Charles Sumner,) "is, that by the constitution and laws of Massachusetts, all persons without distinction of age or sex,
birth or color, origin or condition, are equal before the law. . . . But, when
this great principle comes to be applied to the actual and various conditions
of persons in society, it will not warrant the assertion, that men and women
are legally clothed with the same civil and political powers, and that children
and adults are legally to have the same functions and be subject to the same
treatment; but only that the rights of all, as they are settled and regulated
by law, are equally entitled to the paternal consideration and protection of
the law for their maintenance and security." It was held that the powers of the
committee extended to the establishment of separate schools for children of
different ages, sexes and colors, and that they might also establish special
schools for poor and neglected children, who have become too old to attend
the primary school, and yet have not acquired the rudiments of learning, to
enable them to enter the ordinary schools. Laws forbidding the intermarriage
of the two races may be said in a technical sense to interfere with the freedom
of contract, and yet have been universally recognized as within the police
power of the State.

The distinction between laws interfering with the political equality of the
negro and those requiring the separation of the two races in schools, theatres
and railway carriages has been frequently drawn by this court. Thus in

Strauder v. West Virginia, 100 U.S. 303, it was held that a law of West Virginia limiting to white male persons, 21 years of age and citizens of the State, the right to sit upon juries, was a discrimination which implied a legal inferiority in civil society, which lessened the security of the right of the colored race, and was a step toward reducing them to a condition of servility. Indeed, the right of a colored man that, in the selection of jurors to pass upon his life, liberty and property, there shall be no exclusion of his race, and no discrimination against them because of color, has been asserted in a number of cases. . . .

It is claimed by the plaintiff in error that, in any mixed community, the reputation of belonging to the dominant race, in this instance the white race, is property, in the same sense that a right of action, or of inheritance, is property. Conceding this to be so, for the purposes of this case, we are unable to see how this statute deprives him of, or in any way affects his right to, such property. If he be a white man and assigned to a colored coach, he may have his action for damages against the company for being deprived of his so called property. Upon the other hand, if he be a colored man and be so assigned, he has been deprived of no property, since he is not lawfully entitled to the reputation of being a white man.

In this connection, it is also suggested by the the learned counsel for the plaintiff in error that the same argument that will justify the state legislature in requiring railways to provide separate accommodations for the two races will also authorize them to require separate cars to be provided for people whose hair is of a certain color, or who are aliens, or who belong to certain nationalities, or to enact laws requiring colored people to walk upon one side of the street, and white people upon the other, or requiring white men's houses to be painted white, and colored men's black, or their vehicles or business signs to be of different colors, upon the theory that one side of the street is as good as the other, or that a house or vehicle of one color is as good as one of another color. The reply to all this is that every exercise of the police power must be reasonable, and extend only to such laws as are enacted in good faith for the promotion for the public good, and not for the annoyance or oppression of a particular class.

So far, then, as a conflict with the Fourteenth Amendment is concerned, the case reduces itself to the question whether the statute of Louisiana is a reasonable regulation, and with respect to this there must necessarily be a large discretion on the part of the legislature. In determining the question of reasonableness it is at liberty to act with reference to the established usages, customs and traditions of the people, and with a view to the promotion of their comfort, and the preservation of the public peace and good order. Gauged by this standard, we cannot say that a law which authorizes or even requires the separation of the two races in public conveyances is unreasonable, or more obnoxious to the Fourteenth Amendment than the acts of Congress requiring separate schools for colored children in the District of Columbia, the constitutionality of which does not seem to have been questioned, or the corresponding acts of state legislatures.

We consider the underlying fallacy of the plaintiff's argument to consist in the assumption that the enforced separation of the two races stamps the colored race with a badge of inferiority. If this be so, it is not by reason of anything found in the act, but solely because the colored race chooses to put that construction upon it. The argument necessarily assumes that if, as has been more than once the case, and is not unlikely to be so again, the colored race should become the dominant power in the state legislature, and should enact a law in precisely similar terms, it would thereby relegate the white race to an inferior position. We imagine that the white race, at least, would not acquiesce in this assumption. The argument also assumes that social prejudices may be overcome by legislation, and that equal rights cannot be secured to the negro except by an enforced commingling of the two races. We cannot accept this proposition. If the two races are to meet upon terms of social equality, it must be the result of natural affinities, a mutual appreciation of each other's merits and a voluntary consent of individuals. When the government, therefore, has secured to each of its citizens equal rights before the law and equal opportunities for improvement and progress, it has accomplished the end for which it was organized and performed all of the functions respecting social advantages with which it is endowed. Legislation is powerless to eradicate racial instincts or to abolish distinctions based upon physical differences, and the attempt to do so can only result in accentuating the difficulties of the present situation. If the civil and political rights of both races be equal one cannot be inferior to the other civilly or politically. If one race be inferior to the other socially, the Constitution of the United States cannot put them upon the same plane.

It is true that the question of the proportion of colored blood necessary to constitute a colored person, as distinguished from a white person, is one upon which there is a difference of opinion in the different States, some holding that any visible admixture of black blood stamps the person as belonging to the colored race, others that it depends upon the preponderance of blood, and still others that the predominance of white blood must only be in the proportion of three fourths. But these are questions to be determined under the laws of each State and are not properly put in issue in this case. Under the allegations of his petition it may undoubtedly become a question of importance whether, under the laws of Louisiana, the petitioner belongs to the white or colored race.

The judgment of the court below is, therefore,

Affirmed.

MR. JUSTICE HARLAN dissenting.

. . . In respect of civil rights, common to all citizens, the Constitution of the United States does not, I think, permit any public authority to know the race of those entitled to be protected in the enjoyment of such rights. Every true man has pride of race, and under appropriate circumstances when the rights of others, his equals before the law, are not to be affected, it is his privilege to express such pride and to take such action based upon it as to him seems proper. But I deny that any legislative body or judicial tribunal may have regard to the race of citizens when the civil rights of those citizens are involved. Indeed, such legislation, as that here in question, is inconsistent not only with that equality of rights which pertains to citizenship, National and State, but with the personal liberty enjoyed by every one within the United States. . . .

It was said in argument that the statute of Louisiana does not discriminate against either race, but prescribes a rule applicable alike to white and colored citizens. But this argument does not meet the difficulty. Every one knows that the statute in question had its origin in the purpose, not so much to exclude white persons from railroad cars occupied by blacks, as to exclude colored people from coaches occupied by or assigned to white persons. Railroad corporations of Louisiana did not make discrimination among whites in the matter of accommodation for travellers. The thing to accomplish was, under the guise of giving equal accommodation for whites and blacks, to compel the latter to keep to themselves while travelling in railroad passenger coaches. No one would be so wanting in candor as to assert the contrary. . . .

It is one thing for railroad carriers to furnish, or to be required by law to furnish, equal accommodations for all whom they are under a legal duty to carry. It is quite another thing for government to forbid citizens of the white and black races from travelling in the same public conveyance, and to punish officers of railroad companies for permitting persons of the two races to occupy the same passenger coach. If a State can prescribe, as a rule of civil conduct, that whites and blacks shall not travel as passengers in the same railroad coach, why may it not so regulate the use of the streets of its cities and towns as to compel white citizens to keep on one side of a street and black citizens to keep on the other? Why may it not, upon like grounds, punish whites and blacks who ride together in street cars or in open vehicles on a public road of street? Why may it not require sheriffs to assign whites to one side of a court-room and blacks to the other? And why may it not also prohibit the commingling of the two races in the galleries of legislative halls or in public assemblages convened for the considerations of the political questions of the day? Further, if this statute of Louisiana is consistent with the personal liberty of citizens, why may not the State require the separation in railroad coaches of native and naturalized citizens of the United States, or of Protestants and Roman Catholics?

The answer given at the argument to these questions was that regulations of the kind they suggest would be unreasonable, and could not, therefore, stand before the law. Is it meant that the determination of questions of legislative power depends upon the inquiry whether the statute whose validity is questioned is, in the judgment of the courts, a reasonable one, taking all the circumstances into consideration? . . .

The white race deems itself to be the dominant race in this country. And so it is, in prestige, in achievements, in education, in wealth and in power. So, I doubt not, it will continue to be for all time, if it remains true to its great heritage and holds fast to the principles of constitutional liberty. But in view of the Constitution, in the eye of the law, there is in this country no superior, dominant, ruling class of citizens. There is no caste here. Our Constitution is color-blind, and neither knows nor tolerates classes among citizens. In respect of civil rights, all citizens are equal before the law. The humblest is the peer of the most powerful. The law regards man as man, and takes no account of his surroundings or of his color when his civil rights as guaranteed by the supreme law of the land are involved. It is, therefore, to be regretted that this high tribunal, the final expositor of the fundamental law of the land, has reached the conclusion that it is competent for a State to regulate the enjoyment by citizens of their civil rights solely upon the basis of race.

In my opinion, the judgment this day rendered will, in time, prove to be quite as pernicious as the decision made by this tribunal in the Dred Scott case. . . . The present decision, it may well be apprehended, will not only stimulate aggressions, more or less brutal and irritating, upon the admitted rights of colored citizens, but will encourage the belief that it is possible, by means of state enactments, to defeat the beneficent purposes which the people of the United States had in view when they adopted the recent amendments of the Constitution, by one of which the blacks of this country were made citizens of the United States and of the States in which they respectively reside, and whose privileges and immunities, as citizens, the States are forbidden to abridge. Sixty millions of whites are in no danger from the presence here of eight millions of blacks. The destinies of the two races, in this country, are indissolubly linked together, and the interests of both require that the common government of all shall not permit the seeds of race hate to be planted under the sanction of law. What can more certainly arouse race hate, what more certainly create and perpetuate a feeling of distrust between these races, than state enactments, which, in fact, proceed on the ground that colored citizens are so inferior and degraded that they cannot be allowed to sit in public coaches occupied by white citizens? That, as all will admit, is the real meaning of such legislation as was enacted in Louisiana. . . .

For the reasons stated, I am constrained to withhold my assent from the opinion and judgment of the majority.

■ ■ ■

BROWN ET AL. V. BOARD OF EDUCATION OF TOPEKA ET AL.

No. 1. APPEAL FROM THE UNITED STATES DISTRICT COURT
FOR THE DISTRICT OF KANSAS
Argued December 9, 1952—Reargued December 8, 1953—
Decided May 17, 1954
Syllabus

Segregation of white and Negro children in the public schools of a State solely on the basis of race, pursuant to state laws permitting or requiring such segregation, denies to Negro children the equal protection of the laws guaranteed by the Fourteenth Amendment—even though the physical facilities and other "tangible" factors of white and Negro schools may be equal. Pp. 486–96.

(a) The history of the Fourteenth Amendment is inconclusive as to its intended effect on public education. Pp. 489–90.

(b) The question presented in these cases must be determined, not on the basis of conditions existing when the Fourteenth Amendment was adopted, but in the light of the full development of public education and its present place in American life throughout the Nation. Pp. 492–93.

(c) Where a State has undertaken to provide an opportunity for an education in its public schools, such an opportunity is a right which must be made available to all on equal terms. P. 493.

(d) Segregation of children in public schools solely on the basis of race deprives children of the minority group of equal educational opportunities, even though the physical facilities and other "tangible" factors may be equal. Pp. 493–94.

(e) The "separate but equal" doctrine adopted in Plessy v. Ferguson, 163 U.S. 537, has no place in the field of public education. P. 495.

(f) The cases are restored to the docket for further argument on specified questions relating to the forms of the decrees. Pp. 495–496.

Counsel for Parties

Robert L. Carter argued the cause for appellants in No. 1 on the original argument and on the reargument. *Thurgood Marshall* argued the cause for appellants in No. 2 on the original argument and *Spottswood W. Robinson III,* for appellants in No. 4 on the original argument, and both argued the causes for appellants in Nos. 2 and 4 on the reargument. *Louis L. Redding* and *Jack Greenberg* argued the cause for respondents in No. 10 on the original argument and *Jack Greenberg* and *Thurgood Marshall* on the reargument.

On the briefs were *Robert L. Carter, Thurgood Marshall, Spottswood W. Robinson III, Louis L. Redding, Jack Greenberg, George E. C. Hayes, William R. Ming Jr., Constance Baker Motley, James M. Nabrit Jr., Charles S. Scott, Frank D. Reeves, Harold R. Boulware,* and *Oliver W. Hill* for appellants in Nos. 1, 2 and 4 and respondents in No. 10; *George M. Johnson* for appellants in Nos. 1, 2, and 4; and *Loren Miller* for appellants in Nos. 2 and 4. *Arthur D. Shores* and *A. T. Walden* were on the Statement as to Jurisdiction and a brief opposing a Motion to Dismiss or Affirm in No. 2.

Paul E. Wilson, Assistant Attorney General of Kansas, argued the cause for appellees in No. 1 on the original argument and on the reargument. With him on the briefs was *Harold R. Fatzer,* Attorney General.

John W. Davis argued the cause for appellees in No. 2 on the original argument and for appellees in Nos. 2 and 4 on the reargument. With him on the briefs in No. 2 were *T. C. Callison,* Attorney General of South Carolina; *Robert McC. Figg Jr.; S. E. Rogers; William R. Meagher;* and *Taggart Whipple.*

J. Lindsay Almond Jr., Attorney General of Virginia, and *T. Justin Moore* argued the cause for appellees in No. 4 on the original argument and for appellees in Nos. 2 and 4 on the reargument. On the briefs in No. 4 were *J. Lindsay Almond Jr.,* Attorney General, and *Henry T. Wickham,* Special Assistant Attorney General, for the State of Virginia, and *T. Justin Moore, Archibald G. Robertson, John W. Riely,* and *T. Justin Moore Jr.* for the Prince Edward County School Authorities, appellees.

H. Albert Young, Attorney General of Delaware, argued the cause for petitioners in No. 10 on the original argument and on the reargument. With him on the briefs was *Louis J. Finger,* Special Deputy Attorney General.

By special leave of Court, *Assistant Attorney General Rankin* argued the cause for the United States on the reargument, as amicus curiae, urging reversal in Nos. 1, 2, and 4 and affirmance in No. 10. With him on the brief were *Attorney General Brownell, Philip Elman, Leon Ulman, William J. Lamont,* and *M. Magdelena Schoch. James P. McGranery,* then Attorney General, and *Philip Elman* filed a brief for the United States on the original argument, as amicus curiae, urging reversal in Nos. 1, 2, and 4 and affirmance in No. 10.

Briefs of amici curiae supporting appellants in No. 1 were filed by Shad Polier, Will Maslow, and Joseph B. Robison for the American Jewish Congress; by Edwin J. Lukas, Arnold Forster, Arthur Garfield Hays, Frank E. Karelsen, Leonard Haas, Saburo Kido, and Theodore Leskes for the American Civil Liberties Union et al.; and by John Ligtenberg and Selma M. Borchardt for the American Federation of Teachers. Briefs of amici curiae supporting appellants in No. 1 and respondents in No. 10 were filed by Arthur J. Goldberg and Thomas E. Harris for the Congress of Industrial Organizations and by Phineas Indritz for the American Veterans Committee, Inc.

MR. CHIEF JUSTICE WARREN delivered the opinion of the Court.

These cases come to us from the States of Kansas, South Carolina, Virginia, and Delaware. They are premised on different facts and different local conditions, but a common legal question justifies their consideration together in this consolidated opinion.[1]

In each of the cases, minors of the Negro race, through their legal representatives, seek the aid of the courts in obtaining admission to the public schools of their community on a nonsegregated basis. In each instance, they had been denied admission to schools attended by white children under laws requiring or permitting segregation according to race. This segregation was alleged to deprive the plaintiffs of the equal protection of the laws under the Fourteenth Amendment. In each of the cases other than the Delaware case, a three-judge federal district court denied relief to the plaintiffs on the so-called "separate but equal" doctrine announced by this Court in *Plessy v. Ferguson*, 163 U.S. 537. Under that doctrine, equality of treatment is accorded when the races are provided substantially equal facilities, even though these facilities be separate. In the Delaware case, the Supreme Court of Delaware adhered to that doctrine, but ordered that the plaintiffs be admitted to the white schools because of their superiority to the Negro schools.

The plaintiffs contend that segregated public schools are not "equal" and cannot be made "equal," and that hence they are deprived of the equal protection of the laws. Because of the obvious importance of the question presented, the Court took jurisdiction.[2] Argument was heard in the 1952 Term, and reargument was heard this Term on certain questions propounded by the Court.[3] Reargument was largely devoted to the circumstances surrounding the adoption of the Fourteenth Amendment in 1868. It covered exhaustively consideration of the Amendment in Congress, ratification by the states, then existing practices in racial segregation, and the views of proponents and opponents of the Amendment. This discussion and our own investigation convince us that, although these sources cast some light, it is not enough to resolve the problem with which we are faced. At best, they are inconclusive. The most avid proponents of the post-War Amendments undoubtedly intended them to remove all legal distinctions among "all persons born or naturalized in the United States." Their opponents, just as certainly, were antagonistic to both the letter and the spirit of the Amendments and wished them to have the most limited effect. What others in Congress and the state legislatures had in mind cannot be determined with any degree of certainty.

An additional reason for the inconclusive nature of the Amendment's history, with respect to segregated schools, is the status of public education at that time.[4] In the South, the movement toward free common schools, supported by general taxation, had not yet taken hold. Education of white children was largely in the hands of private groups. Education of Negroes was almost nonexistent, and practically all of the race were illiterate. In fact, any education of Negroes was forbidden by law in some states. Today, in contrast, many Negroes have achieved outstanding success in the arts and sciences as well as in the business and professional world. It is true that public school education at the time of the Amendment had advanced further in the North, but the effect of the Amendment on Northern States was generally ignored in the congressional debates. Even in the North, the conditions of public educa- tion did not approximate those existing today. The curriculum was usually rudimentary; ungraded schools were common in rural areas; the school term was but three months a year in many states; and compulsory school atten- dance was virtually unknown. As a consequence, it is not surprising that there should be so little in the history of the Fourteenth Amendment relating to its intended effect on public education.

In the first cases in this Court construing the Fourteenth Amendment, decided shortly after its adoption, the Court interpreted it as proscribing all state-imposed discriminations against the Negro race.[5] The doctrine of "separate but equal" did not make its appearance in this Court until 1896 in the case of *Plessy v. Ferguson, supra,* involving not education but trans- portation.[6] American courts have since labored with the doctrine for over half a century. In this Court, there have been six cases involving the "sepa- rate but equal" doctrine in the field of public education.[7] In *Cumming v. County Board of Education,* 175 U.S. 528, and *Gong Lum v. Rice,* 275 U.S. 78, the validity of the doctrine itself was not challenged.[8] In more recent cases, all on the graduate school level, inequality was found in that specific benefits enjoyed by white students were denied to Negro students of the same educational qualifications. *Missouri ex rel. Gaines v. Canada,* 305 U.S. 337; *Sipuel v. Oklahoma,* 332 U.S. 631; *Sweatt v. Painter,* 339 U.S. 629; *McLaurin v. Oklahoma State Regents,* 339 U.S. 637. In none of these cases was it necessary to re-examine the doctrine to grant relief to the Ne- gro plaintiff. And in *Sweatt v. Painter, supra,* the Court expressly reserved decision on the question whether *Plessy v. Ferguson* should be held inapplicable to public education.

In the instant cases, that question is directly presented. Here, unlike *Sweatt v. Painter,* there are findings below that the Negro and white schools involved have been equalized, or are being equalized, with respect to buildings, curri- cula, qualifications and salaries of teachers, and other "tangible" factors.[9] Our decision, therefore, cannot turn on merely a comparison of these tangible factors in the Negro and white schools involved in each of the cases. We must look instead to the effect of segregation itself on public education.

In approaching this problem, we cannot turn the clock back to 1868 when the Amendment was adopted, or even to 1896 when *Plessy v. Ferguson* was written. We must consider public education in the light of its full development and its present place in American life throughout the Nation. Only in this way can it be determined if segregation in public schools deprives these plaintiffs of the equal protection of the laws.

Today, education is perhaps the most important function of state and local governments. Compulsory school attendance laws and the great expenditures for education both demonstrate our recognition of the importance of education to our democratic society. It is required in the performance of our most basic public responsibilities, even service in the armed forces. It is the very foundation of good citizenship. Today it is a principal instrument in awakening the child to cultural values, in preparing him for later professional training, and in helping him to adjust normally to his environment. In these days, it is doubtful that any child may reasonably be expected to succeed in life if he is denied the opportunity of an education. Such an opportunity, where the state has undertaken to provide it, is a right which must be made available to all on equal terms.

We come then to the question presented: Does segregation of children in public schools solely on the basis of race, even though the physical facilities and other "tangible" factors may be equal, deprive the children of the minority group of equal educational opportunities? We believe that it does.

In *Sweatt v. Painter, supra,* in finding that a segregated law school for Negroes could not provide them equal educational opportunities, this Court relied in large part on "those qualities which are incapable of objective measurement but which make for greatness in a law school." In *McLaurin v. Oklahoma State Regents, supra,* the Court, in requiring that a Negro admitted to a white graduate school be treated like all other students, again resorted to intangible considerations: ". . . his ability to study, to engage in discussions and exchange views with other students, and, in general, to learn his profession."

Such considerations apply with added force to children in grade and high schools. To separate them from others of similar age and qualifications solely because of their race generates a feeling of inferiority as to their status in the community that may affect their hearts and minds in a way unlikely ever to be undone. The effect of this separation on their educational opportunities was well stated by a finding in the Kansas case by a court which nevertheless felt compelled to rule against the Negro plaintiffs:

> Segregation of white and colored children in public schools has a detrimental effect upon the colored children. The impact is greater when it has the sanction of the law; for the policy of separating the races is usually interpreted as denoting the inferiority of the negro group. A sense of inferiority affects the motivation of a child to learn. Segregation with the sanction of law, therefore, has a tendency to [retard] the educational and mental development of negro children and to deprive them of some of the benefits they would receive in a racial[ly] integrated school system.[10]

Whatever may have been the extent of psychological knowledge at the time of *Plessy v. Ferguson,* this finding is amply supported by modern authority.[11] Any language in *Plessy v. Ferguson* contrary to this finding is rejected.

We conclude that in the field of public education the doctrine of "separate but equal" has no place. Separate educational facilities are inherently unequal. Therefore, we hold that the plaintiffs and others similarly situated for whom the actions have been brought are, by reason of the segregation complained of, deprived of the equal protection of the laws guaranteed by the Fourteenth Amendment. This disposition makes unnecessary any discussion whether such segregation also violates the Due Process Clause of the Fourteenth Amendment.[12]

Because these are class actions, because of the wide applicability of this decision, and because of the great variety of local conditions, the formulation of decrees in these cases presents problems of considerable complexity. On reargument, the consideration of appropriate relief was necessarily subordinated to the primary question—the constitutionality of segregation in public education. We have now announced that such segregation is a denial of the equal protection of the laws. In order that we may have the full assistance of the parties in formulating decrees, the cases will be restored to the docket, and the parties are requested to present further argument on Questions 4 and 5 previously propounded by the Court for the reargument this Term.[13] The Attorney General of the United States is again invited to participate. The Attorneys General of the states requiring or permitting segregation in public education will also be permitted to appear as amici curiae upon request to do so by September 15, 1954, and submission of briefs by October 1, 1954.[14]

FOOTNOTES

PRIOR HISTORY: Together with No. 2, *Briggs et al. v. Elliott et al.,* on appeal from the United States District Court for the Eastern District of South Carolina, argued December 9–10, 1952, reargued December 7–8, 1953; No. 4, *Davis et al. v. County School Board of Prince Edward County, Virginia, et al.,* on appeal from the United States District Court for the Eastern District of Virginia, argued December 10, 1952, reargued December 7–8, 1953; and No. 10, *Gebhart et al. v. Belton et al.,* on certiorari to the Supreme Court of Delaware, argued December 11, 1952, reargued December 9, 1953.

1. In the Kansas case, *Brown v. Board of Education,* the plaintiffs are Negro children of elementary school age residing in Topeka. They brought this action in the United States District Court for the District of Kansas to enjoin enforcement of a Kansas statute which permits, but does not require, cities of more than 15,000 population to maintain separate school facilities for Negro and white students. Kan. Gen. Stat. § 72-1724 (1949). Pursuant to that authority, the Topeka Board of Education elected to establish segregated elementary schools. Other public schools in the community, however, are operated on a nonsegregated basis. The three-judge District Court, convened under 28 U. S. C. §§ 2281 and 2284, found that segregation in public education has a detrimental effect upon Negro children, but denied relief on the ground that the Negro and white schools were substantially equal with respect to buildings, transportation, curricula, and educational qualifications of teachers. 98 F.Supp. 797. The case is here on direct appeal under 28 U. S. C. § 1253.

In the South Carolina case, *Briggs v. Elliott,* the plaintiffs are Negro children of both elementary and high school age residing in Clarendon County. They brought this action in the United States District Court for the Eastern District of South Carolina to enjoin enforcement of provisions in the state constitution and statutory code which require the segregation of Negroes and whites in public schools. S. C. Const., Art. XI, § 7; S. C. Code § 5377 (1942). The three-judge District Court, convened under 28 U. S. C. §§ 2281 and 2284, denied the requested relief. The court found that the Negro schools were inferior to the white schools and ordered the defendants to begin immediately to equalize the facilities. But the court sustained the validity of the contested provisions and denied the plaintiffs admission to the white schools during the equalization program. 98 F.Supp. 529. This Court vacated the District Court's judgment and remanded the case for the purpose of obtaining the court's views on a report filed by the defendants concerning the progress made in the equalization program. 342 U.S. 350. On remand, the District Court found that substantial equality had been achieved except for buildings and that the defendants were proceeding to rectify this inequality as well. 103 F.Supp. 920. The case is again here on direct appeal under 28 U. S. C. § 1253.

In the Virginia case, *Davis v. County School Board,* the plaintiffs are Negro children of high school age residing in Prince Edward County. They brought this action in the United States District Court for the Eastern District of Virginia to enjoin enforcement of provisions in the state constitution and statutory code which require the segregation of Negroes and whites in public schools. Va. Const., § 140; Va. Code § 22–221 (1950). The three-judge District Court, convened under 28 U. S. C. §§ 2281 and 2284, denied the requested relief. The court found the Negro school inferior in physical plant, curricula, and transportation, and ordered the defendants forthwith to provide substantially equal curricula and transportation and to "proceed with all reasonable diligence and dispatch to remove" the inequality in physical plant. But, as in the South Carolina case, the court sustained the validity of the contested provisions and denied the plaintiffs admission to the white schools during the equalization program. 103 F.Supp. 337. The case is here on direct appeal under 28 U. S. C. § 1253.

In the Delaware case, *Gebhart v. Belton,* the plaintiffs are Negro children of both elementary and high school age residing in New Castle County. They brought this action in the Delaware Court of Chancery to enjoin enforcement of provisions in the state constitution and statutory code which require the segregation of Negroes and whites in public schools. Del. Const., Art. X, § 2; Del. Rev. Code § 2631 (1935). The Chancellor gave judgment for the plaintiffs and ordered their immediate admission to schools previously attended only by white children, on the ground that the Negro schools were inferior with respect to teacher training, pupil-teacher ratio, extracurricular activities, physical plant, and time and distance involved in travel. 87 A. 2d 862. The Chancellor also found that segregation itself results in an inferior education for Negro children (see note 10, infra), but did not rest his decision on that ground. Id., at 865. The Chancellor's decree was affirmed by the Supreme Court of Delaware, which intimated, however, that the defendants might be able to obtain a modification of the decree after equalization of the

Negro and white schools had been accomplished. 91 A. 2d 137, 152. The defendants, contending only that the Delaware courts had erred in ordering the immediate admission of the Negro plaintiffs to the white schools, applied to this Court for certiorari. The writ was granted, 344 U.S. 891. The plaintiffs, who were successful below, did not submit a cross-petition.

2. 344 U.S. 1, 141, 891. 3. 345 U.S. 972. The Attorney General of the United States participated both Terms as *amicus curiae.*

4. For a general study of the development of public education prior to the Amendment, see Butts and Cremin, A History of Education in American Culture (1953), Pts. I, II; Cubberley, Public Education in the United States (1934 ed.), cc. II-XII. School practices current at the time of the adoption of the Fourteenth Amendment are described in Butts and Cremin, *supra,* at 269–275; Cubberley, *supra,* at 288–339, 408–31; Knight, Public Education in the South (1922), cc. VIII, IX. See also H. Ex. Doc. No. 315, 41st Cong., 2d Sess. (1871). Although the demand for free public schools followed substantially the same pattern in both the North and the South, the development in the South did not begin to gain momentum until about 1850, some twenty years after that in the North. The reasons for the somewhat slower development in the South (e. g., the rural character of the South and the different regional attitudes toward state assistance) are well explained in Cubberley, *supra,* at 408–423. In the country as a whole, but particularly in the South, the War virtually stopped all progress in public education. *Id.,* at 427–28. The low status of Negro education in all sections of the country, both before and immediately after the War, is described in Beale, *A History of Freedom of Teaching in American Schools* (1941), 112–32, 175–95. Compulsory school attendance laws were not generally adopted until after the ratification of the Fourteenth Amendment, and it was not until 1918 that such laws were in force in all the states. Cubberley, *supra,* at 563–65.

5. *Slaughter-House Cases,* 16 Wall. 36, 67–72 (1873); *Strauder v. West Virginia,* 100 U.S. 303, 307–08 (1880): "It ordains that no State shall deprive any person of life, liberty, or property, without due process of law, or deny to any person within its jurisdiction the equal protection of the laws. What is this but declaring that the law in the States shall be the same for the black as for the white; that all persons, whether colored or white, shall stand equal before the laws of the States, and, in regard to the colored race, for whose

protection the amendment was primarily designed, that no discrimination shall be made against them by law because of their color? The words of the amendment, it is true, are prohibitory, but they contain a necessary implication of a positive immunity, or right, most valuable to the colored race,—the right to exemption from unfriendly legislation against them distinctively as colored,—exemption from legal discriminations, implying inferiority in civil society, lessening the security of their enjoyment of the rights which others enjoy, and discriminations which are steps towards reducing them to the condition of a subject race." See also *Virginia v. Rives,* 100 U.S. 313, 318 (1880); *Ex parte Virginia,* 100 U.S. 339, 344–45 (1880).

6. The doctrine apparently originated in *Roberts v. City of Boston,* 59 Mass. 198, 206 (1850), upholding school segregation against attack as being violative of a state constitutional guarantee of equality. Segregation in Boston public schools was eliminated in 1855. Mass. Acts 1855, c. 256. But elsewhere in the North segregation in public education has persisted in some communities until recent years. It is apparent that such segregation has long been a nationwide problem, not merely one of sectional concern.

7. See also *Berea College v. Kentucky,* 211 U.S. 45 (1908).

8. In the *Cumming* case, Negro taxpayers sought an injunction requiring the defendant school board to discontinue the operation of a high school for white children until the board resumed operation of a high school for Negro children. Similarly, in the *Gong Lum* case, the plaintiff, a child of Chinese descent, contended only that state authorities had misapplied the doctrine by classifying him with Negro children and requiring him to attend a Negro school.

9. In the Kansas case, the court below found substantial equality as to all such factors. 98 F.Supp. 797, 798. In the South Carolina case, the court below found that the defendants were proceeding "promptly and in good faith to comply with the court's decree." 103 F.Supp. 920, 921. In the Virginia case, the court below noted that the equalization program was already "afoot and progressing" (103 F.Supp. 337, 341); since then, we have been advised, in the Virginia Attorney General's brief on reargument, that the program has now been completed. In the Delaware case, the court below similarly noted that the state's equalization program was well under way. 91 A. 2d 137, 149.

10. A similar finding was made in the Delaware case: "I conclude from the testimony that in our Delaware society, State-imposed segregation in education itself results in the Negro children, as a class, receiving educational opportunities which are substantially inferior to those available to white children otherwise similarly situated." 87 A. 2d 862, 865.

11. K. B. Clark, Effect of Prejudice and Discrimination on Personality Development (Midcentury White House Conference on Children and Youth, 1950); Witmer and Kotinsky, Personality in the Making (1952), c. VI; Deutscher and Chein, The Psychological Effects of Enforced Segregation: A Survey of Social Science Opinion, 26 J. Psychol. 259 (1948); Chein, What are the Psychological Effects of Segregation Under Conditions of Equal Facilities?, 3 Int. J. Opinion and Attitude Res. 229 (1949); Brameld, Educational Costs, in Discrimination and National Welfare (MacIver, ed., 1949), 44–48; Frazier, The Negro in the United States (1949), 674–681. And see generally Myrdal, An American Dilemma (1944).

12. See *Bolling v. Sharpe*, post, p. 497, concerning the Due Process Clause of the Fifth Amendment.

13. "4. Assuming it is decided that segregation in public schools violates the Fourteenth Amendment

"(a) would a decree necessarily follow providing that, within the limits set by normal geographic school districting, Negro children should forthwith be admitted to schools of their choice, or

"(b) may this Court, in the exercise of its equity powers, permit an effective gradual adjustment to be brought about from existing segregated systems to a system not based on color distinctions?

"5. On the assumption on which questions 4 (a) and (b) are based, and assuming further that this Court will exercise its equity powers to the end described in question 4 (b),

"(a) should this Court formulate detailed decrees in these cases;

"(b) if so, what specific issues should the decrees reach;

"(c) should this Court appoint a special master to hear evidence with a view to recommending specific terms for such decrees;

"(d) should this Court remand to the courts of first instance with directions to frame decrees in these cases, and if so what general directions should the decrees of this Court include and what procedures should the courts of first instance follow in arriving at the specific terms of more detailed decrees?"

14. See Rule 42, Revised Rules of this Court (effective July 1, 1954).

■ ■ ■

FROM BARACK OBAMA'S KEYNOTE ADDRESS AT THE DEMOCRATIC NATIONAL CONVENTION

Tuesday, July 27, 2004, 11:09 PM

Candidate for U.S. Senate in Illinois, Barack Obama, delivered the keynote address at the Democratic National Convention in Boston Tuesday night. Here is a transcript of his remarks.

On behalf of the great state of Illinois . . . crossroads of a nation, land of Lincoln, let me express my deep gratitude for the privilege of addressing this convention. Tonight is a particular honor for me because, let's face it, my presence on this stage is pretty unlikely.

My father was a foreign student, born and raised in a small village in Kenya. He grew up herding goats, went to school in a tin-roof shack. His father, my grandfather, was a cook, a domestic servant to the British.

But my grandfather had larger dreams for his son. Through hard work and perseverance my father got a scholarship to study in a magical place, America, that's shone as a beacon of freedom and opportunity to so many who had come before him.

While studying here my father met my mother. She was born in a town on the other side of the world, in Kansas.

Her father worked on oil rigs and farms through most of the Depression. The day after Pearl Harbor, my grandfather signed up for duty, joined Patton's army, marched across Europe. Back home my grandmother raised a baby and went to work on a bomber assembly line. After the war, they studied on the GI Bill, bought a house through FHA and later moved west, all the way to Hawaii, in search of opportunity.

And they too had big dreams for their daughter, a common dream born of two continents.

My parents shared not only an improbable love; they shared an abiding faith in the possibilities of this nation. They would give me an African name,

Barack, or "blessed," believing that in a tolerant America, your name is no barrier to success.

They imagined me going to the best schools in the land, even though they weren't rich, because in a generous America you don't have to be rich to achieve your potential.

They're both passed away now. And yet I know that, on this night, they look down on me with great pride.

And I stand here today grateful for the diversity of my heritage, aware that my parents' dreams live on in my two precious daughters.

I stand here knowing that my story is part of the larger American story, that I owe a debt to all of those who came before me, and that in no other country on Earth is my story even possible.

Tonight, we gather to affirm the greatness of our nation not because of the height of our skyscrapers, or the power of our military, or the size of our economy; our pride is based on a very simple premise, summed up in a declaration made over two hundred years ago: "We hold these truths to be self-evident, that all men are created equal . . . that they are endowed by their Creator with certain inalienable rights, that among these are life, liberty and the pursuit of happiness."

That is the true genius of America, a faith . . . a faith in simple dreams, an insistence on small miracles; that we can tuck in our children at night and know that they are fed and clothed and safe from harm; that we can say what we think, write what we think, without hearing a sudden knock on the door; that we can have an idea and start our own business without paying a bribe; that we can participate in the political process without fear of retribution; and that our votes will be counted—or at least, most of the time.

This year, in this election, we are called to reaffirm our values and our commitments, to hold them against a hard reality and see how we are measuring up, to the legacy of our forebears and the promise of future generations.

And fellow Americans, Democrats, Republicans, Independents, I say to you, tonight, we have more work to do . . . more work to do, for the workers I met in Galesburg, Illinois, who are losing their union jobs at the Maytag plant that's moving to Mexico, and now they're having to compete with their own children for jobs that pay 7 bucks an hour; more to do for the father I met who was losing his job and choking back the tears wondering how he would pay $4,500 a month for the drugs his son needs without the health benefits that he counted on; more to do for the young woman in East St.

Louis, and thousands more like her who have the grades, have the drive, have the will, but doesn't have the money to go to college.

Now, don't get me wrong, the people I meet in small towns and big cities and diners and office parks, they don't expect government to solves all of their problems. They know they have to work hard to get ahead. And they want to.

Go into the collar counties around Chicago, and people will tell you: They don't want their tax money wasted by a welfare agency or by the Pentagon. Go into any inner-city neighborhood, and folks will tell you that government alone can't teach kids to learn.

They know that parents have to teach, that children can't achieve unless we raise their expectations and turn off the television sets and eradicate the slander that says a black youth with a book is acting white. They know those things.

Author's Note
and Acknowledgments

What I sought to undertake with *Acting White: The Curious History of a Racial Slur* was both a historical narrative tracing the evolution of the slight as well as a present call to arms and action to eradicate a supposition held by many blacks and whites alike that blacks who excel at and participate in certain activities are doing nothing more than acting white.

There are far too many people to thank and insufficient space to do so. Let me acknowledge the heroic efforts of pioneers such as Frederick Douglass, Booker T. Washington, W. E. B. Du Bois, Dr. Martin Luther King Jr., and countless others who risked their lives so that future generations of blacks would live in a world filled with greater promise and prosperity than their own—a world where blacks would one day be judged by the content of their character and accomplishments rather than the color of their skin.

I merely stand on the shoulders of such brave trailblazers such as Justice Clarence Thomas, Thomas Sowell, Shelby Steele, John McWhorter, Juan Williams, Bill Cosby, and Dr. Condoleezza Rice, who sought to question the status quo of how blacks should think and act in contemporary society. I particularly wish to acknowledge the support and encouragement given me by President George W. Bush as I completed this manuscript—he is someone I am honored to call both a mentor and a friend. Only with open eyes and open hearts will we combat the soft bigotry of low expectations that the acting white slur only seeks to perpetuate.

I wish to thank my literary agents, Shawn Coyne and Eric Lupfer from William Morris Endeavor, for believing in this project as well Senior Editor Rob Kirkpatrick from St. Martin's Press/Thomas Dunne Books for his sage counsel, while his assistant, Margaret Smith, helped keep this train on the rails and on time. I am especially grateful to my publishers, Thomas Dunne and Sally Richardson, for their vision and encouragement to tackle this project.

I remain grateful to my parents, Carl and Mattie Christie, as well as my big brother, Carl II, for their love and for pushing me to seek my dreams—even when doing so defied conventional expectations of what a young black student from the San Francisco Bay Area should be doing and thinking in his life. I also would be remiss if I didn't acknowledge the unconditional love and support offered at all times by my beloved nieces and nephew, Taylor, Elizabeth, and Andrew Owens. Further thanks to Dr. Glenn Owens for his steady support and encouragement as well.

And most important, I remain in love with and in awe of my amazing wife, Jennifer Kay Christie. Your love, patience, consideration, and support are endless. Our life together is the best gift I could have ever hoped for.

Notes

PROLOGUE: A NEW DAY OR DÉJÀ VU?

1. Booker T. Washington, *Up from Slavery: An Autobiography* (New York: Doubleday, 1902), 228.
2. "Jesse Jackson Says Barack Obama 'Acting White' in Case of Six Blacks Accused in Assault Case," Foxnews.com, September 19, 2007.

1. *UNCLE TOM'S CABIN*: THE GENESIS
OF ACTING WHITE

1. The Ohio Historical Society, "Stowe House," http://ohsweb.ohiohistory.org/places/sw18/index.shtml (accessed February 13, 2010).
2. Henry Louis Gates Jr., introduction to Harriet Beecher Stowe, *The Annotated "Uncle Tom's Cabin,"* ed. Henry Louis Gates Jr. and Hollis Robbins (New York: Norton, 2007), xliii.
3. Stowe, *Annotated "Uncle Tom's Cabin,"* 8.
4. Ibid., 250.
5. See chapter 3.
6. Stowe, *Annotated "Uncle Tom's Cabin,"* 21.
7. Ibid., 110.
8. Ibid., 17.
9. Ibid., 243.
10. Ibid., 122.
11. Ibid., 150.

12. Ibid., 258.
13. Ibid., 226.
14. Ibid., 251.
15. Gates, introduction, xi.
16. Stowe, *Annotated "Uncle Tom's Cabin,"* 106.
17. Ibid., 107.
18. Ibid., 323.
19. Gates, introduction, xii.

2. BOOKER T. WASHINGTON: A TURN-OF-THE-CENTURY UNCLE TOM ACTING WHITE?

1. Booker T. Washington, *Up from Slavery: An Autobiography* (New York: Doubleday, 1902), 112–13.
2. Ibid., 206.
3. Ibid., 210.
4. Ibid.
5. W. E. B. Du Bois, "Of Mr. Booker T. Washington and Others," in *W.E.B. Du Bois: A Reader,* ed. David Levering Lewis (New York: Holt, 1995), 319.
6. Ibid., 319.
7. Ibid., 325.
8. Ibid., 323.
9. Quoted in Washington, *Up from Slavery,* 216.
10. Ibid., 217.
11. Debra Dickerson, chapter X, in *Uncle Tom or New Negro? African Americans Reflect on Booker T. Washington and "Up from Slavery" 100 Years Later,* ed. Rebecca Carroll (New York: Harlem Moon, 2006), 93.
12. "Grover Cleveland on Negro Problem," *New York Times,* April 15, 1903.
13. Theodore Roosevelt, quoted in Kenneth O'Reilly, *Nixon's Piano: Presidents and Racial Politics from Washington to Clinton* (New York: Free Press, 1995), 67.
14. James K. Vardaman, quoted in O'Reilly, *Nixon's Piano,* 68.
15. O'Reilly, *Nixon's Piano,* 68.
16. Ibid., 67.
17. Henry Monroe Trotter, quoted in O'Reilly, *Nixon's Piano,* 67.
18. Rebecca Carroll, introduction to *Uncle Tom or New Negro? African Americans Reflect,* 3.

3. *PLESSY V. FERGUSON:* A LONG JOURNEY TOWARD EQUALITY

1. C. Vann Woodward, *American Counterpoint: Slavery and Racism in the North-South Dialogue* (Boston: Little, Brown, 1971), 213–14.
2. Quoted in *The Nation,* November 3, 2008.

3. Ibid.
4. Doris Kearns Goodwin, *Team of Rivals* (New York: Simon & Schuster, 2005), 747.

4. W. E. B. DU BOIS: *THE SOULS OF BLACK FOLK* AND THE ROAR OF THE NIAGARA MOVEMENT

1. David Levering Lewis, *W. E. B. Du Bois: Biography of a Race 1868–1919* (New York: Holt, 1993), 297.
2. Ibid., 225.
3. Ibid., 226.
4. W. E. B. Du Bois, "Of Mr. Booker T. Washington and Others," in *W. E. B. Du Bois: A Reader,* ed. David Levering Lewis (New York: Holt, 1995), 323.
5. Lewis, *Biography,* 260.
6. Ibid., 234.
7. Ibid.
8. Ibid., 239.
9. Ibid.
10. Ibid., 241.
11. Ibid.
12. Ibid., 236.
13. Ibid., 237.
14. Ibid., 276.
15. W. E. B. Du Bois, "Of Our Spiritual Strivings," in *W. E. B. Du Bois: A Reader,* 29.
16. W. E. B. Du Bois, "Of Mr. Booker T. Washington and Others," 320.
17. Ibid., 323.
18. Ibid., 322–23.
19. Ibid. 327–28.
20. Lewis, *Biography,* 293.
21. Ibid., 293.
22. Ibid., 292.
23. Ibid.
24. Lewis, *Biography,* 300.
25. Ibid., 301.
26. Ralph Waldo Emerson, *Concord Hymn,* 1837. Taken from the National Center for Public Policy Research Archive of Historical Documents (www.nationalcenter.org/concord hymn.html.
27. Lewis, *Biography,* 301.
28. W. E. B. Du Bois, "Credo," in *W. E. B. Du Bois: A Reader,* 106. Taken from *The Independent,* 57 (October 6, 1904): 787.
29. Lewis, *Biography,* 312.

5. THE RISE OF MARCUS GARVEY VERSUS THE ROAR
OF THE NIAGARA MOVEMENT: WHO BEST
TO LEAD BLACKS FORWARD AT THE DAWN
OF THE HARLEM RENAISSANCE?

1. Amy Jacques Garvey, *Garvey and Garveyism* (New York: Collier, 1970): 308, quoted in Introduction, *Selected Writings and Speeches of Marcus Garvey,* ed. Bob Blaisdell (Mineola, NY: Dover, 2004), iii.
2. Robert A. Hill, ed., Barbara Bair, associate ed., *Marcus Garvey, Life and Lessons: A Centennial Companion to The Marcus Garvey and Universal Negro Improvement Association Papers* (Berkeley: University of California Press, 1987), lxiii.
3. Ibid., xx.
4. Marcus Garvey, "Articles," in *Marcus Garvey: Life and Lessons,* 37–38.
5. Ibid., 42.
6. Ibid., 41.
7. Ibid.
8. Ibid., 45–48.
9. W. E. B. Du Bois, "Marcus Garvey and the NAACP," in *W. E. B. Du Bois: A Reader,* ed. David Levering Lewis (New York: Holt, 1995), 343. Originally published in *The Crisis,* February 1928.
10. Marcus Garvey, "Articles," 37–38.
11. Du Bois, "Marcus Garvey and the NAACP," 344.
12. Marcus Garvey, *Philosophy and Opinions of Marcus Garvey,* ed. Amy Jacques Garvey, with an introduction by Robert A. Hill (1923, 1992), 1:29, quoted in Randall Kennedy, *Sellout: The Politics of Racial Betrayal* (New York: Vintage, 2008), 44.
13. Marcus Garvey, "Calls Own Race 'Black and Ugly,' Judging from the White Man's Standard of Beauty: Trick of National Association for the Advancement of Colored People to Solve Problem by Assimilation and Color Distinction," in *The Philosophy and Opinions of Marcus Garvey; or, Africa for the Africans,* vol. 2, quoted in *Selected Writings and Speeches of Marcus Garvey,* 111.
14. Ibid.
15. W. E. B. Du Bois, "Back to Africa," in *W. E. B. Du Bois: A Reader,* 333. Originally published in *Century,* February 1923.
16. Blaisdell, ed., *Selected Writings and Speeches of Marcus Garvey,* 112.
17. Ibid.
18. Ibid., 117.
19. Ibid., 118.
20. Du Bois, "A Lunatic or a Traitor," in *W. E. B. Du Bois: A Reader,* 340. Originally published in *The Crisis,* May 1924.
21. Ibid., 341.
22. Ibid., 342.

6. *BROWN V. BOARD OF EDUCATION*: A MILESTONE TO EQUALITY

1. Smithsonian National Museum of American History, "Separate Is Not Equal: *Brown v. Board of Education*," http://americanhistory.si.edu/Brown/history/3-organized/charles-houston.html (accessed February 15, 2010).
2. The five school cases Marshall would consolidate for consideration by the Supreme Court to overrule *Plessy v. Ferguson* were *Briggs v. Elliott, Brown v. Board of Education, Davis v. County School Board, Gebhart v. Belton,* and *Bolling v. Sharpe.*
3. Kai Wright, ed., *The African American Experience: Black History and Culture Through Speeches, Letters, Editorials, Poems, Songs, and Stories* (New York: Black Dog and Leventhal Publishers, 2009), 485.
4. Library of Congress, "With an Even Hand: *Brown v. Board* at Fifty," www.loc.gov/exhibits/brown/brown-brown.html (accessed February 14, 2010).
5. Juan Williams, *Eyes on the Prize; America's Civil Rights Years, 1954–1965* (New York: Penguin, 1987), 20.
6. Ibid., 19.
7. Ibid., 20.
8. *Brown v. Board of Education,* 347 U.S. 483 (1954), at 493–95.
9. *Brown v. Board of Education,* 349 U.S. 294 (1955), at 295.
10. Charles J. Ogletree Jr., *All Deliberate Speed: Reflections on the First Half-Century of Brown v. Board of Education* (New York: Norton, 2004), 10.
11. Ann Zimmerman, "Are Mattel's New Dolls Black Enough?" *Wall Street Journal,* December 3, 2009, http://online.wsj.com/article/SB10001424052748704533904574544442926160228.html (accessed February 14, 2010).

7. HAWK V. DOVE? MALCOLM X V. MARTIN LUTHER KING AND THE STRUGGLE FOR NEW BLACK LEADERSHIP

1. Martin Luther King Jr., *The Papers of Martin Luther King, Jr.,* ed. Clayborne Carson, Peter Holloran, Ralph Luker, and Penny A. Russell (Berkeley: University of California Press, 1992), 135–36.
2. Martin Luther King Jr., *I Have a Dream: Writings and Speeches That Changed the World,* ed. James M. Washington (San Francisco: Harper, 1992), 43. Originally published in "My Trip to the Land of Gandhi," *Ebony,* July 1959.
3. Ibid., 44.
4. King, *I Have a Dream,* 35. Taken from "Speech Before the Youth March for Integrated Schools."
5. Ibid., 35.
6. Henry Louis Gates Jr. and Cornel West, *The African American Century: How Black Americans Have Shaped Our Country* (New York: Simon & Schuster, 2000), 269.
7. Ibid., 270.
8. *American Experience,* "Citizen King: Three Perspectives," PBS, www.pbs.org/wgbh/amex/mlk/sfeature/sf_video.html (accessed February 13, 2010). Taken from the transcript of the

interview conducted between Dr. Kenneth Clark and Malcolm X during the spring of 1963.

9. King, *I Have a Dream,* 103. Taken from introductory remarks preceding the reprinting of the "I have a dream" speech.

10. Ibid.

11. Ibid., 104.

12. Ibid., 101.

13. Malcolm X, "Message to the Grass Roots," in *Malcolm X Speaks: Selected Speeches and Statements,* ed. George Breitman (New York: Grove Press, 1990), 4.

14. Ibid., 9.

15. Ibid., 12.

16. Ibid., 13.

17. Ibid., 16.

8. BLACK POWER, MORAL RELATIVISM, AND RADICAL CHIC

1. Robert L. Harris Jr. and Rosalyn Terborg-Penn, "Black Power / Black Consciousness, 1965–75," in *The Columbia Guide to African American History Since 1939,* 61–74 (New York: Columbia University Press, 2006), 63.

2. Ibid.

3. Ibid.

4. Ibid.

5. Taken from http://en.wikipedia.org/wiki/Stokely_Carmichael.

6. John McWhorter, *Authentically Black* (New York: Gotham Books, 2003), 49.

7. Ibid., 51.

8. Roland G. Fryer Jr. and Steven D. Levitt, "The Causes and Consequences of Distinctively Black Names," *Quarterly Journal of Economics* 119.3 (2004): 787–805.

9. Ibid., 767.

10. Ibid., 770.

11. Ibid.

12. Robert J. Barro, "What's in a Name for Black Job Seekers?" *BusinessWeek,* November 3, 2003.

13. Ibid.

14. Oakland school board resolution taken from www.jaedworks.com/shoebox/oakland-ebonics.html; also *San Francisco Chronicle,* January 2, 1997, A18.

15. John McWhorter, *Losing the Race: Self-Sabotage in Black America* (New York: Harper, 2000–01), 196–97.

16. David Austen-Smith and Roland G. Fryer Jr., "An Economic Analysis of 'Acting White,'" *Quarterly Journal of Economics* 120:2 (May 2005): 5.

17. Ibid., 16.

18. Ibid.

9. AFFIRMATIVE ACTION

1. U.S. Equal Opportunity Employment Commission, "Executive Order 10925: Establishing the President's Committee on Equal Employment Opportunity," http://eeoc.gov/eeoc/history/35th/thelaw/eo-10925.html (accessed February 15, 2010).
2. Ibid.
3. Robert L. Harris Jr. and Rosalyn Terborg-Penn, "Black Power / Black Consciousness, 1965–75," in *The Columbia Guide to African American History Since 1939*, 61–74 (New York: Columbia University Press, 2006), 71.
4. Ibid.
5. Ibid.
6. Ibid.
7. Fox Butterfield, "At Rally, Jackson Assails Harvard Law School," *New York Times*, May 10, 1990, www.nytimes.com/1990/05/10/us/at-rally-jackson-assails-harvard-law-school.html (accessed February 22, 2010).
8. Ibid.
9. Ibid.
10. www.leginfo.ca.gov/.const/.article_1.
11. Eryn Hadley, "Did the Sky Really Fall? Ten Years After California's Proposition 209," *BYU Journal of Public Law* 20 (2005): 103, 105.
12. Ibid., 128.
13. Ibid., 129–30.
14. Shelby Steele, *The Content of Our Character* (New York: Harper, 1990), 113.
15. Ibid., 116–18.
16. John McWhorter, *Winning the Race: Beyond the Crisis in Black America* (New York: Gotham Books, 2005), 266–67.

10. THE DIVIDE: UPWARDLY MOBILE BLACK AMERICA AND THE URBAN POOR

1. "A History of Poison Ivy, Shock Slay Taints NY Scholar," *New York Post*, July 26, 2009.
2. Signithia Fordham and John Ogbu, "Black Students' Success: Coping with the 'Burden of Acting White,'" *Urban Review* 18 (1986): 176–206.
3. Mark Harris, "Saving TV: The Near-Total Control of Mass Culture by Three Omnipotent Networks: Gone. If This Is the End of Television as We Know It, Maybe It's also the Beginning of Something Else," *Conde Nast Portfolio*, September 2008.
4. www.americanrhetoric.com/speeches/billcosbypoundcakespeech.htm.
5. Ibid.
6. Ibid.
7. *Tavis Smiley*, "Bill Cosby: Airdate May 26, 2004," PBS, www.pbs.org/kcet/tavissmiley/archive/200405/20040526_cosby.html (accessed February 14, 2010).
8. www.washingtonpost.com/wp-dyn/articles/A1975102004Jul27.html.
9. "Transcript: Illinois Senate Candidate Barack Obama," *Washington Post*, www.washingtonpost.com/wp-dyn/articles/A19751-2004Jul27.html (accessed February 14,

2010). Keynote address to the Democratic National Convention, July 27, 2004, Boston, Massachusetts.

10. Henry Louis Gates Jr., "Breaking the Silence," *New York Times,* August 1, 2004, www .nytimes.com/2004/08/01/opinion/01gates.html (accessed February 22, 2010).

11. Clarence Page, "Essay: Acting White," *A NewsHour with Jim Lehrer Transcript, On-line Newshour,* PBS, September 27, 2004, www.pbs.org/newshour/essays/july-dec04/page_9-27.html (accessed February 13, 2010).

12. Ibid.

13. Paul Tough, "The 'Acting White' Myth," *New York Times,* December 12 2004, www .nytimes.com/2004/12/12/magazine/12ACTING.html (accessed February 22, 2010).

14. Ibid.

15. John McWhorter, *Winning the Race: Beyond the Crisis in Black America* (New York: Gotham Books, 2005), 274.

16. Michael Eric Dyson, *Is Bill Cosby Right? (Or Has the Black Middle Class Lost Its Mind?)* (New York: Basic Civitas, 2005), 64–86.

17. "Acting White: One Professor Studies the Fight Between Identity and Achievement; One Student Copes with It," *City* (Rochester, NY), February 6, 2006, www.rochester citynewspaper.com/archives/2006/2/Acting+white (accessed February 22, 2010).

18. Ibid.

19. Ibid.

20. McWhorter, *Winning the Race,* 269.

21. Ibid., 296.

22. Shelby Steele, *A Dream Deferred: The Second Betrayal of Black Freedom in America* (New York: Harper, 1998), 44.

11. JUSTICE CLARENCE THOMAS: AN UNCLE TOM ACTING WHITE BY SELLING OUT?

1. Shelby Steele, *A Dream Deferred: The Second Betrayal of Black Freedom in America* (New York: Harper, 1998), 34.

2. Ibid., 7.

3. J. C. Watts, quoted in Steele, *Dream Deferred,* 44.

4. Harper Lee, *To Kill a Mockingbird,* quoted in Clarence Thomas, *My Grandfather's Son* (New York: Harper, 2007), 268.

5. Thomas, *My Grandfather's Son,* 271.

6. Ibid., 274.

7. Randall Kennedy, *Sellout: The Politics of Racial Betrayal* (New York: Vintage Books, 2008), 87.

8. Ibid.

9. "Can Black Congressional Members Survive Supreme Court Blow?" *Jet,* July 25, 1995.

10. Major R. Owens, quoted in Kennedy, *Sellout,* 88. Taken from *Senate Committee on the Judiciary: S. Hrg 102-1084, Pt. 2, Nomination of Judge Clarence Thomas to Be Associate Justice of the Supreme Court of the United States,* www.gpoaccess.gov/congress/senate/judiciary/sh102-1084pt2/browse.html (accessed February 15, 2010).

11. John Lewis, quoted in Kennedy, *Sellout,* 92.
12. Louis Stokes, quoted in Kennedy, *Sellout,* 92.
13. "A Nomination That Will Divide," *Milwaukee Journal Sentinel*, October 31, 2005.

12. THE PRESIDENT WHO HAPPENS TO BE BLACK VERSUS A BLACK PRESIDENT: THE COMING RISE OF COLORLESS VALUES—OR NOT?

1. "Jesse Jackson: Obama Needs to Bring More Attention to Jena 6," *CNN.com,* September 19, 2007, www.cnn.com/2007/POLITICS/09/19/jackson.jena6/index.html (accessed February 22, 2010).
2. Ibid.
3. Ibid.
4. M. E. Sprengelmeyer, "Nader: Obama Trying to 'Talk White,'" *Rocky Mountain News,* June 25, 2008, www.rockymountainnews.com/news/2008/jun/25/nader-critical-of-obama-for-trying-to-talk-white/?printer=1/ (accessed February 22, 2010).
5. Ibid.
6. John McWhorter, *Authentically Black: Essays for the Black Silent Majority* (New York: Gotham Books, 2004), 2.
7. Ibid., 6.
8. Matt Bai, "What Would a Black President Mean for Black Politics Post Race," *New York Times Magazine,* August 10, 2008, 37.
9. Ibid.
10. Ibid, 37–38.
11. "Attorney General Eric Holder at the Department of Justice African American History Month Program," www.justice.gov/ag/speeches/2009/a9-speech-090218.html.
12. Helene Cooper, "Attorney General Chided for Language on Race," *New York Times,* March 7, 2009, www.nytimes.com/2009/03/08/us/politics/08race.html (accessed February 22, 2010).
13. Walter E. Williams, "A Nation of Cowards," *Townhall.com,* February 25, 2009, http://townhall.com/columnists/WalterEWilliams/2009/02/25/a_nation_of_cowards (accessed February 22, 2010).
14. Cooper, "Attorney General Chided."
15. "Black Panther Intimidation at the Polls?" *MichelleMalkin.com,* November 4, 2008, http://michellemalkin.com/2008/11/04/black-panther-intimidation-at-the-polls/ (accessed February 22, 2010).
16. John Fund, "Holder's Black Panther Stonewall," *Wall Street Journal,* August 21, 2009.
17. Ibid.
18. Ibid.
19. Ibid.
20. www.sodahead.com/blog/136397/is-this-post-racialobama-protecting-black-panther-criminals/.
21. Krissah Thompson, "Scholar Says Arrest Will Lead Him to Explore Race in Criminal

Justice," *Washington Post,* July 22, 2009, www.washingtonpost.com/wp-dyn/content/article/2009/07/21/AR2009072101771.html?hpid=artslot (accessed February 22, 2010).

22. "News Conference by the President, East Room, July 22, 2009," The White House, Office of the Press Secretary, www.whitehouse.gov/the_press_office/News-Conference-by-the-President-July-22-2009/ (accessed February 15, 2010).

13. THE DEATH OF A RACIAL SLUR: THE NEW UNDERGROUND RAILROAD—TRANSPORTING BLACK PEOPLE TO REAL EQUALITY

1. "How No Child Left Behind Benefits African Americans," Department of Education, www.ed.gov/print/nclb/accountability/achieve/nclb-aa.html (accessed February 15, 2010).

2. www.americanrhetoric.com/speeches/billcosbypoundcakespeech.htm.

3. Gwen Ifill, *The Breakthrough: Politics and Race in the Age of Obama* (New York: Anchor Books, 2009), 161.

4. Ibid., 160.

5. Marc Morano, "Harry Belafonte Calls Black Republicans 'Tyrants,'" *CNSNews.com,* August 8, 2005, http://archive.newsmax.com/archives/ic/2005/8/8/102152.shtml (accessed February 22, 2010).

6. Ibid.

7. Ifill, *The Breakthrough,* 18–19.

8. Maureen Dowd, "Boy, Oh, Boy," *New York Times,* September 13, 2009, www.nytimes.com/2009/09/13/opinion/13dowd.html (accessed February 22, 2010).

9. Ibid.

10. John Bresnahan, "For CBC, the Joy Is Tempered by Worry," *Politico,* September 23, 2009, 24.

11. Diana West, "Political Opposition Isn't Racism," *Washington Examiner.com,* September 20, 2009. www.washingtonexaminer.com/opinion/columns/Political-opposition-isn_t-racism-8264660-59759582.html.

12. Kathleen Parker, "Playing the Racial Deck," *Washington Post,* September 20, 2009.

13. John Heilemann and Mark Halperin, *Game Change* (New York: Harper, 2010), 36.

Index